Crime Fiction and Film
in the Sunshine State

Crime Fiction and Film in the Sunshine State:
Florida Noir

edited by

Steve Glassman
and
Maurice O'Sullivan

Bowling Green State University Popular Press
Bowling Green, OH 43403

Copyright © 1997 Bowling Green State University Popular Press

Library of Congress Cataloging-in-Publication Data
Crime fiction and film in the Sunshine State : Florida noir / edited by
    Steve Glassman and Maurice O'Sullivan.
        p.   cm.
    Includes bibliographical references (p.).
    ISBN 0-87972-749-7 (cloth). -- ISBN 0-87972-750-0 (pbk.)
    1. Detective and mystery stories, American--History and criticism.
    2. Florida--In literature. 3. Crime in literature. 4. American fic-
    tion--Florida--History and criticism. 5. Detective and mystery
    films--United States--History and criticism. 6. Detective and mys-
    tery television programs--United States--History and criticism.
    I. Glassman, Steve. II. O'Sullivan, Maurice, 1944- .
    PS374.D4C74   1997
    813'.08720932759--dc21   97-15074
                                                                  CIP

Cover design by Dumm Art

Contents

Acknowledgments

Any endeavor such as this owes its genesis and development to a vast number of friends and colleagues. Front and center among those stands Ira Jacobson, vice-president of Academics at Embry-Riddle University, whose grant of release time materially advanced the publication date and quality of this book. We also deeply appreciate the support of our colleagues at Embry-Riddle and Rollins. The Florida College English Association has proved an important source of talent and support. Karen Slater, administrative assistant to the English Department at Rollins, provided her usual excellent work in coordinating the typing and guiding the editors through the wonders of Windows. Foremost in the ranks of the secret helpers of any volume such as this, the reference librarians, are Laura Robbins and her colleagues at Embry-Riddle. Wayne Matthews, Katherine R. Gardiner, Alice Haldeman, Gayle Harmon and Anne Potter of the Volusia County library system gave unstintingly of their time and, in Wayne Matthews's case, advice. We also appreciate the help of Dianne Walton of the Rollins Library, and the staffs of the Orange County and Winter Park libraries. Last and by no means least, we must thank Betsy Willeford for her helpful early guidance on this project.

Introduction

Back in the early days of the movies, when films like *Public Enemy* and *Scarface* lionized New York and Chicago gangsters, Florida produced nothing more glamorous than the Ashley-Mobley gang. That gang of farmboy cousins would occasionally emerge from the pine-palmetto scrub on embarrassingly inept crime sprees. Once when robbing a train, Florida's Bonnie and Clyde wannabes left the mail car without forcing the safe because they had no idea that a safe even existed.

In those days the rest of America still considered Florida the sticks. Sporadic bursts of development in the late nineteenth and early twentieth century inevitably died as waves of natural disasters rolled through the state. Although by the twenties and early thirties Palm Beach had enticed the wealthy and Key West had seduced such diverse writers as Wallace Stevens, Robert Frost, and Ernest Hemingway, most Americans regarded the whole region as a vaguely exotic Eden on the fringe of the United States. Now, the better part of a century later, Florida has become the fourth most populous state in the Union. Perhaps not surprisingly—given the booming growth in population—according to FBI statistics, this state, shaped roughly like a handgun, leads the country in the percentage of criminals in its population. Again perhaps predictably, popular culture, which glamorized western outlaws and northern gangsters in an earlier era, has recently shifted southeast. In the past decade or so, more than a hundred crime novels have been set in the Miami area alone. Indeed, shortly before his retirement, *New York Times Book Review* crime columnist Newgate Callendar bemoaned the floodtide. He had seen enough books set in Florida. He feared drowning.

The collection of essays presented here, which we have labeled *Florida noir*, is the first attempt to deal critically with this phenomenon. Every first-year film major knows that film noir developed out of the Hollywood of the forties and early fifties. As the "noir" (French for dark or black) implies, these films, shot in black and white, had a hard-nosed tone that matched their film stock. Framed against nocturnal exteriors and hard angled, minimalist interiors, chain-smoking, alienated protagonists picked their way sparely but relentlessly through a nihilistic world of violence and sexual obsession. With roots in existentialism, German expressionism, and nineteenth-century English gothic fiction (called by

1

French critics "le roman noir"), film noir captured the fragmented uncertainty of postwar urban America. Although the period of the unselfconscious film noir ended by the late fifties, the form influenced such outstanding (if no longer always black and white) movies as *In Cold Blood* in the sixties, *Chinatown* and *Taxi Driver* in the seventies, and *Body Heat* and *The Big Easy* in the eighties.

Purists like Kurt Vonnegut and Gore Vidal who decry the influence of cinema on the novel would no doubt object to our choice of title as well as to our using "noir" as a catch-all definition of the subject matter. It seems doubtful that many popular writers—and by definition noir novelists are popular writers—would make many such objections. More important, the noir characterization encompasses a variety of works that cannot easily be defined using any other categorization. And in popular culture "noir" has become associated not only with crime but with the violence, bleakness, and conflict associated with the American hard-boiled mystery.

Many of the old noir movies could be called crime films—whether the protagonist attempted to unravel the mystery like Humphrey Bogart's Philip Marlowe in *The Big Sleep* or to commit the crime like Fred MacMurray and Barbara Stanwyck in *Double Indemnity*. But many of the best examples do not fit neatly into the crime category. *Casablanca* and *Sunset Boulevard* leap readily to mind. Similarly, in one entire category, the prison movie, in which, ironically, the grim situation of men pressed together engenders an eminently noir situation, no crime is required. Presumably—but by no means certainly—most of the inmates have done something to merit incarceration; their crimes, however, need have no relevance to the plot of the movie. *The Shawshank Redemption* with Tim Robbins and Morgan Freeman suggests a recent incarnation of the genre.

In sum, then, we take the broadest possible definition of noir in these essays on Florida's detective novels. A crime, usually a murder, has been committed and a sleuth, whether a cop on the public payroll, a private eye, a salvage consultant, or some private citizen, is called on to sort through the increasingly involved plotline as through the leaves of an artichoke for the succulent corruption at its heart. But we have expanded the term to include writers of a number of hues. Some of the works have comic undertones, while others read more like adventures. Some, like John D. MacDonald's *Flash of Green*, focus more on moral and social corruption, while still others, like Thomas McGuane's *Ninety-two in the Shade*, explore the individual psyche.

Hundreds of novels that meet these criteria—and a fair number of films—have been set in Florida. Naturally, no critical study could hope to deal with them all. We have focused chiefly on the important works, generally by authors who have produced more than one book of note, of the past few years going back to about the time when John D. Mac-Donald first began mapping crime in Florida. In order to deal with all this material in some sort of systematic basis, we have broken the state up geographically.

It will come as a surprise to few readers to learn that more titles have been set in the Miami area than in any other part of the state. Dade and Broward counties, which the Miami megalopolis takes in, account for the greater part of three chapters of this book and claim part of a fourth. The towering figure in Florida's detective fiction, Travis McGee, moored his houseboat in Bahia Mar Marina in Fort Lauderdale; almost every subsequent Florida mystery writer has had to deal with the challenge of being hailed as "the next John D. MacDonald." Edgar Hirshberg, who played liar's poker on Friday afternoons with MacDonald during the years when McGee was being conceived, discusses the character and the man who created him. The peculiar humor of Miami writers Carl Hiaasen and Charles Willeford deserves a complete chapter, and Julie Brannon talks about their relationship to the tradition of the southern grotesque. Sarah Fogle explores the distinctive contributions to the genre by women both in the greater Miami area and elsewhere in the state.

Elmore Leonard first came to Florida prominence with novels set in the Miami area. Now he seems to have moved a bit farther north in the southeast Florida megalopolis to Palm Beach county. In the interests of avoiding congestion, we asked Anna Lillios to discuss Leonard as well as Palm Beach's Lawrence Sanders and two Orlando-based writers, John Lutz and Kevin Robinson, in her chapter.

The Keys come in second to Miami in the number of mystery novels and novelists in residence. Susan and Harold Nugent, in their chapter, discuss the work of James Hall, Laurence Shames, Thomas Sanchez, Jim Harrison, and Thomas McGuane. Maurice O'Sullivan investigates the ecothrillers of Randy Wayne White and the myth-laden series by Ed McBain set along the southwest coast. Finally, Steve Glassman examines novelists such as Mickey Friedman and Geoffrey Norman who choose to write about the other Florida, the more traditionally southern part of the state located, ironically, in Florida's northern tiers of counties.

In addition to these geographically oriented chapters, three others deal with the state in more holistic fashion. Ellen Smith discusses the surprisingly small number of Florida films noir. However, Smith notes that what Florida may lack in numbers it makes up for in quality from the early classic *Key Largo* to Lawrence Kasdan's *Body Heat*. Bill Brubaker painstakingly details about two dozen early works, many of which, he notes, bear only the faintest resemblance to their modern counterparts.

The first chapter of the book takes on the thorny question of the quality of Florida detective fiction vis-à-vis the classic California masters of the early 1920s through the 1970s. Among other things, this essay points out how the California murder school grew out of the literary tradition of naturalism that earlier mainstream California writers such as Jack London and Frank Norris nourished. That no analogous tradition was identified with Florida goes a long way toward explaining the diversity of styles among the state's best practitioners. As a guide for further reading, Maurice O'Sullivan and Lynne Phillips have compiled a bibliography of Florida mysteries since 1895.

Finally, let us say a word about the utility of this volume. It is self-evident that the student of popular culture will find much of value in the essays we offer here. But this book will be just as valuable to the general reader of mysteries, whether casual dabbler or aficionado. She may want to find out what we say about her favorite writer or he may read this book to learn of new writers. In any case, we invite all our readers to sample these reflections on some of the best writing Florida has yet produced.

1

West Comes East

Steve Glassman

In recent years an impressive amount of crime fiction has been set in Florida, and an equally impressive list of crime writers has begun to impinge on the consciousness of American readers: John D. MacDonald, Elmore Leonard, Charles Willeford, and Carl Hiaasen reflect only a few of the hundreds of authors who have set crime novels in the sunshine state. But whatever their level of popular interest, Florida crime writers carry a particular burden. No matter what their claims to glory, there is always that nagging question about how they really stack up compared to the classic American crime writers of early mid century.

For that reason the best—and perhaps only—place to start a book about Florida crime fiction is California. As shown in the introduction, the modern detective story of the hard-boiled sort was invented and developed in that state. First came Hammett in the late twenties and early thirties. Then followed Cain in the thirties, Chandler in the late thirties through the fifties, and later, Ross Macdonald, whose best work came out in the sixties and seventies. Serious literary critics have made extravagant—and justified—claims for the literary merit of each of them, and their prose has become an essential part of the American canon. But what about this upstart, this parvenu of Florida at the end of the century. Has Florida produced either individual authors or a school of crime writing comparable in merit to California's?

In order to answer that daunting question, we must detour far to the west. Not only will individual California writers be discussed but, most important, the larger matrix from which they came will be examined. Then, we'll slide I-10 completely across the country to investigate Florida writers of detection and finally I'll attempt to make some sort of assessment of Florida crime writing.

It is extravagant to claim that any writer single-handedly invented an art form, but such claims are routinely made for Dashiell Hammett. Before him, it is said, there was no detective fiction in the modern sense of the word. "Hammett gave murder back to the kind of people that

5

commit it [and] for reasons not just to provide a corpse," Raymond Chandler said in his famous essay "The Simple Art of Murder." "He put these people down on paper as they are, and he made them talk and think in the language they customarily used for these purposes. He had style, but his audiences didn't know it, because it was in a language not capable of such refinements. They thought they were getting a good meaty melodrama, written in the kind of lingo they imagined they spoke themselves" (14-15).

Hammett's background as a Pinkerton detective and, in a wholly different but equally important way, as a Marxist provided the warp and the woof for his fiction. Critics like James Naremore feel that "American fiction of the twenties was generally hard-boiled, and if Hammett had not become the 'father' of the tough detective, someone else would have" (49). Naremore points out that Hammett "like Chandler began by writing verse, and like the other aesthetes of his period he found his true vocation by reacting against the genteel, prettified, vaguely homosexual tone of the nineties."

Although born and reared in Baltimore, Hammett became closely identified with San Francisco. It was in that city that he worked as a Pinkerton operative and it was there that his own Continental Op performed many of his deeds for the benefit of *Black Mask* readers. It was there that *The Maltese Falcon* was set.

It was the San Francisco of the post-earthquake era. The gold rush that birthed the town lay in the past but not that far in the past. It was a town with more cosmopolitan and artistic pretensions than any city west of the Mississippi. The city became the cradle of American naturalism, boasting among its artistic pretenders Jack London and Frank Norris. If Hammett fathered the hard-boiled detective story, Norris, more than anyone else, was the progenitor of American naturalism, that French literary import that rebelled against the escapist tendencies of lesser nineteenth-century works. Taking the model of science, naturalists sought to be objective and detached while giving detailed portraits of their subjects. No sordid detail about their characters, generally drawn from the lower strata of society, was spared. Most importantly, the characters of naturalist fiction were stuck—helpless pawns of greater social and historical forces. Generally, naturalistic writers affected a plain prose style with camera-like objectivity. Norris had studied in France where he had become exposed to the works of Zola and his followers.

Whatever the theoretical provenance for his fiction, Norris's stories were purely American, with a distinctly California flavor. One of the great protagonists in American fiction is Norris's McTeague. The hulking teddy bear of a San Francisco dentist is thrown out of his occupation by a change in the law, reduced to a street person and, in a final futile attempt to gain control of his life, turns robber and killer. McTeague ends—in one of the great conclusions in all fiction—handcuffed to a dead man in Death Valley. Norris, who died at the age of thirty-three, wrote, "I never truckled; I never took off the hat to Fashion and held it out for pennies. By God, I told them the truth" (Norris 699).

It was an epitaph that most readers would agree could have been Hammett's. In many other particulars—especially in style—Hammett's fiction bears a striking resemblance to naturalism. As Naremore notes, "[T]he plainness of the language contributes to the illusion of realism and honesty, especially when Hammett combines spectacular events with documentary detail or accounts of the more quotidian aspects of the Op's job." In his later novels, particularly *The Maltese Falcon*, "[T]hird-person narration . . . presents everything from the detective's point of view without ever telling us what the detective is thinking. The narrator stands outside the character, like a camera watching an actor, describing only his movements."

Much has been made of Hammett's Marxism. Naturalism and Marxism share several important philosophical assumptions. The universe in both doctrines is mechanistic and materialistic, devoid of a providence. Both doctrines posit a social hierarchy in which the higher social classes feed lustily on the lower. Naturalism, however, offers a purely literary view while Marxism is a political philosophy that has literary side effects. Both theories acquired large followings during the early years of this century, especially with the disillusionment of the Great War followed by the unequal prosperity of the twenties and the devastating economic collapse of the Depression.

Hammett was by no means the only Marxist with a naturalistic bent. Theodore Dreiser, author of *Sister Carrie* (1900) and *An American Tragedy* (1925), America's leading novelist in the very early years of the century, provides a much purer example of naturalism (if a somewhat less obvious Marxist than Hammett who was dragged before the cameras in the post–World War II communist witch hunts). In any case, it is astonishing that literary critics have not made more of the obvious naturalistic elements in the tough-guy style. For our purposes, let's note that Hammett's formative years included immersion in a city with a literary as well as a criminal milieu, an immersion that inevitably affected his prose style—and the prose style of many other detective writers after him.

Like Hammett, James M. Cain hailed originally from Maryland. But unlike his model, Cain arrived in California in the early thirties as a middle-aged man with a new wife and two young children. Although hardly a failure in his earlier incarnations as a professor of journalism, an editorial writer for Walter Lippmann and a managing editor of *The New Yorker,* Cain went west to make himself over as a storyteller. After a faltering start—he lost his job as a screenwriter after only six months—Cain got down to the business of recasting the hard-boiled novel. That enterprise, too, seemed star-crossed at the beginning. As Cain himself said, "[For] ten years [I] resigned myself to the conviction I couldn't write a novel. . . . My short stories, which were put in the mouth of some character, marched right along. Yet they were very homely characters, and spoke a gnarled and grotesque jargon that didn't seem quite adapted to long fiction; it seemed to me that after fifty pages of ain'ts, brungs and fittens, the reader would want to throw the book at me. But then I moved to California and heard the Western roughneck: the boy who is just as elemental inside as his Eastern colleague, but who has been to high school, completes his sentences, and uses reasonably good grammar. Once my ear had put on this wax, I began to wonder if *that* wouldn't be the medium I could use to write novels" (vii).

Murder, Cain reasoned, "had always been written from its least interesting angle, which was whether the police would catch the" culprit. Drawing on the naturalist tradition, Cain started telling the story from an unusual perspective: the criminals'. The first job was getting the reader to like and sympathize with such characters and their situations. As Tom Wolfe says, "Cain puts you inside the skin of one utterly egocentric heel after another, losers who will stop at nothing—and makes you care about them. Sympathy runs along shank to flank with the horror and disgust. It's strange stuff" (vii). Then Cain put his characters in a pleasant little device he called "the love rack." Two persons hopelessly in love—hopeless in the sense they could not have both each other and a life that would make them happy, unless they do in at least one spouse. Cain said he strove for a rising coefficient of intensity, which he certainly achieved in such early masterpieces as *The Postman Always Rings Twice, Double Jeopardy,* and, to a lesser extent, in *Mildred Pierce* (not strictly speaking a crime novel, although there is a murder in it). As Thomas Lask writes, "Cain's ability to tell more in few words is equalled by no one in the game. If you doubt it, try the first seven pages of *Postman.* The amount of information in them will make a computer card seem as talky as Henry James" (qtd. in "Cain" 120).

Like Hammett (and unlike Cain), Raymond Chandler was an alumnus of the *Black Mask* school. His origins lay in pulp fiction and, like Hammett, he chose to cast his stories through the eyes of a private eye. Although his private eye has the reputation as one of the hardest-boiled eggs around, Chandler actually softened the tough, no-nonsense image:

his detective hardly ever charges a fee and his clients of preference seem to be the defenseless and outcast. And his storylines viewed from a half century later have an old-fashioned flavor, the hunt for a rare doubloon or a bank robber's moll. While the naturalism of Hammett and Cain propelled their characters (and storylines), the deepest philosophical strain that Chandler tapped into was a vague dislike for the moneyed classes.

With the strikes against Chandler, just being a notable failure would seem a solid accomplishment. But of all the writers treated in this chapter, Chandler has received the most serious critical attention. Since 1980, 100 articles have been indexed in the *MLA International Bibliography* on Chandler, as opposed to 75 on Hammett, 38 on Ross Macdonald and 22 on Cain.

So how did he do it? And what did he do right? The Marxist critic Fredric Jameson, puzzled by the power of Chandler's detective fiction, argues that a "case can be made for Chandler as a painter of American life: not as a builder of those large-scale models of the American experience which great literature offers, but rather in fragmentary pictures of setting and place, fragmentary perceptions which are by some formal paradox somehow inaccessible to serious literature" (624). In particular, he claims that Chandler's strength lies in his social criticism. "By an accident of place, his social content anticipates the realities of the fifties and sixties. For Los Angeles is already a kind of microcosm and forecast of the country as a whole; a new centerless city, in which the various classes have lost touch with each other" (624).

Frank MacShane, one of Chandler's biographers, says that "much of Chandler's fiction . . . resembles a Restoration comedy in which the plot is not so important as the picture of life portrayed through its characters and the humor produced by the jokes and situations" (91). In Chandler's hands, D. C. Russell claims, "[W]ords do become beautiful and wonderful things, operating with economy and precision. What a delight it is to come upon a writer who tosses off a good image on almost every page" (123). Getting more specific, George P. Elliot observes, "Surely no American since Mark Twain has invented so many wisecracks as this British-educated classicist. . . . The dialogue when it is not hobbled by plot work, is fast, glittering and tough. . . . The famous language of his style is a fabrication based only in part on the argots of police and criminals" (357). Finally, as Lawrence Clark Powell notes, Chandler himself defined good writing as "any sort of writing that reaches a sufficient intensity of performance to glow with its own heat. 'There must be magic in the writing,' [Chandler] said, 'but I take no credit for it. It just happens, like red hair'" (377).

Ross Macdonald paid homage to Hammett by naming his shamus/protagonist, Lew Archer, after Sam Spade's partner, Miles Archer. Macdonald's southern California–based private cop also developed as his signature device a sort of psychologically predetermined leitmotif that echoed the naturalism of his namesake's San Francisco home base. In short, Archer's clients had the habit of falling eerily prey to the moral and mental collapse occasioned by a crime long buried in the past. As a prose stylist Macdonald earns high marks from many critics although others find his overreliance on metaphor and simile a bit tedious. Although he was the only member of the hard-boiled California fraternity actually born in the state, Macdonald spent his formative years in Canada and the upper Midwest. In any case, he achieved the same sort of reputation for interpreting the social enigma of southern California as Chandler, who was reared and remained in England until a young man, had for his generation. As William Goldman notes, "Nobody writes southern California like Macdonald writes it. All those new rich people, the perfect front lawns where no one but the gardener ever treads, the dustless houses with their huge picture windows facing other picture windows—there's something unalive about it all. And since Macdonald's characters are all dying anyway, that's what makes him their perfect chronicler. His world is every bit as tactile as O'Hara's Pennsylvania" (1).

Individually, these California authors (with the possible inclusion of Jim Thompson) are regarded by serious critics as the cream of crime writers. All have received considerable critical attention. (To keep things in perspective, Faulkner was cited 1,760 times in the *MLA Bibliography* during the last fifteen years, Hemingway 1,151 times, Eudora Welty 371 times, Ralph Ellison 161, and John O'Hara 67.) By contrast, the writers whom we will try to make a case for as a Florida school of crime writing have attracted much less critical attention. John D. MacDonald received serious mention in ten pieces, Elmore Leonard in nine and Carl Hiaasen in none.

John D. MacDonald's protagonist, Travis McGee, was forged in the crucible of pulp fiction as was MacDonald. After receiving an MBA from Harvard and doing a hitch in the India-Burmese theater during the Second World War, MacDonald opted for the independence of supporting himself by grinding out stories for the pulp magazines and, later, novels for the paperback publishers. In the early sixties the idea of a mystery series was broached by his publisher, Fawcett. MacDonald was cautious about getting locked into a series. But "the author of original paperbacks," MacDonald notes, was "in a real squeeze between pornography rising up from the bottom and reprints of block-buster best sellers coming down from the top. A series [was] self-generating; new books

[sent] readers back to the older ones" ("MacDonald"). The name Mac-Donald chose for his lead character, Dallas McGee, did not seem auspicious. Before he finished writing his prototype novels, the president was assassinated in the namesake city and MacDonald hastily renamed his protagonist.

In 1970 McDonald said in an interview with the *Washington Post*, "Most of my published novels are of the folk dancing category, the steps, the patterns traditionally imperative, the retribution obligatory. . . . Within these limits I have struggled for freshness, for what insights I can muster, for validity of characterization and motivation, for the accuracies of method and environment which enhance any illusion of reality" (qtd. in "MacDonald, John D[ann]" 408).

One of MacDonald's biographers, David Geherin, argues that "writing for a mass-market audience and adhering to the general pattern of genre fiction—activities that some would dismiss as second-rate—are in his case no impediments to the creation of first-rate work. . . . MacDonald is a gifted storyteller" (vii).

Although recognizing this gift, *Time* book reviewer John Skow speaks for MacDonald's critics. "This month the reader with a November in his soul is in luck," Skow writes on the issue of *The Scarlet Ruse* and *The Turquoise Lament* (108). "John D. MacDonald, the nation's best writer of no-qual crime fantasies, has turned out two splendid . . . volumes." Skow goes on to call the series "a dream manual about the beachboy Hamlet, Travis McGee. This paladin is a roughneck who lives on a houseboat in Fort Lauderdale, despoiling stewardesses and brooding about the decline of the West. He quests forth, when funds are low, to do battle for the dread forces of reality—a Robin Hood among chattel rustlers who steals loot back from thugs and swindlers and returns it, minus a 50% commission, to the widows and orphans from whom it was taken. The McGee mixture is an agreeable blend of boat lore, suspense, *machismo* and lighthearted sadism."

Skow's commentary is to the thoughtful McGee fan what the mystery of procreation is to a suddenly wised-up child. No matter how much he might want to repair to the fantasy of the stork, there is something that rings true. McGee is credible enough and likable enough, but one never entirely believes in his literary reality. His philosophical soliloquies and his action triumphs come just a tad too easily. The wires controlling the papier mâché mask might not be visible, but the introspective reader can never be entirely blind to their existence.

Unlike many of his mystery-writing colleagues who served their apprenticeship in the pulp magazines, MacDonald was not a frustrated aesthete. His writerly talents are solid, rather than brilliant; he was a craftsman, not an artist. He could develop a character or a scene with economy and empathy, a dead tooth, carelessly applied lipstick, a lop-sided smile. A nice talent, but hardly genius. Likewise, he understood place. Many have called him the best writer about Florida—even if his is a curiously stylized Florida, done over for a TV movie. His plots, are engaging and inventive enough. The reader does not generally mind that pretty much the same thing seems to happen in each one.

McGee storylines are charged by the villain—hardly anyone creates better psychopathic bad guys than John D. MacDonald. They are no-holds thugs who stop at nothing, and the action climaxes at book's end can thrill the most jaded paperback thrill seeker—never minding that it is a foregone certainty that Travis McGee will prevail and almost an equal certainty that his current ladylove will be lost.

MacDonald draws McGee absurdly larger than life, starting with his size—the man is outrageously big—and going on to his ability to endure physical punishment. Charles Champlin once observed that McGee has "been kicked, hammered, beaten, flayed, drugged, immersed, stabbed, jabbed, bent, thrown and shot at so often he has more entry and exit signs than a shopping mall" (qtd. in "MacDonald" 313).

To say that John D. MacDonald is not a literary titan misses the point. He was not one. But neither he nor his work seriously strove for literary acceptance. What he is the best American writer of the classical genre mystery in the postwar era and possibly the century. Jacques Barzun has claimed that the weakness of Chandler and others was that they tried to make the detective genre do things it could not support—and then bemoaned their martyrdom when critics refused to grant them full literary canonization (161). John D. MacDonald transcended the genre by embracing it and all of its conventions and playing them for everything they were worth. While Chandler and others pushed at the frontiers of the medium, ultimately they failed—even if those failures were brilliant failures. John D. MacDonald's prose may not have dared as much, but its full realization of the possibilities within the genre is equally brilliant.

"The question here," Walker Percy asked on the release of *Bandits*, "is why is Elmore Leonard so good? He is as good as the blurbs say: 'The greatest crime writer of our time, perhaps ever.' [Can't put it down,' and so on. It's true enough. But how does he do it? Because he looks like he's thrown away the rules of a noble genre. He doesn't stick to the same guy or the same place" (7).

A secondary question of interest is whether Florida can legitimately claim Elmore Leonard. Following the classic pattern of crime writers,

Leonard was reared elsewhere (in Detroit) and moved, seasonally, to the scene of his fiction-writing later in life. But even Cain, who transplanted himself and his fiction to California when he was forty, was a youngster compared to Leonard whose first Florida book came out when he was fifty-five. It was his eighteenth novel.

Leonard's first book was a western, published in 1953 when he was twenty-eight. Over the next decade and a half he wrote advertising copy in Motown and worked on western stories on the side—Glenn Ford's classic *The 3:10 to Yuma* was adapted from his short story—and sometimes on the job. He would occasionally write fiction in a drawer at work; when a manager would appear the tray would roll into his desk and he'd go back to penning odes to Chevrolets. His first essay into crime fiction, *The Big Bounce* (1969), was generated by the drying up of the western market. The book was rejected eighty-four times before it was picked up as a paperback original. Leonard went back to the western until a reversal in fortune ended both his career as a cowboy poet and his job as a copy writer—*The Big Bounce* was sold to the movies for $50,000.

For the next ten years Leonard concentrated on crime fiction. When he first began attracting critical attention in a big way, notably after *City Primeval: High Noon in Detroit* (1980), reviewers made much of his coming of age in the westerns. They saw or claimed they saw the code of the west transferred to the inner city: the tight-lipped hero, the cowboy knight errant, the struggle between unambiguous good and evil. In actual fact, they were grasping to make sense of a genre writer who, as Walker Percy observed, had thrown away the rule book—and was succeeding superlatively.

Other critics trotted out all the usual sources: Ross Macdonald, Chandler, Hammett, and even John D. MacDonald. Leonard himself credited Hemingway, Steinbeck, and O'Hara for his literary influences. Traces of them are easily seen in his work, as are those of George V. Higgins's dialogue-driven crime novels. Even at that, the parts do not add up to the whole. In fact, Elmore Leonard has made a breakthrough in crime writing of a magnitude that can only be measured on some sort of open-ended instrument like the Richter scale. Whitney Balliett has called him "a poet of the vernacular who . . . makes Chandler and Cain sound Victorian" (106).

J. D. Reed points out that Leonard's world is Dickensian, "where social strata collide, and the gravedigger waits by the charnel house. In this underworld. . . [are] Eddie Moke in *Stick* [who] looked 'like he mainlined cement,' Paco Boza, a Cuban street junkie of *La Brava,* [who] tools around South Miami Beach in a stolen Eastern Airlines wheelchair 'because he didn't like to walk and he thought it was cool.' Cornell

Lewis, a black ex-con houseman for a high roller in *Stick* who explains his boss: 'What the man likes is to rub up against danger without getting any on him. Makes him feel like the macho man. . . . See, he sits there at the club with his rich friends? Say, oh yeah, I go right in the cage with 'em. They don't hurt me none' " (84).

Both Leonard and the critics note that lying below the surface of his fiction is a nice sense of the ridiculous. In *Swag,* a character named Frank tries to recruit another called Earnest as a cohort in crime. " 'What do you think is the fastest and, percentagewise, safest way to make the most money?' " The answer, according to Frank, is armed robbery (21). It is upon this premise that the boys launch a short-lived but eminently funny career as stickup artists.

Stylistically, Leonard has his peculiarities. As Gary Giddins notes: "[S]entences that start in medias res ('You asking me for?' means 'What are you asking me for?'); sentences without conjunctions ('You're the perfect combination I ever saw one'); strangely parsed phrases ('That's all you got a do'). Leonard's classiest technique is the way he shifts the point of view between major and minor, active and passive characters" (4). James W. Hall picks up on that theme: "Early on in *Maximum Bob*, Leonard gives us a glimpse of things from [a] gator's point of view. . . . It's a very strange interlude, going into the gator's mind like that. An odd and risky moment, even for Elmore Leonard, who is used to dipping into some pretty exotic minds" (1).

George Stade agrees that Leonard "is never more entertaining than when one of his villains is stealing a scene. They are inspired hams, these bad actors, so empty inside that they only become themselves when they are playing a part, milking it for all its worth" (11). Rhoda Koenig agrees that "the villains of Elmore Leonard . . . have an almost supernatural awfulness about them" (86). "Leonard's empathy for villains . . . scares the hell out of" Gary Giddins. "They are more energetic, determined, and colorful than his heroes" (4).

Compared to Leonard's characters, Sam Spade and Philip Marlowe look like "kindly nannies, mere bleeding hearts," according to Michael Wood, who postulates that what is "both dated and attractive in Chandler's vision is not the crime in it but the quiet outrage it contains" (1,370). In short, Leonard achieves his killing shots to a large extent by throwing out the genre convention that the good guys will always win in the end. To critics, particularly foreign critics like Wood, Leonard's moral vision—or lack of it—is chilling. "There is no battle," writes Britisher John Sutherland "because the bad guys have won" (16).

As for the question of whether Leonard can legitimately be claimed as a Florida writer, his primary residence is still in the Detroit area.

Recent titles have been set in New Orleans, Hollywood, and back home in Michigan. Nevertheless, it's hard to deny that the novels that propelled him to notoriety were mostly set in south Florida. It is perhaps too facile to argue that transplanting his talents to Miami did for Leonard what going to California did for Cain. After all, the man had been painstakingly building a reputation by producing fiction loaded with many of the techniques he became widely known for once he moved his fiction south. For that, it is the technicolor diversity of south Florida that makes some of his best work shimmer. As John Sutherland notes, Leonard's fictional landscape relied on a real world created by a series of rapid influxes of people, capital and contraband all cooked in the Sun Belt's year-round summer. First came the monied retirees, who triggered off the real-estate boom. . . . Secondly, the mind-boggling sums of money generated by middle-class America's insatiable appetite for prohibited cocaine. Thirdly, the invasion by criminal classes educated in villainy outside the US—in Cuba, Haiti and Colombia. Fidel Castro's exporting his entire population of moral incorrigibles from Mariel in 1980 topped off the anti-social mixture nicely. Until a convincing case is made to the contrary, we will claim Elmore Leonard as our own.

There is no question that Carl Hiaasen is a wrapped in the flag Floridian. His grandfather was lured from the Dakotas to south Florida by the boom of the twenties. Hiaasen himself was born in Florida, raised in Florida, educated in Florida (B.S. University of Florida), and has worked as a journalist first at Cocoa and currently in Miami. His work as an investigative reporter earned him kudos from various local and national organizations, including the Heywood Broun Award from the Newspaper Guild and finalist for the 1981 Pulitzer in public service reporting.

After coauthoring three novels, Hiaasen brought out *Tourist Season*, a detective spoof about a terrorist organization that attempts to depress the Miami tourist economy. Tony Hillerman reviewing the book in the *New York Times Book Review* said *Tourist Season* "is full of . . . quick, efficient, understated little sketches . . . [and] of the sort of subtle truth that leaves you grinning. In fact, Mr. Hiaasen leaves you grinning a lot" (qtd. in Hiaasen).

Other Hiaasen titles have included *Double Whammy*, about skullduggery at a championship bass tournament; *Skin Tight*, which features psychopathic plastic surgeons and TV personalities; and *Native Tongue*, set in the Keys with a love-sick dolphin as one of its main characters. Among Hiaasen's more memorable characters are Skink, a former Florida governor who lives in the woods and subsists on roadkill, an investigative reporter whose stilt house is guarded by a killer barracuda, and a murderer with the head of a pit bull attached to his arm.

The sense of the ridiculous that lies under the surface in Leonard's novels is fully exposed in Hiaasen. In another time, he might not be seriously considered as a noir writer, but as Hiaasen says, "[F]or inspiration, all I had to do was read the daily newspaper. Crime in Miami is so bizarre that no novelist's inventions could surpass true life" ("Hiaasen" 199).

Is it really possible that so disparate a collection of writers as John D. MacDonald, Elmore Leonard, and Carl Hiaasen can be compared to the classic California school? I believe the answer to that question is yes. The Californians' unity of style and subject matter was an accident—an accident as it happened of place and *the times,* but nevertheless an accident. Hammett's development of the hard-boiled detective had as much to with his exposure to the literary milieu of San Francisco as to its criminal milieu. Realist and naturalist writers and the post–World War I ethos had prepared the reading public for more hard-boiled fare; this trend was apparent in literary as well as genre fiction. The social environment of California, the weirdos and grifters and glittery types, contributed too to the development of those writers.

During the last third of the century an altogether different literary climate emerged. After World War II, literary style fragmented. No longer did realism (and its handmaiden, naturalism) dominate fiction. Whereas earlier in the century a predominance of writers seemed to rebel against the sentimentalism of the nineteenth century and develop effects to heighten the sensation of realism (in both literary and genre fiction), almost all serious literary writers in the later twentieth century became experimenters.

John D. MacDonald, utilizing the conventions of the genre to capacity, might not stir the blood of literary critics the way his California namesake or Chandler or others have, but he has left an impressive oeuvre, which will be held up to apprentice crime writers for many decades to come. Elmore Leonard, like his cohorts writing straight literary fiction, is an experimental writer—as far as genre fiction is concerned—even if his electrifying talent and success partially cloak the obviousness of that assertion. Even when his prose is not working completely, he does things other crime writers can only aspire to. The jury is still out on Carl Hiaasen. His treatment of crime fiction, while drawing on the grotesquery of his southern roots is also experimental: fresh and irreverent, perhaps too irreverent to gain him long-term standing in the great hall of crime fiction. On the other hand, he may spawn a whole slew of imitators, without his own work's losing a sense of freshness.

With its fluid population, ethnic diversity, enormous growth, flexible morality, and subtropical setting, Florida has attracted many of the finest—and most popular—people writing crime fiction today. Despite significant differences in approach to character, plot, and style, they share a fascination with the country's southeasternmost state. The palpable presence of Florida is in their work as a myth or an ideal, as vision or nightmare, as Eden or dystopia. It justifies grouping them if not as a school at least as a gang or mob—the Florida Noir Mob.

Works Cited

Balliett, Whitney. "Elmore Leonard in Hollywood." *The New Yorker* 3 Sept. 1990: 106-07.

Barzun, Jacques. "The Illusion of the Real." *The World of Raymond Chandler.* Ed. Miriam Gross. London: Weidenfeld and Nicholson, 1977.

Cain, James M. Preface. *Three of a Kind.* New York: Knopf, 1943. vii-xv.

"Cain, James M(allahan) 1892- ." *Contemporary Authors. First Revision, Vol. 17-20.* Detroit: Gale, 1965.

Chandler, Raymond. *The Simple Art of Murder.* 1950. New York: Vintage, 1988.

Elliot, George P. "Country Full of Blondes." *The Nation* 23 Apr. 1960: 354-56, 358-60.

Geherin, David. *John D. MacDonald.* New York: Ungar, 1982.

Giddins, Gary. "Glitz." *Voice Literary Supplement* Feb. 1985: 4.

Goldman, William. *New York Times Book Review* 1 June 1969: 1.

Hall, James W. "Alligators and Other Reptiles." *Washington Post Book World* 14 July 1991: 1-2.

"Hiaasen, Carl 1953- ." *Contemporary Authors, New Revision Series.* Vol. 45. New York: Gale, 1995.

Jameson, Fredric. "On Raymond Chandler." *The Southern Review* 6.3 (1970): 624-50.

Koenig, Rhoda. "Freaky Deaky." *New York Magazine* 2 May 1988: 86.

Leonard, Elmore. *Swag.* 1976. New York: Penguin, 1984.

MacDonald, John D. *Publisher's Weekly* 21 Sept. 1964.

"MacDonald, John D(ann) 1916—." *Contemporary Authors, New Revision Series.* Vol. 19. Detroit: Gale, 1987.

McShane, Frank. *The Life of Raymond Chandler.* New York: Dutton, 1976.

Naremore, James. "Dashiell Hammett and the Poetics of Hard-Boiled Detection." *Art in Crime Writing: Essays on Detective Fiction.* Ed. Bernard Benstock. New York: St. Martin's, 1983. 49-73.

"Norris, [Benjamin] Frank[lin]." *Benet's Reader's Encyclopedia.* 1987.

Percy, Walker. "There's a Contra in my Gumbo." *New York Times Book Review* 4 Jan. 1987: 7.

Powell, Lawrence Clark. "'Farewell, My Lovely': Raymond Chandler." *California Classics: The Creative Literature of the Golden State.* Los Angeles: Ward Ritchie, 1971. 371-81.

Reed, J. D. "A Dickens from Detroit." *Time* 28 May 1984: 84, 85.

Russell, D. C. "The Chandler Books." *Atlantic Monthly* Mar. 1945: 123-24.

Skow, John. "Tasty No-Qual." *Time* 3 Dec. 1973: 108-09.

Stade, George. "Villains Have the Fun." *New York Times Book Review* 6 Mar. 1983: 11, 41.

Sutherland, John. "No. 1 Writer." *London Review of Books* 5 Sept. 1985: 16.

Wolfe, Tom. Introduction. *Cain x 3: Three Novels by James M. Cain.* New York: Knopf, 1969. v-viii.

Wood, Michael. "Down These Meaner Streets." *Times Literary Supplement* 5 Dec. 1986: 1370.

2

John D. MacDonald and Travis McGee: Heroes for Our Time

Ed Hirshberg

In July 1995, Fawcett Books embarked on the republication of the series of novels by John D. MacDonald about Travis McGee starting with *The Deep Blue Good-by*, which first appeared in 1964 and was closely followed that same year by three more: *Nightmare in Pink, A Purple Place for Dying,* and *The Quick Red Fox.*

These four novels got Travis McGee off to a running start. They established him as a character, introduced the idea of using a different color to distinguish the title of each book, and set the pattern for his stories. Travis calls himself a "salvage expert," who helps people recover large sums of money that have been stolen from them, and keeps half of what he recovers, and returns the rest to the rightful owners. That's his profession, at which he makes a very good living, enabling him to take his retirement "in chunks" as he goes along instead of waiting until he's too old to enjoy it (*Deep Blue* 8). He lives on the *Busted Flush,* a fifty-two-foot barge-type houseboat luxuriously accoutered with a sunken bathtub and plush furnishings, which is moored at the Bahia Mar Marina in Fort Lauderdale. He has won it in a poker game with a rich South American who was afraid to call his bluff, hence the name. He is a superb physical specimen, handsome in a rough sort of way, of that indeterminate age at which he remains attractive to most women of practically any age.

What Travis McGee has, in short, is everything—enough money, a plethora of women, and an interesting job doing good for people—all of which has made him a fascinating figure for millions of readers of both sexes, the kind of guy most women would like to be in love with and most men would like to be. John D. MacDonald wrote twenty-one books about him between 1964 and 1985, the year before he died. They have continued to sell briskly in the bookstores, though not nearly as briskly as they did when MacDonald was alive, despite the efforts of a passionate group of aficionados who hold conferences about him and his work every other year or so, usually at the Bahia Mar, and support a semiannual publication about him called *The JDM Bibliophile*.

Why did Fawcett Books choose this particular time to start republishing the Travis McGee series? The new edition of *The Deep Blue Good-by* includes such extra features as an enthusiastic introduction by successful Fort Lauderdale satirist Carl Hiaasen, a note from John D.'s son Maynard, and testimonials from Mary Higgins Clark, Sue Grafton, Dean Koontz, Jonathan Kellerman, and Donald Westlake. Fawcett also mounted a substantial publicity campaign, complete with radio and TV promotions, bookstore displays, and elaborate information kits for the book editors of most major newspapers. Aside from the fact that there is a new generation of readers who never heard of Travis McGee, the question of Why now? has an obvious and straightforward answer: the United States—and the rest of world—needs heroes. And maybe—just maybe—Travis McGee fills the bill.

Not only is he handsome and successful, he's also on the side of the angels. Despite his weaknesses, and there are many, he is unquestionably one of the good guys. The people he chooses to help regain their stolen property are usually the poor and the put-upon. Invariably what Travis tries to do is help good people recover from injuries inflicted on them by bad people. He usually succeeds, though often at considerable and grievous cost to himself in the form of injuries, insults, and other indignities that result when you try to be a knight in shining—if occasionally tarnished—armor who rides out into an evil world and tries to help people and do good.

Despite his sybaritic and free-wheeling lifestyle, including his daily tot of Plymouth Gin and tonic and the stream of women who pass through the door of the *Busted Flush*'s snug cabin—and occasionally detour into its king-size bed—he is a fundamentally decent as well as heroic man. He is a fit role model for a generation of people who are starved for heroes in an age when the year's most outstanding film concerned a mildly retarded ex-soldier who became a successful shrimper —not that there's anything wrong with being a shrimper, it's just not a very heroic occupation. MacDonald has carefully crafted Travis McGee in a heroic mold. In the tradition of such mythical heroes as Hercules, Achilles, and Theseus, he is of mysterious origins, has great physical strength, and is indefatigable in his amorous exploits.

But he's not just a hero—he also is concerned about his fellow humans. Unlike the ordinary hero, who is usually a strong, silent type, Travis talks a lot. Actually, he is MacDonald's mouthpiece in the expression of his opinions on a host of social issues. MacDonald brought in a sounding board for Travis after his fourth book about him because he felt that Travis was indulging in too many interior monologues. As sidekick, Meyer suddenly appears in *A Deadly Shade of Gold* and plays a vital part in the rest of the series. He is a garrulous, hirsute economist, highly intelligent, with whom Travis can discuss anything. MacDonald once remarked that he felt he had every right to move his suspense novels in the direction of the so-called "legitimate" novels "of manners and morals, despair and failure, love and joy. . . . I shall continue with my sociological asides, with McGee's and Meyer's dissertations on the condition of medicine, retirement, facelifting, earmites, road construction, white collar theft, apartment architecture, magazine editing, acid rain, billyrock, low fidelity, and public service in America today" (All unattributed quotes come from personal interviews with the author).

Wide-ranging and all-embracing as Travis's interests are, his most persistent and passionate opinions have to do with Florida's besieged environment. There are strong statements about what man's greed has done and is doing to despoil the state's natural resources—statements that are just as relevant today as they were when Travis or Meyer made them back in 1965. For example, in *Bright Orange for the Shroud*, the sixth book in the series, Travis speculates about the Everglades. Having failed to subdue it from frontal attack, "[W]e are slowly killing it off by tapping the River of Grass. In the questionable name of progress, the state in its vast wisdom lets every two-bit developer divert the flow into the dragline canals that give him 'waterfront' lots to sell. As far north as Corkscrew Swamp, virgin stands of ancient bald cypress are dying" (*Bright Orange* 58-59). In *Turquoise Lament* there is a vivid description of what pollution already has done to Florida's west coast as Travis views it from the air (166-67). Among the "shocking" changes that he notes along the shore from Venice northward to Siesta Key are the "pale and remarkably ugly high-rises" that are "jammed against the small strip of sand beach, shoulder to shoulder," and the "blooms of effluent" that are "murking the blue waters." He notices the "tiny churchgoing automobiles" that are "stacked up at the lift bridges, winking in the sun, and making a whisky haze that spoiled the quality of the light." Further north are the effects of the "massive and dangerous pollution" that "Big Borden" has spewed into the atmosphere over Bradenton. An unusual addition to the description of these effects is Travis's abrupt, and somewhat disconcerting, suggestion to his readers that they find out who the members of the board of directors of the Borden Company are, and—why not?—"Drop the fellows a line, huh?" MacDonald was particularly dismayed by what was happening to the busy Bradenton sky that is so close to Sarasota's.

Sometimes Travis indulges in long diatribes about what is happening to the ecology of Florida, as he does in the passage above; sometimes he makes brief remarks about it in passing, which in a way are just as effective, as he does in *The Scarlet Ruse,* published in 1973, the same year as *The Turquoise Lament.* As he sits alone on the deck of the *Busted Flush* where it is moored at Bahia Mar in Fort Lauderdale, relaxing after a trying day, Travis notes the mixture of impressions that impinge on his senses: "Car lights, boat lights, dock lights, star lights. Sound of traffic and sound of the sea. Smell of salt and smell of hydrocarbons." And, as he is guiding the *Muñequita,* the *Flush's* tender, out of the marina on a foray at sea, he notes in another masterful juxtaposition of opposites, "Teak baked in the sun, and brightwork shimmered, and toilet-paper danced in my wake in the bourbon-colored water of the boat basin" *(Scarlet Ruse* 55-58). Years later, Travis is still conscious of what is happening to his environment. In *The Empty Copper Sea,* first published in 1978, as he and Meyer sit at their ease on the transom of Meyer's old cruiser, the *John Maynard Keynes,* he remarks that they "are looking at the overhead stars faint through the particulate matter that jams the air of the gold coast night and day, never dropping below twenty thousand particles per cubic centimeter, except when a hurricane sweeps it away briefly, blowing it all into somebody else's sky" *(Copper Sea* 25).

Such observations as these typify what Travis—that is, MacDonald—thinks about what is happening to Florida's environment, and they form a sort of thematic refrain running through all of the Travis McGee books as well as others, such as *Flash of Green, Condominium,* and *Barrier Island.* Certainly MacDonald's vigorous and consistent expression of these opinions still wields considerable influence, and may well form one of the lasting bases of his continuing fame.

II

Concerning himself, MacDonald once said, "At the heart of it all I am a moralist . . . because I believe people must accept responsibility for all those acts that affect the lives of others." Perhaps if we had more heroes who were willing to assume this kind of responsibility for their actions we would be living in a better world. Travis McGee is this kind of hero—he is both strong and good, qualities that don't come together very often. It is tempting to compare him with his creator and, on the surface at least, there seem to be many similarities between the two. Does this mean that McGee is a sort of projection of what MacDonald visualizes himself to be, or would like to be, as some commentators seem to think? After all, both men lived in—or at least worked out of—Florida. Both were tall and rangy and had light, slate-blue eyes. Both liked to fish and go boating. Both were attracted to women. Both were serious and dedicated ecologists, with strong, well-articulated feelings about what has been happening to Florida's environment because of man's greed and rapacity. And both were interested in money, and managed to make enough of it to satisfy most of their conceivable needs and wants.

But do all these similarities prove that Travis McGee really is John D. MacDonald's alter ego? I think not. For though MacDonald, like every author, necessarily drew on his own experience in the act of creating his hero, Travis McGee remains essentially a figment of the imagination, not a reality. MacDonald made him real enough to be believable by weaving around him a complex and ingenious network of events and circumstances that are so vivid and convincing that the reader's propensity not to believe in Travis McGee is largely dissipated. As Coleridge said long ago, the quality that determines whether a play—or any fiction—is worth its salt is its capacity to make you temporarily suspend your disbelief in it, at least while you're watching or reading it. This MacDonald certainly managed to do—by creating in Travis an actual person, backed by all the accouterments of reality—a bizarre kind of reality, perhaps, but certainly one that most of us can accept at least temporarily.

Travis emerges full-blown in 1964, in MacDonald's first book about him, *The Deep Blue Good-by*, describing himself as "that big brown loose-jointed boat bum, that pale-eyed, wire-haired girl-seeker, that slayer of small savage fish, that beach-walker, gin-drinker, quip-maker, peace-seeker, iconoclast, disbeliever, argufier, that knuckly, scar tissued reject from a structured society" (*Deep Blue* 28-29). He describes himself in similar terms in the later novels, gradually changing as he grows older—about half as rapidly as the rest of us do. But just to make sure that you keep believing in him, MacDonald inserted additional details about him into each succeeding episode in order to achieve what he called "a kind of *accumulation* of an illusion of wholeness" (Benjamin 140-41). In so doing, MacDonald gradually built up a fairly substantial body of biographical details which go to form the whole man— or as whole a man as a fictional figure can become—whom the reader can conceptualize, though in slightly differing terms as Travis develops and changes.

For example, though we find out very little about Travis's early childhood, there is one passage in *Turquoise Lament* describing his first encounter, as an eleven-year-old boy, with evil, in the form of a huge sow bear, which utterly terrified him and "colored that whole year of my life with a taste of despair" (*Turquoise* 240). This same association of a bear with absolute evil forms the crux of an earlier short story by Mac-

Donald, "The Bear Trap," first published in *Cosmopolitan* in 1955. A little more light is shed on his early youth by some occasional and very sketchy references to an older brother, who was killed while Travis was away at war, probably in Korea. There are a few brief mentions of service in the military, apparently before he went to college, where he played football. Later he played professionally, so he must have kept himself in good physical condition. His career as a tight end was cut short after two years, when a Detroit rookie middle linebacker named DiCosola messed up his legs (*Turquoise* 170). All of these evidences of what Travis's life was like before the series began comprise a substantial—if vague—idea of what formed his personality and general makeup. Obviously, in the thirty or so years previous to his advent in *Deep Blue Good-by*, he had met a lot of people and done many things. In addition to the differing groups of characters who appear in each story, many of whom reappear or are referred to in some of the other books, there is an interesting array of friends who pop up at opportune times when Travis needs them and are never heard of again. Some of these are Leonard Sibelious, a high-powered lawyer who gets him out of trouble in *Long Lavender Look* (1970); Will Lucci, a gangster type with Mafia connections who enables Travis to survive in *Scarlet Ruse* (1973); Maurie Ragna, a Chicago hood who provides some important help in *Fearful Yellow Eye* (1966); Jake Karlo, a talent scout who is able to find a double when needed for Vangie in *Darker Than Amber* (1970); and Dr. Mike Guardina, a lab pathologist whom Travis consulted in *Pale Grey* (1968) (see Benjamin 143). There are also references to important events in Travis's life that never actually happen in any of the books, like Conan Doyle's untold story of the "giant rat of Sumatra." Travis's allusions to unchronicled episodes in his past and the people who participated in them build up the mystery and fascination of what happened to him before he started writing his autobiography in the form of the twenty-one novels in the series—all written from the "I" point of view, that is, Travis's. (For further elaboration on MacDonald's use of previously created or referred to characters and events, see Lane.)

He reveals more and more about himself in each successive book, developing a credible past, a palpable present and a future that you are kept in suspense about so that you continue wanting to know what happens next. To reinforce your belief in McGee even further, he created a setting for him which, though with one side of your mind you are unable to accept it as credible, actually enhances your ability to do so. Home to Travis McGee, as I mentioned above, is the *Busted Flush,* a fabulous houseboat with a sunken bathtub, and many other evidences that Travis lives in unseamanlike luxury. The factual details surrounding the *Busted*

Flush make it credible: it's moored at a marina that actually exists in Fort Lauderdale, the Bahia Mar, in Slip F-18 where there is now a plaque memorializing McGee and MacDonald. In Travis's heyday letters used to arrive addressed to him there, which were duly forwarded to MacDonald's Sarasota home. As described by Travis, the Bahia Mar was often inundated with an engaging variety of perpetually partying beach girls, usually under the supervision of the Alabama Tiger, a neighboring boat-dweller who supplied inexhaustible quantities of beer and food, which kept everyone happy, including Travis.

The usual starting point for Travis's ventures into the outside world of distressed females and crooked connivers was the *Busted Flush* and its environs, as firmly based on actuality as Sherlock Holmes's lodgings at 221B Baker Street in London. But this setting does not imply any identification between McGee and MacDonald, any more than the Baker Street setting implied one between Holmes and Conan Doyle. Both characters are products of their creators' imaginations, though one might argue that MacDonald resembled McGee more closely than the portly and spiritualistic Doyle did the lathe-thin, science-worshipping Holmes. But McGee's variations from MacDonald, like Holmes's from Doyle, far outweigh similarities in both their personalities and their settings. The *Busted Flush*, luxurious as it is, is a far cry as a place to live from Mac-Donald's plush establishment on the shores of Siesta Key on the outskirts of Sarasota. Though it had a tin roof and only one bedroom, it had two stories, was some 2500 air-conditioned square feet in extent, and afforded around its four wide porches and glassed-in sides some extremely expensive and breath-taking views of the Gulf of Mexico and other natural Florida wonders. And despite the inroads of the builders and developers on other parts of Siesta Key, MacDonald managed to maintain an insulating barricade of mangrove swamp, crabgrass and palm trees around the three sides not directly facing on the water.

Unlike Travis, MacDonald was not gregarious and would not have been a good Alabama Tiger party man. He and his wife, Dorothy, both very private people, preferred to entertain their friends in small groups. This is not to say that MacDonald was a recluse. On the contrary, like Travis, he loved to lift a glass with a friend or two when the circumstances were right. He was simply careful about who the friends were with whom he drank and partied, not necessarily because he was over-choosy, but simply, like most people who work hard and long, because he valued his play times highly.

There are many other ways in which the two differ. Most obvious, perhaps, are the circumstances that govern their approaches to the business of making a living. MacDonald spent eight hours a day at his typewriter, perforce living a sedentary life, except for occasional breakouts, when he and his wife would take a world tour or run off to New Zealand for a family outing. Travis, by the very nature of his business, must travel a lot—he's spent time in Mexico, New York, the Bahamas, and various other places in the western hemisphere, as duty calls. He also has to run around in various Florida localities to chase down local clues. When he's working, then, he is moving; when MacDonald was working, he wasn't.

Travis uses, in his Florida forays, a 1936 Rolls Royce named Miss Agnes, which, because of a long-ago accident that inflicted serious damage to her rear end, has been converted into a pickup truck and is painted a "horrid electric blue." Despite her "brutal surgery," she "retains a family knack of going 80 miles an hour all day long in a kind of ghastly silence," to quote Travis (*Deep Blue* 163). But Miss Agnes did not suit MacDonald as a mode of travel at all—he drove a plushly equipped but undistinguished-looking Dodge van, and was known to remark that "I wouldn't drive that damn car of Travis's around the block."

Also connected with their manner of making their way in the world is their physical condition. Travis has to be rugged, tough and agile in order to deal with the many and various villains who come his way. People like Boone Waxwell, the disagreeable muscleman of *Bright Orange for the Shroud*, the mountainous Ans Terry of *Darker Than Amber*, ex-pug King Sturnevan of *The Long Lavender Look*, and the lithe but oh so nasty Freddy Van Harn of *The Dreadful Lemon Sky* are only a few among that unsavory gang of men of enormous guile and power whom Travis somehow manages to vanquish. He has to be a man of strength and action, then, an athlete who must keep himself in peak physical shape pretty much all the time. And even though we watch him age as the years go by, and some of his lightning-like reactions get a little slower and the whip of his punch gets a little less lethal, he still is fundamentally a creature who must depend heavily on his physical strength to survive.

MacDonald, again, obviously did not. And though he was by no means another Nero Wolfe, his efforts to keep his body in reasonably good shape were like those of the rest of us. He fished, swam, sailed, and managed to stay fairly trim. He may even have played tennis or jogged, at one time or another. But he was not an exceptionally active man. When he was still in high school, he suffered a long and serious illness from which he almost did not recover. He had to stay in bed for nearly a year, much of it spent reading or listening to his mother read to him when he tired. The experience changed him. According to his own account, it resulted in his becoming a much more avid reader than he had been before, and much less interested in physical activity.

There are other differences between McGee and MacDonald, perhaps less fundamental than that between their basic orientations toward the physical aspects of life. McGee is a receptive entertainer of errant females, and most often performs in this function as part of his legitimate business as a salvage expert. On occasion he finds himself in bed with one or the other of them, either by accident or design. The details of what happens on these occasions, always described in good taste, provide welcome relief from the sometimes grim realities of his struggles against the forces of evil. They also afford opportunities for MacDonald to dilate on the mental, physical and moral attributes of many differing types and sizes of women, a subject of which he never seems to weary. But McGee's amatory propensities have nothing apparent to do with MacDonald's own experience; he lived with the same wife he married in 1938 until he died in 1986. His own reactions to a rather stupid question concerning the rich variations in McGee's sex life, as compared to his own, he considered to be one of his "better comments": "DaVinci painted the Last Supper and he didn't get a bite to eat."

Which leaves us with some interesting speculations about what the relationship is or should be between an author and the hero he works hard to create. In a series as long and detailed as the stories about Travis McGee there must be a constant intermingling of the author's experience and his imagination. In some ways Travis is MacDonald; in others he isn't. MacDonald himself acknowledged that Travis often serves as his mouthpiece, and of course he does, perhaps to an even greater extent than MacDonald realized. As someone he liked and admired, he couldn't have McGee saying and thinking things he wouldn't say and think himself. As MacDonald said of this relationship,

If we're talking about a social, ecological, ruin-the-environment area, such as when, for example, in *The Turquoise Lament* . . . he is flying into Sarasota and remarks on the stacks of the mighty Borden Company, up in Bradenton, and says it's known locally as the place where Elsie the Cow coughed herself to death—Why not? That's my comment as well as his. . . . As long as I'm making him a hero, it would be rather grotesque for me to give him an opinion with which I was at odds, like, "Hooray for mighty Borden—they're improving the tax base!"

In personal matters, such as women, on the other hand, Travis is his own man. Or clothes—Travis might wear things that MacDonald wouldn't be caught dead in, and vice versa. The Swedish yachting cap that MacDonald so often had himself photographed in, for example—certainly McGee would reject it out of hand as much too prissy. And he would never veil his keen, flat, light-blue eyes with the huge dark sunglasses that MacDonald often retreated behind. He goes for scruffy shirts and plain bluejeans, not the elegant mixture of Miami tourist and Sarasota beach bum that MacDonald affected, at least in public. On the other hand, as I mentioned above, MacDonald would have no time for Miss Agnes, the Rolls Royce pickup truck, nor would he choose the *Busted Flush* as his mode of water transport. For him these indications of the carefree bachelor life were "a bit of flamboyance on one's exterior" that he can do without. For they mean that "one becomes the observed rather than the observer," and "I prefer to watch and listen and observe; therefore I have a minimum of flamboyance in my personal life because it would obscure—or make more difficult—my function of people-watching" which "is where the stuff comes from for books."

MacDonald assumed, then, the position of the observer rather than the observed, the innocuous bystander who faded into the crowd so that he could gaze steadily on the passing scene and record it for later use in his fiction. This is the time-honored guise of most storytellers, and though it doesn't necessarily fit MacDonald all of the time, his appearance and behavior generally were inconspicuous. But much the same—except for a few irregularities—can be said about Travis. The fact that Travis always tells his stories in the first person lends all the more credibility to the assumption that he is indeed MacDonald. But actually he could be anybody, as long as he and his creator are reasonably congenial with each other. Every writer, MacDonald concluded, "is going to put into the mouths of the people he wants you to respect opinions that he thinks are respectable. It's that simple. That doesn't mean that he's one's mouthpiece in everything he says and everything he does."

I think this is as valid a summation as we can come to of MacDonald's own attitude toward Travis McGee. He liked him. He respected him. Maybe he even envied him a little—don't we all? But he certainly was not McGee, nor would he want to be. MacDonald was his own man, and so is his hero, and never, as somebody said long ago about East and West, the twain shall meet. But, unlike East and West, they're not very far apart much of the time about a great many things. One of the fascinations in reading about Travis McGee is that there is so much of John D. MacDonald in him, because MacDonald himself was a very complex and interesting person indeed, about whom much remains to be studied and discovered.

Works Cited

Note: All unattributed quotes come from personal conversations and interviews from the 1960s until JDM's death in 1986.

Benjamin, David A. "John D. MacDonald and the Life and Death of the Mythic Hero." Diss. Harvard University, 1977.

Lane, Thomas D. "Faulkner and MacDonald: Ending Well." *JDM Bibliophile* 58 (Dec. 1996).

MacDonald, John D. *Bright Orange for the Shroud*. Greenwich: Fawcett Gold Medal, 1965.

——. *The Deep Blue Good-by*. New York: Fawcett Gold Medal, 1964.

——. *The Empty Copper Sea*. Philadelphia: Lippincott, 1978.

——. *The Scarlet Ruse*. Greenwich: Fawcett Gold Medal, 1973.

——. *The Turquoise Lament*. Greenwich: Fawcett Gold Medal, 1973.

3

Florida's Crime and Detective Fiction through 1945

Bill Brubaker

In the national publishing scene of the 1930s, crime and detective fiction had grown into two relatively distinct conventions: those of the puzzle-mystery gent detective and the hard-boiled P.I. The puzzle-mystery traces itself from the Edgar Allan Poe tales of the superlogician Dupin through the British adaptation in Arthur Conan Doyle's Sherlock Holmes stories to its American rebirth among such writers as Melville Davisson Post, S. S. Van Dine, Rex Stout, and Ellery Queen. Among these, Rex Stout's adaptation reflects a fairly characteristic nativist reshaping—the obese and industrially exempt Nero Wolfe engages in elite penthouse pleasures of orchid cultivation while confidant Archie Goodwin does the legwork; and this organization of effort into roles distinguishing brain/body, management/labor appears elsewhere. The tough-guy school in the lineage of *Black Mask* magazine introduced a more socially marginalized solitary male P.I. in an impersonal and criminally tainted urban environment, as in the Continental Op's efforts to survive in the Poisonville of Dashiell Hammett's *Red Harvest* (1929) and Raymond Chandler's vision of Philip Marlowe's peril in the mean Los Angeles streets. The development of series imprints such as the Crime Club of Doubleday, Doran and Red Badge of Dodd, Mead helped define these categories by promulgating the fiction their editors identified as having the right stuff. A Dodd, Mead promotion of 1936 suggests the significance of series imprints in modeling the genre; their Red Badge competition offered a $2,000 prize and a book contract for the best submission written to editorial requirements ("Are You Planning a Murder").

While several Florida mysteries of the 1930s do fall into these confirmed categories, earlier novels reflect the plasticity of developing conventions, particularly those frontier and romance narratives from 1895 to 1920 by writers unconscious of themselves as writing detective fiction but aware of the utility of organizing stories around mysterious deaths

31

and the resolving acts of informal detectives. Later Florida mysteries of the 1920s show greater formal awareness of narrative convention and are marked by a gothic feeling for the mysterious and supernatural that assumes a local coloring. They tell stories about ghostly mansions, tainted legendary wealth, a Florida land and sea so threatening in their tropical natures and alien to human experience and understanding as to seem uncanny. Others seek to merge the detective's pursuit of justice with romantic love interest; and this impulse continues even in tough-guy novels from 1930 to 1945 in which love story and tough-guy story merge either by metamorphoses of the solitary male detective and the femme fatale into truer receptive selves (seeming is not being) or by introducing the tough-guy as a paternalistic, soft-hearted uncle to a romantic pair. Most notably, whatever the genre variation, these Florida crime and detective novels seek to moderate the misogyny and loneliness of the tough-guy by bringing him into human community.

In their representation of Florida, these authors commanded an authenticity of detail relative to their residential experience, from the vagueness of geography in the British author Bessie Marchant's *The Secret of the Everglades* (1902) to the rich cultural and material detail of cypress-mill life on the Suwanee as Baynard Kendrick knew it first hand in *Death beyond the Go-Thru* (1938). Often, the sense of place reflects the writer's contact with an older though still identifiable Florida: the West Palm Beach of Carroll John Daly's *The Hidden Hand* (1929), where public park games of horseshoes distinguish its working/middle class identity from the moneyed class of Palm Beach; the road-work-is-never-done replacement of single-lane brick highways in favor of broader macadam in Baynard Kendrick's *Blood on Lake Louisa* (1934); the Key West Sloppy Joe's bar (albeit of different street address) in Jonathan Latimer's *The Dead Don't Care* (1938); the abrupt elevation from streets onto Miami drawbridges threatening auto undercarriages in Sturges Mason Schley's *Dr. Toby Finds Murder* (1941).

Uniformly, in the novels considered here, the image of Florida is that of hollow, ahistorical space assuming the shapes humans struggle to give it. Most of these writers map the state as an empty shell—a coastal outline marked by rail and highways but a shadowy unknown interior. Their map starts at Jacksonville and traces the peninsula to Miami and the Keys, including fine detail of Florida Bay and the Dry Tortugas, and runs northward to Tampa and more vaguely to the Suwanee River, from whence highways are untrustworthy and make no connection with Tallahassee. For the criminal class—whether the pirates and wreckers of the real and legendary past or the smugglers and crime syndicates of more recent time—Florida is a sandy beach, newly opened territory, a civic vacancy where you can run and you can hide. For the more law-abiding, Florida is empty land developed into pleasure palaces made habitable by outside wealth and entrepreneurial vigor in an uncertainly sustaining and sometimes threatening physical environment. For what seems passive empty nature also has inner agency, a capacity for destruction, demonstrated in floods, lightning, and hurricane season. As Albert Payson Terhune observes in a prose-poem on its geological past, modern Florida rests upon the work of the coral worm, whose creation of reefs nurtures mangrove-land emergence but also smashes ship keels (Foreword, *Black Caesar's Clan*). The sense of the cyclic, creating/decaying natural order—profligate flowering growth and black organic decay—runs through these texts as a motif complementing stories of human disorder; and the pathetic fallacy occurs in an uglier version as cynic nature.

Against these images of Florida space, the story of greatest concern is the control and rightful preservation of wealth. It is the central act of these novels: murder as an agent of conspiracies against wealth by the criminal class or alien conspirators, or the looting of wealth by corrupt members of the moneyed class (dissolute kin, prodigal sons, corporate officers). The social fractures of racial segregation and economic depression suffered elsewhere make little appearance in these Florida stories. Benign paternalism characterizes black-white relations in Eric Levison's three Jacksonville novels (1920, 1921), Mignon Eberhart's *Unidentified Woman* (1943), and Lee Thayer's *Five Bullets* (1944). The discontent Baynard Kendrick observes among sawmill laborers in *Death Beyond the Go-Thru* offers an exceptional view of 1930s hard times. In contrast, the external threat to Florida during World War II found place in several novels about foreign plots to siphon wealth toward fascist powers, develop refueling stations for axis submarines, or introduce saboteurs among refugees.

II

In the early juvenile and romance fiction considered here, sentimentality and uplift ameliorate the reality of crime and qualify their authors' adaptations of detective fiction convention. Wilmer Ely's Florida Boy Chums series gives us a Charley West and friends who comprise in microcosm the social system within which boys can become successful men (a patriarchial mentor, the likely boy-apprentice Charley, his underclass crew—one white, one black—of buddy-workers). In *The Boy Chums Cruising in Florida Waters* (1914) Charley enters the fishing business at Clearwater; and Ely assigns to him the word "detective" when the Chums find a fisherman murdered by the Hunter gang, who threaten the success of the fishing industry; but in a few chapters the Chums take care of the Hunter gang and move on to other adventure-tests of equal value toward certifying their development of adult power.

The village of Opie Read's romance *On the Suwanee River* (1895) demonstrates frontier extremes—brawling land speculation, a barroom murder, and born-again piety; but the Reverend (detective) Avery's efforts to determine the truth of the rumors that Rose Sibley is a murderess find closure in proof of their falsity (her "murdered" boyfriend actually committed suicide in her presence) and the happy betrothal of detective and suspect. In Bessie Marchant's weeper *The Secret of the Everglades* (1902) James Kavanaugh may have murdered his business partner John Osney and certainly inflicts suffering on the Osney family; but Kavanaugh dies in an accidental death of poetic justice and Osney is restored not from the tomb but Seminole captivity. In Edward H. Hurst's *Mystery Island* (1907) the drunken Lindsay flees unfaithful Effie by sailing from Tampa only to shipwreck and wander into an Everglades hunting camp. There he falls in love with Muriel and as detective finds the murderer of her father in Carrington, who in remorse conveniently commits suicide.

Although these narratives may *seem* like detective fiction, their treatment of crime promotes evasion: the murdered aren't murdered (not even certifiably dead), those deserving punishment commit suicide, it was all a misunderstanding (wasn't it?), and moral authority can transform the fallen world. In contrast, valid detective fiction persuades us of the intransigence and immanence of evil held at bay for the time being in narrative closures, of the inner kinship of tainted mirrored selves displayed by detective protagonists and criminal antagonists.

Nevertheless, what survives from these early Florida novels is the detective as male apprentice-at-life, the engagement with crime as quest, and the woman as ambiguous locus of crime and power. Certain Florida crime novels of the second and third decades continued to develop narratives in which lovers identify each other and their true interests in detective quests. Two novels of 1922, Absalom Martin's *Kastle Krags: A Story of Mystery* and Albert Payson Terhune's *Black Caesar's Clan*, take up Florida legends of ill-gotten treasure hordes, their continuing effect upon powerful families, and the purging influence of love. In *Kastle Krags* the narrator Kildare is a graduate teaching assistant in biology at the state university who takes a summer job as overseer of hunting grounds on the Grover Nealman estate. Nealman's brooding mansion overlooks the meeting of the Ochakee (the Suwanee?) with the Gulf of Mexico; living with him is the butler Florey and Nealman's niece Edith, perhaps innocent, perhaps tainted. Martin develops gothic themes: the identity of mysterious forest, mansion, and inhabitant; the conflict of supernaturalism with the science of the redeeming biology grad student. The murder of a houseguest switches Kildare into the informal detective mode; he solves a cryptogram, discovers a sunken treasure horde in the harbor before the house, determines its source in a royal fratricide of Spanish colonial history connected with the Nealman genealogy, and uncovers the butler Florey (yes, the butler did it) as a murderous descendant of a branch of the family seeking to regain control of its wealth. Kildare restores vigor to the gene pool by marrying the surviving (and innocent) heiress Edith and giving Kastle Krags a spiritual renovation of "homely charm and cheer" (Martin 267).

Terhune's novel takes up the Florida legend of the escaped slave Black Caesar and his pirate treasure; and the efforts of the Secret Service agent Gavin Brice, like those of Absalom Martin's Kildare, end in a wealthy marriage. However, Terhune's treatment of the Miami and Keys setting offers a more recognizable Florida. The opening chapter places Gavin Brice undercover as a tourist in a public park listening to William Jennings Bryan sermonize on the theme of Florida realty. The Standish family wealth comes from its citrus corporation which is threatened within by one of its officers, Rodney Hade. On corporation property Hade has recovered a million 1804 Black Caesar silver dollars now worth $3,000 each. Gavin perseveres against Hade, whom Gavin recognizes as a World War I turncoat; shields the interests of the Standish family and state and federal treasuries; and acquires blond Claire Standish.

Octavus Roy Cohen's *Child of Evil* (1936) associates sex with death in the story of the redneck fundamentalist Jeff Butler's preoccupation with the sexuality of Kay Forrest. The setting is Cathedral Gardens, a tourist development of the Hamilton family displaying botanical gardens and natural springs. There a New York City art photographer is engaged in a series of nude studies of the beautiful young woman. Jeff Butler's prurient peeping and moral condemnation manifest the conflict between rural Florida conservatism and the liberal moneyed pleasure culture of northern tourists and developers. Kay is forced into a marriage by the violent local boy Kirk Reynolds when on a date she witnesses him commit murder during a traffic confrontation. In his failure to consummate the marriage with Kay but his retention of the hairdresser Sadie Henkel as mistress, the narrative provides a further example of male sexual confusion; and it seems appropriate that Kirk becomes Jeff's murder victim. In closure, the resistance of the Cathedral Gardens developer's son Barney to further acts of violence defines him as Kay's true advocate and natural lover. In *Child of Evil* Cohen finds gothic energy in the demonic provincial social environment that threatens the new Adam and Eve in their modern Florida garden.

Both Octavus Roy Cohen and Theodore Pratt were prolific writers of series detective fiction, crime fiction, and other trade-fiction novels. Though Cohen's *Child of Evil* is anomalous in his use of a Florida setting, *Mercy Island* (1941) reflects Pratt's adoption of the state as residence; and various sites appear as settings in Pratt's Anthony Adams puzzle-mysteries as well as his historical novels. In *Mercy Island* lawyer Warren Ramsay seizes control of Captain Lowe's boat and runs it aground in pursuit of his wife Leslie's hooked tarpon. That circumstance maroons the crew, Warren and Leslie Ramsay, and their friend Clay Foster on an isolated Keys island, where they discover the self-sufficient squatter Richard Powell. Claire is impressed by this young-old man's inner peace and the simple pattern of his life, which has found organic connection with such a beautiful but dangerous place. When Ramsay discovers that Powell is a physician who fled prosecution for a mercy-killing, he insists upon the fugitive's return to the mainland to stand trial (with himself as the defense attorney in yet another courtroom success). While they seek to repair the damaged boat, Ramsay and Clay Foster enter a sexual competition for Claire, who has blossomed into strength and knowledge in contact with the exiled doctor. The lawyer's predatory behaviors make him the fitting victim of a crocodile attack; and the boat crew and the lovers Claire and Clay leave the benign Jehovah-doctor to reign in this terrible Florida Eden.

III

Detective novels by Earl Derr Biggers, Eric Levison, and Carroll John Daly trace out the diminishing appropriation of sentimental romance and the developing centrality of hard-boiled sensibility. Biggers hadn't yet found his series character Charlie Chan when he conceived of the insurance detective Richard Minot of *Love Insurance* (1914), who travels by rail to Florida to oversee a Lloyd's of London contract ensuring the marriage of Lord Harrowby to the American heiress Cynthia Meyrick. The writer's descriptions of "San Marco" seem certainly to point to St. Augustine as his model, and Twainian satire dominates his approach to its winter visitors. The magnet of wealth attracts a wonderfully caricatured body of wannabe's and phonies: Minot's old college chum-turned-gigolo-writer of smart dinner repartee for his current benefactress; the advertising booster Henry Trimmer's use of sandwich boards to denounce the fraudulent Lord Harrowby; tabloid journalists; and the appearance of the real George Harrowby, who has long rejected his title and assimilated to American culture as a Chicago automaker.

Minot sees Cynthia as an innocent or conspirator; his conflict between love and duty becomes characteristic of the relation between many detectives and their ladies; and the cynical tone of the novel otherwise echoes the deflating realism of hard-boiled style.

Eric Levison's three Jacksonville novels establish the series character Dr. Edward Lester, whose life model was the physician Herrman H. Harris, the dedicatee of *Hidden Eyes* (1920). Dr. Lester plays the mentor to the lesser, mostly younger men who make use of the doctor's remote, brainy analysis to solve crimes against wealthy self-made Jacksonville bankers or industrialists. The premise of *Hidden Eyes* seems shaky—that realtor Morton Ralby has planted a post-hypnotic suggestion leading the physics major Halvey Thornton to rob a bank. *The Eye Witness* (1921) makes clearest use of the mentor-apprentice relationship as Dr. Lester helps Secret Service agent Courtney Gillian decode criminal letters and preserve Jacksonville banks (and the federal system) against counterfeiters. In each of these novels, including *Ashes of Evidence* (1921), the closures exculpate promising young men who marry and enter adult life with unsentimentalized women. Although his introduction of local detail may pique the reader, regrettably Levison's flatly efficient style does not sustain that interest.

The fifth of Carroll John Daly's detective novels, *The Hidden Hand* (1929), gives us Race Williams, a P.I. who promotes his detective skills as a small entrepreneur independent of corporate or civil authority. This disaffiliation and his embarrassment about his underclass origins distinguish him from such elite agency ops as Biggers's Richard Minot or Levison's Courtney Gillian. Even so, his subcontracting of services to the wealthy, avuncular, and loquacious Howard Quincy Travers places Race Williams under the probative judgment of an elite senior male whom Race wishes to please; and his relation to the ambiguous Tina Sears ultimately draws Race to the reward of the woman's love in her true identity as Tina King, daughter of wealth. Employed by Travers to use his toughness and weapon accuracy to destroy the Hidden Hand gang, Race travels by ship to Miami. There the special operative Gregory Ford has also been hired by the state's attorney in Tallahassee to rid Florida of the shadowy group. Daly's command of crime argot and the detail of streets and suburbs proves persuasive; it's not, however, the representation of objective reality that is central to Daly's success in this novel, since the dark interiors of ship's cabins, Miami warehouses, abandoned houses, fast cars, and Palm Beach mansions situate all the action and provide the objective correlative to Race's persistent inner confusion, auditory hallucinations, and paranoia. Characters' names echo patronymic greatness and power in politics and business: Howard

Quincy Travers, Gregory Ford, Tina Sears. The conspirators Race seeks have legendary criminal histories conferring such nicknames of archetypal malice as the gas man and the giant Swede. Race's sequential tracking and execution of the Hidden Hand conspirators provide the episodic order of the novel; and the detective is forever on dark stairways, in other rooms, hallways, sensing—like the child who fears the ubiquity and omniscience of the parent—that the Hidden Hand is eminently *there* and sees, knows his thoughts and movements. And it's true, and Race murders the father and gets the wealthy daughter, and this Howard Quincy Travers whom the detective has named informally Old Benevolence *is* in fact THE HIDDEN HAND (never mind H.Q.T.'s death confession of desire to purge his guilt from having made a criminal "Frankenstein's monster") (Daly 315).

IV

Walking from Daly's marvelous house of comic-book detective fiction to puzzle mysteries and cozies takes hardly any time but requires an abrupt turn into a nice suburb where the architecture is uniform, no rusted jalopies are permitted, and in a well appointed bungalow readers are invited into Parlor A or Parlor B. If Parlor A, listen to a tweedy talking head who synthesizes the teaching method of Socrates and the logic of Aristotle. If Parlor B, it's sherry with a slightly dotty lady who's in command of terrific gossip.

Theodore Pratt's *Murder Goes in a Trailer* (1937) gives us Lord Peter Wimsey–like Anthony Adams and his man Thurber. Pratt's dedication observes his own sometime manner of living in a Delray Beach trailer park; and his detail generates a certain humor by placing the mystery in a swishy Palm Beach County trailer park where the perquisites and eccentricities of the retired wealthy must be maintained. (Anthony Adams lives undercover in one, his man Thurber in another Aeroyacht). Aside from that, there's not much action—everybody despised the victim General Warner for good cause (including the physician brother who gassed him)—and the novel takes its shape from a series of interviews with suspects and a formal denouement by the riddlemeister.

Rufus King, Canadian by birth and Floridian by choice, set his four Lieutenant Valcour novels in Miami, Keys, and Caribbean settings. Although in the bloodless tradition of the superior, detached puzzle-mystery detective (despite his ID as a New York City police detective), Valcour receives permission from his creator to move around. Somewhat. *Murder Masks Miami* (1939) takes up the plight of the New York City and Palm Beach socialite Mrs. Justin Waring, whose widowhood has placed her in the prospect of hard times from which she hopes to extricate herself by marrying off her daughter, Sophrina. Meanwhile she is dependent upon her sister-in-law, Theodessa, who dies in the presence of Valcour and companion Constance, accused of murder by the victim's last words. Or was the "she" Mrs. Justin Waring's dissolute son Robert dressed as a woman? King's treatment of Miami Beach culture generates fragile Noel Coward humor, though the opening scene is a howler—the Hollywood mogul Mr. Lipkovitz enters a beach cabana expecting an assignation with Lola, Robert Waring's curb-service girlfriend. Regrettably, Valcour quits moving and starts interviewing.

Two cosies—Mignon G. Eberhart's *Unidentified Woman* (1943) and Lee Thayer's *Five Bullets* (1944)—tell stories of mature women whose comfortable lives have been altered by the deaths of strong males; and these mysteries by women authors have an inviting fullness of detail and characterization. Eberhart's Victoria Steane might well be daughter by affinity and setting of one of the Jacksonville writer Eric Levison's promising young men saved for marriage and success by the detective work of Dr. Edward Lester. The Steane estate sits on the St. Johns River in the neighborhood of Jacksonville, "Ponte Verde" (Ponte Vedra Beach?), and "Camp Blakoe" (Camp Blanding?); and the time is the months before the entry into World War II. The decease of Victoria's father leaves her heiress to the Steane papermill fortune but also the center of a family struggle for its control. Only recently having been acquitted of murder in the suspicious drowning of the interim Steane CEO, Victoria will marry Michael Bayne. Eberhart's themes—summer country-house pleasures of the old Florida elite, spy hysteria, rapid development of the officer corps and military infrastructure, sudden money for the privileged as well as the working class who crowd local towns—make this a significant record of time and place; and the writer's investing these energies in the male who subverts and the male who defends Victoria's interest gives the narrative a persuasive structure.

Lee Thayer's *Five Bullets* takes its setting in "Sweetwater College" on a pretty lake (Rollins College?) in the Florida lake country close to Tavares and Eustis and a few hours drive from "Homalusa (Homosassa?) Spring." The narrator, Zingara Hartley, is visiting her old friend Rowena, whose developer-husband's death and the failure of a promising housing development have led Rowena to open a tourist-boarding house. There Zingara meets German refugees, Professor Liebling and student Knopf. In one of Professor Liebling's psychology experiments, Rowena's son Douglas accidentally kills fellow student (but personal enemy) Ted Rockwell. Zingara invites Thayer's series detective, Peter Clancy, to find the real murderer; and the writer's handling of the complexities of personality, relationships, and motive give the narrative a charming richness. Adding to this fullness are details of wartime shortages and rationing, small-town class differences, and a treatment of black-white relationships that neither condescends nor sentimentalizes. Unfortunately, the two final chapters seem forced in their development of a foreign conspiracy behind local events (realtor Bergenstein is actually Colonel August Heimlich) and the writer's point of view shifts from Zingara's delightful common sense and social sensitivity to Peter Clancy's suave heroics. But Thayer's feel for the details of narrow yet complex small-college and Florida town culture is dead on and evokes a lost, provincial innocence.

V

Hard-boiled 1930s and 1940s Florida detective fiction collects its toughest guys in novels by Wesley Price, Whitman Chambers, and Jack DeWitt. Each introduces hostile natural settings (a Caribbean island, the stormy Dry Tortugas, a Keys hurricane) that test the physical virtue of detective heroes.

Price's indebtedness to Dashiell Hammett echoes constantly in *Death Is a Stowaway* (1933). The solitary Miami PD detective James Wick takes no emotional prisoners; and as with Sam Spade's obligation to his murdered partner Miles Archer, the premise of Wick's dogged pursuit of whoever is killing all the guests on the yacht Carib is professional loyalty to the first victim, Wick's old friend Francis X. Moloy, murdered trying to serve a warrant and last seen dressed in snappy Florida style with "tan-and-white shoes, brown striped flannels, and a straw hat the color of a pale egg yolk" (Price 13). The group aboard the Carib relate to the elite Theodore Cogswell as a quasi-family, just as Gutman's adherents relate to him. Like Hammett's characters, they are engaged in an obsessive search for a mythic treasure, the history of which is recounted in a manner like that of the falcon. Like Sam Spade, Wick coaxes information from others through shrewd analysis of words and body language and shows facility for sardonic comebacks, as when he chides Cogswell's alcoholic son Charlie: "Your dad's a great kidder. He ought to be arrested for impairing the intelligence of minors." Miss Chasten— Cogswell's girlfriend and actually the stripper Ada La Marr—repeats Bridget O'Shaughnessy's request of Spade to Wick: "Be kind" (Price 212, 220). Price's rather utilitarian style can nonetheless strike fire; and the narrative succeeds generally in uniting action, character, and clue except for a point of view shift to journalist Eddie Briggs, which the author needed for backwriting to make the closure work.

A spy conspiracy draws the attention of Whitman Chambers in *Dry Tortugas* (1940). In the Key West bar Tiny's Cantina, the series character and Miami journalist Jack Eldridge meets his friends George Bell, a "redheaded cocky attorney," and Dodd Zerker, "one of the most famous novelists in the country" (Chambers 1, 5). Also present are gigolo Peter Channing with Lilith Patterson Pordo, whose yacht sits in Key West harbor and whose Bund-advocate husband, Levot Pordo, is under investigation by the Dies Committee. Musicians Sandra and Tommy Lawrence enter, seeking work. Channing's murder and Eldridge's lust for Sandra draw the journalist-detective into the efforts of federal agents to thwart international weapons sales at the Dry Tortugas. This is real tough-guy stuff, with laconic male talk, adultery, bloody assaults, knifings, and murders single and multiple; and the characters are mostly engaged in violent private quests for sex, money, and success. Chambers's style is direct, focused, and persuasively vernacular, however implausible his hero's physical endurance may sometimes be. Curiously enough, an idealistic aspect of Jack Eldridge's personality unites his efforts—his schoolboy faith in the possibility of Sandra's love—and their love affair starts in just the right way, with the two parked at night on a Key West jetty.

Jack DeWitt's *Murder on Shark Island* (1941) narrates the effort of a German spy ring in south Florida to silence Baron von Lichten, an anti-Nazi refugee who has sought entry into the United States through Cuba. The P.I. Clint Walsh oftens finds himself slipping into foul language; has clubby, hairy fingers; and feels defensively underclass in elite company. Though drawn in the tough-guy mode, Clint's affection for his wife, Letty, reveals his heart of gold. Undercover as tourists they accompany the baron's daughter Anna to Shark Island. Despite his stereotyping of the German nasties and Cuban smugglers, DeWitt's treatment of commercial fishermen and their lifestyle rings true. The hook-armed fisherman Stub Watkins has become an alcoholic because of his injury and the economic losses he has suffered; he alternates between stupor and activity; his catharsis of anger in avenging the murder of his daughter and her simple home funeral are modestly drawn. So is Tom Kelly's mother, who takes simple pleasure in the flowers and garden her self-providence delivers. A long history of smuggling engages the fishermen as one of the activities of their struggle to survive; what they want most of all is to be left alone by outsiders, including federal authority. It's appropriate, therefore, that the conspiracy Clint uncovers should be organized by Commodore Fairhaven, whose spy disguise has been that of developer seeking to buy up the island and install tract housing while at the same time installing a fuel depot facility for submarines and selectively murdering the politically incorrect among the aliens smuggled by the fishermen.

Novels by Jonathan Latimer, Sturges Mason Schley, Courtney Riley Cooper, Raymond Knotts, and Brett Halliday offer softer boiled heroes. Collectively, these detectives have social refinement if not respectable profession. The crimes they investigate bring them into contact with wealthy south Florida families whose difficult kids are implicated as agents or victims in efforts to extort wealth. In *The Dead Don't Care* (1938), Jonathan Latimer removed his series character, Chicago P.I. William Crane, to Miami and the Keys to take advantage of the setting the author knew well from his residence on Key West (1935-1936). Crane's paternalistic mentor Colonel Black has assigned him to protect Camelia and Penn Essex, who has received death threats; but it is the tanned summer-girl Camelia who is kidnapped and held for ransom. For Crane, Florida is a puzzle. The Essex mansion on Marathon seems like a white marble castle and a prison. Flamingos frighten him. The interior of a Miami nightclub looks like a real tropical garden; and real tropical spaces—the flowering abundance of Key West and its sunsets—have the gaudy artificiality of Samuel Goldwyn technicolor films. These conflicted feelings come to focus in his attraction to the femme fatale Imago Paraguay, whose ambiguous sexual orientation and layered ethnicity (Cuban, Mayan) lead the two into the most direct sex scene of these novels and Crane's horror in awaking with Imago's corpse in a closed-room murder. In time, Crane understands that young Penn has set up a kidnap-ruse without his sister's knowledge to extort money from their guardian Major Eastcomb; and Camelia is rescued from the cruiser where thugs hold her.

In *Dr. Toby Finds Murder* (1941), Sturges Mason Schley places his psychiatrist Quentin Toby in Miami, where he is to marry interior decorator Olive Palmer after she has completed the renovation of the Baldrich house. Olive's sympathy for Janice, suffering as daughter in a dysfunctional family, draws Dr. Toby's interest to the efforts of Dr. Walter Best to care for the ill parents. A murder attempt upon Dr. Toby's friend Jack La Master and the murder of Janice push the psychiatrist detective into an investigation of the Baldrich past. Schley's success lies in deep characterization and shifting narrative point of view. Perhaps Dr. Toby's training as physician and psychiatrist accounts for his complexity: he possesses scientific insight, common sense without dogmatism, and decent human pity unswerved by sentimentality. Shifting the narrative point of view reveals the mindset of distinct characters so that what is narrowly a *clue* in less competent writing firmly indexes history and personality. For example, Janice's obsessive reading of *Hamlet* becomes an act that reflects her sense of parental betrayal and disharmony. Schley's Miami is objectively detailed in docks, waterside restaurants, rough drawbridges, the old fisherman Miller, and the Miami horse trainer Siesta Smith. Having developed the secret past of his characters so successfully, Schley serves only current history by tacking on the fascist conspiracy that has precipitated the Baldrich terminal illness.

An anomalous book in his career, Courtney Riley Cooper's *Action in Diamonds* (1942) benefits from the investigative research characteristic of his many popularized accounts of the FBI, circuses, Alaska travel, the gold rush, prostitution, and famous criminals; for his detective novel makes a virtually documentary use of how the FBI organizes its fieldwork. *Action*'s hero is lawyer and FBI school grad Phil McNally who hopes to be accepted as an agent under the mentoring of the retired bureau officer John Justin. Meanwhile McNally captains the *Tarpon Queen* out of Everglades City, and in that capacity is chartered by Hallie Kent to take her to her jewel merchant father's yacht on Whitewater Bay. Cooper's writing benefits from its continuing authenticity of local detail, as exemplified in McNally's technique of splashing water on a reel to retard backlash and wrapping line under a milk bottle to mark the strike of tarpons. McNally falls in love with Hallie, who may have participated in a jewel heist carried out by a criminal ring including her father; and the narrative develops the inner collapse of the conspiracy through betrayals and murders. Like Schley, Cooper makes effective use of shifting narrative point of view, and Hallie Kent's meditations upon physical nature are striking examples of the recurrent view in these novels of Florida space as a creating/decaying continuum of beautiful surface overlying dark energies (Cooper 31, 250).

Perhaps Raymond Knotts knew *The Dead Don't Care* since the premise of his *And the Deep Blue Sea* (1944) is almost precisely that of Jonathan Latimer's novel: wastrels Judie and Orring decide to extort money from their rich dad, Breckinridge Polk, through a kidnap ruse that displays Murphy's Law when a wandering depression becomes a hurricane that blows into Miami and sinks Orring's escape cruiser, which leads Orring to steal a neighboring yacht and kill its owner during a boat theft, which draws inept Orring into a vain coverup attempt on the life of his sister. The newspaperman detective Jim Hale manages to piece all this out and along the way encounter some rather sharply drawn types: Congresswoman Cayples, who manages to transform political threats into capital; the self-absorbed singer Velma Martine; and the protofeminist Marcia Lansing. It's an interesting twist when Raymond Knotts lets his detective journalist understands what the police don't—that the criminal pasts of neighbor Kelrayne, chauffeur Pavich, and millionaire Quillimire are red herrings; and, of course, the whole thing proves an exclusive for Jim Hale's Chicago paper.

Under the pseudonym of Brett Halliday, Davis Dresser's Michael Shayne mysteries became a self-perpetuating industry of novels written by others after 1958 (Gardner, Hubin). The first Shayne novel *Dividend on Death* (1939) establishes Miami as the most recurrent setting of the 1940s novels. Mapped with surface accuracy, Halliday's city serves as a commodified tropical site of moneyed prey and criminal predators; and Shayne's own interest in money identifies him as true cohort. The P.I. has a men's mag feeling for good dress, Martell and Hennessy cognac, art, culture; inside knowledge of the connections between city politics and crime; and a P.I.'s animosity to police authority as embodied in the chief of detectives, Peter Painter. Preferring pleasure to pain, Shayne can deal violence as well as take it, when necessary, and has remarkable recuperative powers. He's also a lanky, red-haired innate bachelor who marries the nice (wealthy) girl, Phyllis Brighton, of *Dividend* after solving the conspiracy against her family. In the early series novels their marriage and her death places her memory in the narratives as an ideal of fidelity. Later, his secretary, Lucy Hamilton, takes the place of the chaste lady against whom Dresser contrasts the many women who hit upon Shayne as if drawn by pheromones, such as the underclass blonde Natalie Briggs or the femme fatale Estelle Morrison in *Blood on Biscayne Bay* (1946). However improbably coincidences place his P.I. at the center of events, Dresser's efficient narratives gave his reader the savvy male of power and control who keeps his cool and survives.

VI

This terminal place is reserved for two admirable novels by Baynard Kendrick, *Blood on Lake Louisa* (1934) and *Death beyond the Go-Thru* (1938), that do not take place in the exotic Florida of tourism and wealth. Unlike mysteries that demonize criminals or import crime from another place, both of Kendrick's novels define crime as an inner expression of provincial, coherent societies; both explore evil in benign persons of trust representative of the status quo; and both enter a conflicted sense of an older Florida resisting cultural change. Baynard Kendrick had a diverse and prolific writing career, including the Duncan Maclain and Miles Standish Rice mystery series, nonseries mysteries, historical novels, and books treating Florida history.

Doctor Ryan, the narrator of *Blood on Lake Louisa,* serves the small town of Orange Crest in the heart of Florida's citrus industry. He enjoys his role as sole practitioner, has a good marriage, knows most Orange Crest residents, and participates fully in civic life. He is also an advocate of Manasaw County backwardness that preserves the wild natural character of the place from tourism; and Kendrick's feel for telling detail renders a rich sense of security and isolation. Bass fishing on Lake Louisa, the doctor finds the body of the town banker but can't believe that any local person could be a murderer since the only crime in Manasaw county involves local crackers hunting out of season. The doctor's role as confidant to the informal detective lawyer Marvin Lee makes him the register of clues and confusion; his benign role as the good physician imperils and preserves him on two occasions when local members of a counterfeiting ring might have murdered him but can't because he is Doctor Ryan and they know him. It's a sad occasion for the good doctor when a person of public trust like himself—Deputy Sheriff Brown—is uncovered as coconspirator with jeweler Tim Reig in a counterfeiting operation.

The go-thru in *Death beyond the Go-Thru* refers to the breaks in seawalls that access channels and the harbor of the Drenner family cypress-mill operation at "Cypress Key" (Cedar Key?) south of the Suwanee River. On a boat beyond the go-thru, Drenner has died of insulin shock (or is it murder?). Undercover as sport-fisherman, Stan Miles investigates. Kendrick's command of detail generates persuasive realism and the cultural stew that promotes crime. Attempting to take control of her father's ailing company, Connie Drenner's education and self-confidence clash with the patriarchal culture. Hoping to work his way up, college grad David Slade—with New Deal enthusiasm—means to rebuild the company with better wages and housing for the workers. The intellectual physician Doctor Kellogg and the pragmatic interim executive Pop Talbot counsel wisdom, knowing the resistance of the workers to change. Both exercise a benign, fatherly authority toward Connie that may be subversive of her interests. As a mild former sheriff, now state's attorney investigator, Stan Rice has to sort this out. And though at points it looks as if the good doctor may have betrayed his trust, it's Pop Talbot who lies behind the effort to wrest control from Connie, in the closure freed with David Slade to carry out their reforms and to move this part of Florida into the modern era.

Works Cited

"Are You Planning a Murder?" *Forum* 95 (Apr. 1936): 260.

Biggers, Earl Derr. *Love Insurance*. New York: Collier, 1914.

Chambers, Whitman. *Dry Tortugas*. New York: Doubleday, Doran, 1940.

Cohen, Octavus Roy. *Child of Evil*. New York: Appleton-Century, 1936.

Cooper, Courtney Riley. *Action in Diamonds*. New York: Random, 1942.

Daly, Carroll John. *The Hidden Hand*. New York: Clode, 1929.

46   Crime Fiction and Film in the Sunshine State

DeWitt, Jack. *Murder on Shark Island.* New York: Liveright, 1941.

Dresser, Davis, as Brett Halliday. *Dividend on Death.* New York: Holt, 1939.

Eberhart, Mignon. *Unidentified Woman.* New York: Random, 1943.

Ely, Wilmer M. *The Boy Chums Cruising in Florida Waters.* New York: Burt, 1914.

Gardner, Janette C. *Florida Fiction 1801-1980.* Saint Petersburg: Little Bayou Press, 1980.

Hubin, Allen J. *Crime Fiction II.* 2nd ed. 2 vols. New York: Garland, 1994.

Hurst, Edward H. *Mystery Island.* Boston: Page, 1907.

Kendrick, Baynard. *Blood on Lake Luisa.* 1934. New York: Triangle, 1943.

——. *Death beyond the Go-Thru.* New York: Doubleday, Doran, 1938.

King, Rufus. *Murder Masks Miami.* New York: Doubleday, Doran, 1939.

Knotts, Raymond, as Gordon Volk. *And the Deep Blue Sea.* New York: Farrar, 1944.

Latimer, Jonathan. *The Dead Don't Care.* New York: Doubleday, Doran, 1938.

Levison, Eric. *Ashes of Evidence.* Indianapolis: Bobbs-Merrill, 1921

——. *The Eye Witness.* Indianapolis: Bobbs-Merrill, 1921.

——. *Hidden Eyes.* Indianapolis: Bobbs-Merrill, 1920.

Marchant, Bessie. *The Secret of the Everglades.* London: Blackie, 1902.

Martin, Absalom. *Kastle Krags: A Story of Mystery.* New York: Duffield, 1922.

Pratt, Theodore. *Mercy Island.* New York: Knopf, 1941.

—— as Timothy Brace. *Murder Goes in a Trailer.* New York: Dutton, 1937.

Price, Wesley. *Death Is a Stowaway.* New York: Godwin, 1933.

Read, Opie. *On the Suwanee River.* Chicago: Laird, 1895.

Schley, Sturges Mason. *Dr. Toby Finds Murder.* New York: Random, 1941.

Thayer, Lee. *Five Bullets.* New York: Dodd, 1944.

4

The Rules Are Different Here:
South Florida Noir and the Grotesque

Julie Sloan Brannon

Anything that comes out of the South is going to be called grotesque
by the Northern reader, unless it is grotesque, in which case it is
going to be called realistic.

>—Flannery O'Connor, "Some Aspects
> of the Grotesque in Southern Fiction"

In a city where Santeria rituals clog up the courthouse steps with
chicken carcasses and judges are indicted on an almost yearly basis, few
of Miami's homicides rate the front page. It's as if something happens to
people when they reach the Florida border, as if they think reasonable
behavior is suddenly not necessary anymore: witness any given Spring
Break in a coastal Florida town. As a recent tourist slogan stated: "The
rules are different here." One literary trip through the South Florida of
writers like Charles Willeford and Carl Hiaasen will show that the rules
aren't just different, they're downright bizarre.

It is only fitting that, in order to get to the Florida border, most
people have to trek through the Georgia clay that provides a foundation
for Flannery O'Connor's writing. The grotesquery in O'Connor's short
stories is intertwined with their very "Southern-ness"; moral corruption
provides the underpinnings to the physical deformity of her characters.
But could those characters exist anywhere outside the South? Her stock
answer to why Southern writers dwell so much on freaks was that they
"are still able to recognize one" (44), and she states that a novelist must

know how far he can distort without destroying. . . . He will have to descend far
enough into himself to reach those underground springs that give life to his
work. This descent into himself will . . . be a descent into his region. I hate to
think that in twenty years Southern writers too may be writing about men in
grey flannel suits and may have lost their ability to see that these gentlemen are
even greater freaks than what we are writing about now. (50)

While O'Connor's 1969 essay, read at Wesleyan College, in Macon, Georgia, in the fall of 1960, addressed the future of Southern literary tradition, her comments also reflected the very disappearance of that tradition as the South began entering the urban age. It is doubtful now that the citizens of Atlanta or Charlotte or Jacksonville differ much from their Cleveland or Detroit counterparts, other than in their accents. And even that is not a certainty in Florida, since the majority of our citizens are not natives of this region; you are just as likely to hear a Midwestern twang as a Southern drawl. The "men in grey flannel suits" are to be found everywhere except in the most rural regions. It seems strange that, in the thirty-five years since she made these remarks, O'Connor's ideas have come to be reflected in the works of two crime novelists who focus on the very thing she decried; yet her fear that Southern writers will have lost their ability to detect the freakishness in the grey flannel men is not borne out.

Like O'Connor, both Willeford and Hiaasen use the grotesque as a commentary on amorality, but it is the Miami area and not the rural South that breathes the foul air into each author's stories and characters . The pestilential nature of "lawyers, guns, and money"[1] overrunning South Florida provides rich material for both authors, yet each utilizes the Miami grotesque in ways peculiar to their own styles: Hiaasen paints his world in wildly comic strokes, with the weirdness happening at full-tilt like O'Connor on speed, piling on one eccentric event or character after another; Willeford in contrast describes, almost celebrates, the blasé attitude that greets even the most bizarre events in Miami, flatly outlining the grotesque in the same tone as he describes a suit jacket.

Richard Gehr describes Willeford's style as "evocative neutrality" ("Pope of Psychopulp" 30); like bas relief, the grotesquery is all the more visible for its seemingly bland surface. For example, in *New Hope for the Dead*, the protagonist, Sergeant Hoke Moseley, attempts to get a house-sitting job and meets the homeowner and his very amorous dog:

The dog released Hoke's leg at once and jumped to a chair, then onto the kitchen table, which still held the dirty dishes from Mr. Ferguson's lunch. Mr. Ferguson reached between the dog's legs, above the red, pencil-sized penis. "Old Rex gets horny living here without a mate, but if you jack him off once or twice a day, he stays mighty quiet." The dog climaxed, and Ferguson wiped the table with a paper napkin. Rex jumped to the chair, then to the floor, and crossed to a corduroy cushion under the stove. (25-26)

Moseley and Ferguson continue their conversation as if nothing untoward has happened, and then Moseley declines the house-sitting job. Ferguson replies: "That's too bad. Rex liked you a lot. I could tell" (26).

The real-estate agent who sent Moseley to Mr. Ferguson is desperate to find someone, and asks Moseley how long it takes to masturbate the dog; when he tells her less than one minute, she replies, "What's the big deal then, Sergeant? It seems to me that getting a lovely home to live in free, and five dollars a day besides, should be worth a minute of your time every day" (27). No one behaves as if it were the least bit unusual for a dog owner to masturbate his pet. Although Moseley is a bit unsettled, he conducts himself as if it were perfectly normal for someone to jack off his dog on the dining table.

Willeford's Miami fiction operates on a subtle level of grotesquery; the strangeness is not the main event, just the environment in which the story happens. During an introductory description of Moseley's office, Willeford slips in a dig at the high crime rate in Miami by mentioning a poster on one wall: "A hand holding a pistol, with the pistol pointed at the viewer, was in the center of the wall. The message, in bold black letters beneath the pointing pistol, read "MIAMI—SEE IT LIKE A NATIVE" (*Miami Blues* 22-23). There are two things going on with this poster: the first is obviously the joke on Miami's reputation for violent crime; the second, and more subtle, is the implication that Miami natives are under siege by forces outside their control—exploding immigration, overdevelopment, the drug trade. None of this is emphasized by Willeford; the reader has to pick it up from dialogue throughout the book. Later, in *New Hope for the Dead*, the poster has changed: it is now a "masked man holding a pistol" and the caption is a Miami Chamber of Commerce slogan, "MIAMI'S FOR ME!" (29). The only people Miami is for, the poster implies, are criminals. But in a fashion typical of Willeford's style, the poster is given no more emphasis than the ashtray on Moseley's desk or the files piled up on the chair. The poster, and its wry implication, is just another piece of background for the reader to absorb.

The Miami grotesque in Willeford's Moseley novels is merely "business as usual" and the crimes in the books reflect this. In *Miami Blues* the villain, Freddy Frenger, Jr., a "blithe psychopath from California," gets into an altercation with a Hare Krishna at the Miami airport. After the Krishna pins a flower into Frenger's suede jacket, Freddy, in a rage over the resultant hole in his coat, bends and breaks the Krishna's middle finger. The screaming Krishna collapses and ultimately dies from shock. While murder by broken finger is strange enough, the carnivalesque atmosphere of Miami becomes apparent in the crowd's reaction to the whole scene:

[T]wo men, obviously related, who had watched the whole encounter, broke into applause and laughed. When a middle-aged woman wearing a Colombian poncho heard one of the tourists say "Hare Krishna," she took a Krishna Kricket out of her purse and began to click the metal noisemaker in the pain-racked Krishna's face. The injured Krishna's partner . . . came over from the line he was working at Aeromexico and began to berate the woman for snapping the Kricket. The elder of the two laughing men came up behind him, snatched off his wig, and threw it over the heads of the gathering crowd. (3)

We find out in a later chapter that a "Krishna Kricket" is a noise-maker provided free of charge to airport patrons by a man who hated the Krishnas; people clicked the device at them until it drove the Krishnas to another panhandling target. A comic blood-lust infuses this passage, with the onlookers actually finding humor in the man's suffering and exhibiting absolutely no pity for his condition. The distinct indifference to humanity shown here makes it difficult indeed to decipher just who the freaks are at the airport. Of course, the Krishna himself is somewhat of a low-life who would do O'Connor proud: he is one Martin Waggoner, late of Okeechobee, Florida, a boy from a God-fearing rural family who just happens to be having an affair with his own sister. He had escaped to Miami with her and joined the Krishna commune, skimming money from his daily haul at the airport and supporting his sister's enrollment at Miami-Dade Community College. She also works as a prostitute at a local hotel. Between the murderer Frenger, the Krishna victim, his prostitute sister, and the airport crowd, the reader is left to wonder just who is more bizarre. It would seem that Willeford, at least, has not lost his ability to recognize a freak when he sees one: they're everywhere in Miami.

Painting the city as morally corrupt is, of course, not a new ploy; detective fiction has mined this particular vein effectively since its inception. In fact, the urban scene as amoral wasteland is a necessary part of crime fiction in order to give the detective his impetus as Chandler's justice-seeking individual ("The Simple Art of Murder"). Willeford simply points out through his deadpan style that what Chandler calls a "world gone wrong" has no referent in a place like Miami. Gone wrong from what? To what? How is murder to be judged in a place where a dying man can be jeered and "kricketed"?

The answer, of course, in Chandler's fiction and just about all other hard-boiled detective stories, is to be found in the person of the detective himself. He is the man of honor who judges how retribution is to be administered (whether outside the law or not), the one who sets the world right. Willeford does not toy with this formula—much. Hoke Moseley in particular is a sorry excuse for a hero; balding, middle-aged, and toothless with a horrible set of dentures, he makes a comical literary heir to Mike Hammer. Detective heroes often smoke and drink, but they rarely hack or smell bad or wear second-hand yellow leisure suits. Rather than taking a "warts and all" approach to Moseley, Willeford concentrates on the warts. Moseley deals with much more than just catching criminals: "The crimes he solves are almost incidental . . . to the existential quandaries of his Miami existence" (Gehr 31). For example, Moseley doesn't let a little thing like murder derail his search for a place to live; he solves a case and, instead of arresting the perpetrator, he arranges to let her escape in return for the use of her house. The victim was a junkie and chronic small-time offender, and Hoke desperately needs a house inside the city limits. In Moseley's scale, letting this particular criminal escape is worth solving his own domestic dilemmas, with the added bonus of one less junkie in Miami.

Of course, Moseley might have operated differently if the political problems of the police chief had not forced him to find new living arrangements in the first place; the chief had instituted a policy that all Miami cops had to live inside Miami, which makes sense except that no police officer wanted to live in Miami. Willeford describes the "white flight" syndrome which not only operates in black areas but in Hispanic areas as well. In fact, racial tensions form a constant theme in Willeford's Moseley novels: affirmative action forces the department to do some creative hiring and personnel shifting, black youth are constantly throwing bricks at the white cops' cars, and Hispanic people refuse to speak English even though they know the language well. Moseley himself adds to the racial tension in the books. He espouses a WASP ethnocentrism, which causes him to assume that anyone with a Spanish name is Cuban; he insults a banker named Lhosa-Garcia by threatening to call the DEA to investigate the bank. The banker gives Moseley the information he wants, but when Moseley compliments him on his English the banker sets him straight:

I was born in Evanston, Illinois—not Cuba, where you think. My surname helped me get this job, but it also makes me vulnerable to pricks like you. . . . If you told your DEA friend you suspected a Latin banker of laundering, he'd be down here interrupting our work, even though we have nothing to hide. But if you'd gone to Bruce Waterman with this crap instead of coming to me, he'd've called the Coral Gables chief of police. (*New Hope* 220)

Moseley learns nothing from this encounter; he continues to make the same mistake with others having Spanish surnames, assuming they are all Cuban immigrants. On the surface this seems puzzling, but the exchanges only underscore the reality of life in Miami: his stereotype is completely arrogant and presumptuous, but it is somewhat understandable because there are so many first-generation Americans there. This sort of assumption leads to a great deal of tension at times in South Florida, and Willeford illustrates a kind of survivalist self-absorption through Moseley. There is often a feeling of assault in the non-Hispanic population in South Florida, a paranoia that things are changing too fast for them to assimilate. The recent movement to amend the Florida constitution to declare English as the primary language of the state is symptomatic of a larger, vaguely amorphous concern that Miami isn't quite part of Florida anymore. This, of course, is not true; but Moseley's racial insensitivity subtly illustrates another source of tension and oddity in Miami.

In a reversal of the usual racial stereotypes, the criminal elements in Willeford's Hoke Moseley books are usually white lower-class psychopaths rather than blacks or Hispanics, and Gehr traces this tendency back to Willeford's days in the army. Gehr quotes Willeford: "'A good half of the' men you deal with in the Army are psychopaths.' What are these men good for afterward? Willeford asks. Eight hours a day in a 7-Eleven?" (30). Willeford seemingly asks the same question of those men who are processed by our criminal justice system. Freddy Frenger was not in the army, but a lifelong resident of the penal system of California. He tested as a sociopath, as does Troy Louden of *Sideswipe*. As Louden explains it to another character, "I'm a professional criminal, what the shrinks call a criminal psychopath. What it means is, I know the difference between right and wrong and all that, but I don't give a shit" (50).

Willeford's criminals are often deformed physically as well as psychically; Louden bears a striking resemblance to a lizard, and Frenger has a slight build but has pumped so much iron in jail that his arms are of "grotesque proportions" (*Miami Blues* 11). In *The Way We Die Now*,[2] Tiny Bock, the overweight owner of a produce farm in Southwest Florida, hires illegal Haitian immigrants to harvest his fields, then kills them instead of paying them. Bock is missing a finger and has a "sun cancer the size of a half-dollar on his right cheek, bordered by a quarter-inch of gray stubble" (135-36). When his foreman, a Mexican who tortures the Haitians before killing them, discovers Moseley investigating their operation, the Mexican brutally beats him and attempts to rape him as well. Each of these criminals is extremely casual about murdering people, shooting and stabbing without losing stride. They are indifferent as to their choice of victims, often killing for trifling reasons, as Frenger does the Hare Krishna for putting a hole in his jacket.

Moseley is quite normal compared to these sociopathic criminals, even though he operates under his own fairly antisocial, numbing haze. He lives in pseudodomestic bliss with his two daughters, who were dumped on his doorstep ten years after his divorce when his wife went off to marry a wealthy black ballplayer (another source of Moseley's ethnic sensitivity problems). He also shares his home with his former partner, Ellita Sanchez, pregnant from her first and only one-night stand. Her Cuban parents threw her out of the house—which she was paying rent for—because she had dishonored them. Moseley takes her in, but not entirely out of altruism. He needs someone to look after his teenaged daughters.

For the most part, however, Moseley is a dilapidated version of the chivalric noir detective, operating under a code of honor that dictates that justice should prevail—even if it means torching the scum, as he does to Tiny Bock's farm. To prevent serious legal repercussions for undertaking a secret operation outside his jurisdiction, Moseley tells the chief that the farm had already burned down when he got there. The chief, who sent Moseley as a favor to an old college friend, can do nothing to investigate Moseley's story since it would uncover his own role in the affair. In Moseley's view, Bock and Chico got what they deserved, the Haitians were released from their slavery, and that's the end of it. Many critics have remarked on the similarity of Westerns and detective fiction;[3] Moseley's brand of swamp justice is no different from the frontier justice of John Wayne or Clint Eastwood.

Perhaps Willeford's best-known work is *The Burnt Orange Heresy*, a noir novel set in West Palm Beach. This book is not a detective novel in the usual sense, for the murder happens late in the book and there is no mystery to solve. The narrative takes place inside the mind of James Figueras, an art critic who will do anything to advance his career. He is sent by a collector to interview Jacques Debierue, a "Nihilistic Surrealist" painter near the end of his reclusive life, and in return for the opportunity he is to steal a painting. He leaps at the chance because he knows that an interview with the old hermit will seal his own career aspirations.

Figueras is an egomaniac, amoral to the core, but we only realize this slowly. Willeford gives us small glimpses of his personality, such as his annoyance at having salad dressing instead of mayonnaise on his sandwich, or noticing that his girlfriend Berenice's lipstick is a shade too orange and contributes a slight imperfection to her appearance. Early in the novel, he breaks up with Berenice, but then welcomes her back to the apartment they shared, primarily because "Berenice makes much better coffee" than he does (36). Berenice wonders how she is supposed to be impressed by Debierue's fame when she's never seen his work to judge for herself, and Figueras tells her that she isn't "qualified" to judge for herself (62).

These glimpses of Figueras's personality compound subtly, so that by the end of the novel we are readily prepared for his actions. When he discovers that the kindly old Debierue has no paintings to steal—in fact, has not painted anything at all—he steals a canvas and paints one himself, calling it the "Burnt Orange Heresy." He signs Debierue's name to it, and types up his "interview" and critique of the old Surrealist's "work." Berenice discovers his ploy and he kills her. He is never caught, and his career (as well as Debierue's reputation) soars.

Like Wilde's Dorian Gray, Figueras achieves an outer appearance of success and glory but only through theft, deception, and murder. Instead of Dorian Gray's painting, which shows his soul growing uglier and older with each new depravity, Figueras has Berenice's finger, wrapped in a handkerchief and desiccating in the bottom of a dresser drawer. Underscoring his amoral megalomania, he does not finally confess to the murder because he feels guilty, but because he realizes that there "was no place for [him] to go as an art critic." Figueras turns himself in to the police, but he doesn't divulge the secret of the Debierue painting; rather, he confesses to a "crime of passion" because "[t]he man who achieves success in America must pay for it. It's the American way, and no one knows this fact better than I, a de-islanded Puerto Rican" (143-44).

In *The Burnt Orange Heresy* the grotesquery is even more subtle than usual, except for the gothically charged element of Berenice's severed finger, which serves as Figueras's "Picture of Dorian Gray." Since we are actually inside the mind of the sociopathic Figueras, there is no referent for grotesquery. Willeford's focus seems to be the artificial and mercurial nature of the art world in general, where a man can have a worldwide reputation based on absolutely nothing at all. Debierue was a Parisian picture framer crowned the father of Nihilistic Surrealism by the art world because of one work, the infamous "No. One." This work, a baroque gilded frame hung over a crack in the wall of a maid's bedroom, ignited a flurry of interpretation and posturing in the art world and sealed Debierue's reputation, even though he did nothing after this. Figueras further mocks the art criticism he takes so seriously by forging the painting that reignites Debierue's fame. And yet it is his love for the art world that drives him to forge the painting in the first place; he cannot bear the thought of Debierue's being exposed as a fraud, nor the critics as fools for their part in creating this fraudulent reputation. His "crime of passion" is not Berenice's murder, but rather his forgery and subsequent critique of "Debierue's" painting.

The question then becomes, why set this novel in South Florida? It could have just as easily been set in New York or Los Angeles or anywhere with a flourishing art community. The answer possibly lies in the illusions at the core of South Florida culture. There is an air of unreality about West Palm Beach, with its seasonal occupancy and vast amounts of moneyed WASPs, and the artificiality of the art world finds a winter home in West Palm's whirlwind of parties and superficial schmoozing. The alien nature of the Palm Beach inhabitants is mirrored in Figueras, who is only there to cover the winter art scene for a New York publication. But a deeper reflection of the alienation is seen in Figueras's identity as a "de-islanded Puerto Rican." His father, whom he never knew, was a blond Puerto Rican and his mother was a dark-haired Scots-Irish woman. Figueras moves with his mother to the United States and rapidly drops not only the Spanish spelling of his name for James but also his Spanish accent. He makes up a father in his mind, an *hombre duro* or hard man, and judges his own actions by what this nonexistent father would have done. In essence, his entire moral code is based on something he made up himself: "A boy who doesn't have a father around doesn't develop a superego, and if you don't get a superego naturally you've got to invent one." When Berenice scoffs at this notion and tells him that "everybody's got a conscience," Figueras replies: "Right. At least I've got one intellectually, if not emotionally, because I was smart enough to create an imaginary father" (37).

There is a sort of dark humor in this exchange, because it is precisely Figueras's super ego that demolishes his conscience. He feels little moral culpability for forging the painting or killing Berenice to cover it up. His "repentance" at the end of the novel only comes with his intellectual realization that his career has topped out, that the ride is over. He feels no emotional remorse, but rather a sense of logic, which propels him to confess to Berenice's murder: in America, you have to pay for your success. Figueras is Gatsby, making his own fame in a land where making something from nothing is a revered way of life. Like Fitzgerald's self-made man, Figueras must "pay" for his success, but unlike Gatsby he is never found out as a fraud. Even his Faustian fall is suspect, because the "crime of passion" he confesses to at the end of the novel is an ambiguous phrase; we are left with the image of Berenice's finger on the policeman's desk, but the real passion of Figueras's life has always been the art world, and it was for that he committed his crime. Presenting Figueras's story in the South Florida milieu merely places this crime in a region that would seem to be a natural backdrop for oddity and horror.

Willeford, with a poker face, presents the grotesquery of South Florida as completely taken for granted by the residents; he makes very little direct comment upon the weirdness, preferring to let the events weave a slightly psychedelic nausea around and throughout the stories. He reflects the residents' acceptance of the bizarre by routinizing it and making the reader complicit in accepting it as well. We begin to become just as numb to the freaks as South Floridians are; it's just business-as-usual in Miami. In contrast, Hiaasen not only foregrounds the grotesque, he makes it a central focus of his works. The carnivalesque is not incidental to the detective story for Hiaasen; it is the story, and it takes place within a framework of political corruption and environmental destruction. If Willeford's books extol being "a thriving asshole [rather] than a dead dork" (Gehr 30), then Hiaasen shows what happens when there are so many thriving in one place.

In a phone interview conducted in 1992, Hiaasen discussed what he called the "geek factor," the level of ease at which freaks are accepted as part of the landscape. Many times throughout his works, the refrain of "Hey—it's Miami" encourages the reader to go along with the "anything could happen" attitude. In *Skin Tight*, one of the villains works as a bouncer at a club called the Gay Bidet; he stops a man from bringing an Ingram submachine gun into the club, and the man replies as if puzzled, "But this is Miami" (120). Anywhere else, someone trying to bring an automatic weapon into a nightclub would be met with incredulity; somehow, in Miami, it seems the natural thing to do. Moseley's poster comes to life in Hiaasen's books, and seeing Miami like a native becomes all too possible.

But in Hiaasen's Miami the weirdness is not just comic relief or plot device; it manifests the true grotesquery of what's been done to the environment in pursuit of money. Hiaasen continually foregrounds the irony of selling a pristine tropical paradise that no longer exists. In *Skin Tight*, he describes "Gables-by-the-Sea, a ritzy but misnomered neighborhood" that was

nowhere near the ocean but fronted a series of man-made canals that emptied into Biscayne Bay. No one complained about this marketing deception, as it was understood by buyers and sellers alike that Gables-by-the-Sea sounded much more tony than Gables-on-the-Canal. The price of the real estate duly reflected this exaggeration. (28)

This is a Florida where "fleecing a snowbird in such a way that he came back for more" is a "dream concept" (*Native Tongue* 39). A carnivalesque atmosphere permeates Hiaasen's Florida, and he lampoons both the rube and the shill with equal vigor.

The catalyst for the plot of *Tourist Season*, Hiaasen's first solo novel, is Skip Wiley's mania for saving Florida from the "odious reality" of being "a peninsula stolen from the Indians, plundered by carpetbaggers, and immorally occupied by Yankee immigrants who arrive at the rate of one thousand per day, Okies in BMWs" (238). Wiley, a columnist for a large Miami newspaper, goes on a holy crusade to rid Florida of its tourists, lending the pun to the title and carrying a current of warning underneath the absurdities in the novel: Florida's unchecked growth is creating an environmental disaster. The murders in *Tourist Season* seem to be fit retribution, in a warped way: a tourist promoter is found crammed inside a Samsonite suitcase floating in the Atlantic, dressed in Bermuda shorts, slathered with suntan lotion and choked to death by a toy alligator; a retired, condo-dwelling Jewish woman from up north is fed to a huge American crocodile, of which there are only about thirty in the state due to habitat loss. But the real crimes in Hiaasen novels aren't necessarily the ones perpetrated against humans; the world of detective fiction is turned upside down, and the true injustices are those committed against nature. Miami is a place where "crimes against the landscape are simply good business" (Jordan 63). The inhabitants of Miami have no love for the land they plunder, because they have no connection to it (Hiaasen, phone interview). They see the natural world as grotesque, when in Hiaasen's view it is their own avarice and corruption that truly deserve the label.

Hiaasen gives an abbreviated history of Miami's development from Fort Dallas, "a mucky, rutted, steaming, snake-infested settlement of two hundred souls" existing in a time "when the local obsession was sur-vival, not square footage, when the sun was not a commodity but a blis-tering curse" (229). The transformation from mosquito-plagued outpost to glitzy international hotspot was undertaken by "rabid opportunists" who "seized as much land as they could, swapped it, platted it, sold it. Where there was no land they dredged it from the bottom of Biscayne Bay, manufactured an island . . . and peddled it as a natural oasis. All this was done with great efficiency and enthusiasm, but with no vision what-soever" (*Tourist* 238). This is the history Wiley attempts to balance, and his crusade in one sense seems to be Hiaasen's; the similarity between Wiley and Hiaasen should not go unnoticed, since Hiaasen's works all hinge on the same themes that push Wiley over the edge. The author has stated that he has been "fighting the bulldozers all [his] life" (phone interview).

It would seem, however, that by *Double Whammy* (1987) and *Native Tongue* (1991) the possibility of turning back the clock on devel-opment is remote at best; instead, small blows are struck for the environ-ment, targeting specific developers and their respective businesses. In *Double Whammy*, Hiaasen lampoons bass fishing and televangelism, and in *Native Tongue* he sets his sights on amusement parks and a sloppy criminal justice system. His most recent work, *Stormy Weather*, details the aftermath of Hurricane Andrew and the booming tourist industry that grew even out of this tremendously tragic event. Florida's tourism hucksters miss no opportunity to turn anything into a money-making franchise. What could illustrate the depravity of the human race more than a man who cuts short his honeymoon in Disney World to drive to Miami and make home movies of South Florida's devastation after the hurricane?

In these books, Hiaasen introduces an environmental crusader named Skink, who embodies a retreat-but-don't-surrender mentality. Skink stands about six feet four, has long braided hair, a beard and a glass eye, wears a flowered shower cap and a fluorescent orange rainsuit, and has incredibly handsome teeth. He lives off roadkill, reads Dostoevsky, and loves Puccini. Skink is a man in communion with nature, Thoreau on acid; his eyes are not just "hazel or olive, but deep green, like Rocky Mountain evergreens" (*Double Whammy* 33). We discover that Skink is none other than Clinton Tyree, former governor of Florida who disappeared from office never to be heard from again. After fighting vainly to prevent the destruction of Florida's environment by greedy land developers and the equally greedy state legislators in the pockets of those land developers, Tyree abandons his crusade and becomes a reclusive hermit deep in what's left of Florida's wilderness. His bizarre behavior stems from his fiery passion for the natural beauty of the state. In *Stormy Weather*, he lashes himself to the Card Sound bridge during a hurricane so he can feel it firsthand; he stops two hung-over fraternity boys on their way out of Key West during the evacuation, tosses a dead squirrel into the back of their car, and then has them tie him to the bridge. Skink has been waiting for a great hurricane to wash away the sins of South Florida, and he revels in the sheer magnitude of nature's destructiveness. He sees the hurricane as a purge, a way to redress the damage done to the environment. He's not without sympathy for the hurricane victims; he just sees it as a sort of Darwinian balancing of nature's scales: "Fuck with Mother Nature and she'll fuck back." When Bonnie Lamb tries to make him understand why people continue to move to Florida by comparing them to the "settlers of the Old West," Skink replies with a sigh, "Oh, child . . . tell me what's left to settle" (224-25).

The nemesis in *Stormy Weather* is a true sociopath with a grotesque appearance to match his killer's soul, the paroled convict Lester Maddox Parsons, named by his KKK parents after the famous gubernatorial racist. He got his nickname "Snapper" from his crooked jaw, punched by a game warden to "approximately thirty-six degrees out of alignment" (96). He bears similarities to Louden and Frenger, in that he doesn't care about the difference between right and wrong. Skink doles out his fate by fitting a car-theft prevention device to his jaws: "The Club exaggerated Snapper's pre-exaggerated features. It pushed the top half of his mug into pudgy creases, like a shar-pei puppy; the eyes were moist slits, the nose pugged nearly to his brow. The rest was all maw" (306). Skink underscores his Darwinian sense of justice by leaving Snapper to fend for himself in the midst of a wildlife refuge: "If he gets out of here, he deserves to be free. . . . [But] he'll go the wrong way. That's his nature. It's the arc of all life. For Lester we merely hasten the sad promenade. Tonight we are Darwin's elves" (329-30).

On the surface, Skink is an oddball, an outsider with a quick trigger finger and more love for animals than for people. In the South Florida Hiaasen paints, the animals deserve love far better than the people: in *Double Whammy*, he describes "the Human Sludge Factor—it all drips to the South" (151); in *Native Tongue,* he calls Miami the "prime relocation site for scores of scuzzy federal snitches (on the theory that South Florida was a place where just about any dirtbag would blend in smoothly with the existing riffraff)" (47). As Rudy Graveline, the malpracticing plastic surgeon in *Skin Tight*, proclaims, "One of the wondrous things about Florida . . . was the climate of unabashed corruption: There was absolutely no trouble from which money could not extricate you" (101). The only difference between the professional riffraff in Hiaasen's books and the rest of Miami is that the killers exhibit their moral deformity in physical grotesquery, and the grey flannel men hide their corrupt natures behind a bland public official's smile.

One of the most memorable of Hiaasen's killer freaks is Chemo in *Skin Tight*:

[H]e truly did appear to be in the final grim stages of chemotherapy. Black hair sprouted in random wisps from a blue-veined scalp. His lips were thin and papery, and the color of wet cement. Red-rimmed eyes peered back at gawkers with a dull and chilling indifference; the hooded lids blinked slowly, pellucid as a salamander's. Chemo's skin looked like breakfast cereal, like somebody had glued Rice Krispies to every square centimeter of his face. (51-52)

Chemo met with an unfortunate electrolysis accident early in his life, and his deformed features only manifest his sociopathic soul. During the course of events Chemo loses an arm to a barracuda and replaces it with a weed-eater. Other grotesque villains include Pedro Luz of *Native Tongue*, who is so addicted to steroids that he hooks up a portable IV to pump them directly into his veins. Pedro chews off his own foot at one point, and ends up drowning in the dolphin tank at the Amazing Kingdom of Thrills while Dickie the dolphin tries to mate with him: "As he was pulled underwater for the final time, terror gave way to abject humiliation: he was being fucked to death by a damn fish" (383). Hiaasen did not invent this bizarre dolphin behavior; in fact, (as the disclaimer at the front of the novel indicates) incidents of dolphins attempting to mate with humans have been widely documented. But after several reports of near-injury from amorous dolphins in tourist attractions that invited people to swim with semiwild dolphins, the legislature shut most of them down and strictly regulated the rest. Truth in South Florida is indeed stranger than fiction.

Hiaasen's novel *Strip Tease* deals with two seemingly disparate industries that generate big money in South Florida: adult entertainment and big sugar. The link between these two worlds comes in the form of one Congressman Davey Dilbeck, whose weakness "is of the fleshly nature." He is also on a subcommittee that determines price supports for the sugar industry, and his is the deciding vote that would continue these price supports. The other congressmen on the committee are preparing to vote against them, not because they are against the price supports, but because big sugar (in the form of the Rojo family, owners of a vast sugar operation in South Florida) filled Dilbeck's election coffers, and Dilbeck had drunkenly voted against a pay raise for the House. "Rather than admit the truth—that full credit for the deed belonged to the distillers of Barbancourt rum—David Dilbeck went on 'Nightline' and said he was proud of voting the way he did, said it was no time for Congress to be picking the public's pocket" (14). Hiaasen exposes the hypocrisy in a society which deems the stripper to be a whore and the congressman to be an upstanding citizen. Hiaasen takes aim not only at dirty congressional politics, but also lawyers, cops, divorce judges, and the entire male sex in general. For the first time Hiaasen gives us a female protagonist, Erin Grant; as a stripper, she finds herself in the midst of a grotesquery that is not confined to South Florida, but the Fort Lauderdale location lends a suitably "spring break" atmosphere. Fort Lauderdale is, after all, "where the boys are," and any place that can come up with creamed corn wrestling as an adult entertainment attraction is definitely grotesque.

Hiaasen steers away from the usual freakish killers in *Strip Tease*. Instead, the real villains wear Armani suits and expensive Italian cologne. Malcolm J. Moldowsky, also known as Moldy, is a "distractingly short" man with a smile that reveals "the small and pointed dentition of a lesser primate" and he wears an imported Italian musk heavily enough "to gas termites" (11). Moldy is a fixer who idolizes John Mitchell and who believes "in influence for the sake of influence" (112). He arranges to have three people killed, all of whom tried at one time or other to blackmail the congressman over his involvement in an assault at the strip club where Erin works. Outwardly, however, Moldowsky is polished and smooth. His death ironically comes at the hands of Erin's ex-husband, Darrell, who starts off as a small time convict and pillhead but winds up a drug crazed, one-armed psychopath. The only person in this novel who has a truly freakish appearance is Shad, the bouncer who befriends Erin. Shad is tall, bald, and his sharp nose and overbite make him look like a snapping turtle. He occupies his spare time in dreaming up product liability suits so that he can get out of the strip business. His latest scam involves placing a roach in a container of Delicato yogurt so that he can sue the company for his trauma at "discovering" the insect in his food. Shad's grotesquery is finally overshadowed not only by his unswerving loyalty to Erin, but also by the even larger grotesquery of the congressman.

David Dilbeck outwardly appears like any other middle aged politician who, if his peccadilloes were confined merely to going to strip clubs and getting drunk, would not raise an eyebrow. But Dilbeck is, by the words of his own aide Erb Crandall, a "sick puppy," and he has Erb steal lint from Erin's clothes dryer so he can (as he tells Erin later) "make love" to it. On another occasion, Dilbeck asks him to steal Erin's razor. When he returns with the pilfered item, Crandall finds the congressman "flat on the bed. He wore a black cowboy hat, a white towel around his waist and a pair of green lizardskin boots. Using handkerchiefs, the congressman had tied one arm and both feet to the bedposts. Above the boots, his pale shins gleamed, as if shellacked" (202). Dilbeck has covered himself and filled his boots with Vaseline. Witnessing this scene and filling with disgust, Crandall tells Dilbeck, "Even that jizzbag Nixon wouldn't have pulled something like this" (203). Even Moldowsky is exasperated at the congressman's antics: "Insanity was one thing he could not fix, spin, twist or obscure. Rep. David Dilbeck had no inkling of the drastic steps that had already been taken to save his worthless hide" (207-10).

Dilbeck and his cronies represent all that is corrupt in the political game not only of South Florida but of the entire United States. The influence of Big Sugar over federal government has long been a thorn in the sides of Florida environmentalists and migrant labor groups, since the huge amount of money made by artificially supported sugar prices allows the industry to lavish incredible attention on key members of Congress. Dilbeck loses no sleep over this situation:

It was enough that the Rojos were nice people, well-bred and so generous. The Congressman saw no injustice in the price supports that had made multimillionaires of the Rojos. The grain, dairy and tobacco interests had soaked the taxpayers for years by melodramatically invoking the plight of the "family farmer." Why not sugar, too? Nor did the congressman agonize over the far-reaching impact of cane growers flushing billions of gallons of waste into the Everglades. Dilbeck didn't understand what all the fuss was about. In truth, he didn't care much for the Everglades; it was torpid, swampy, crawling with bugs. (319-20)

In the climax of the novel, Erin forces Congressman Dilbeck at gunpoint to go out to the fields off of Tamiami Trail and cut sugar cane in the middle of the night wearing nothing but his boxer shorts: "After less than a minute, the congressman stopped. His face was flushed, his chest heaved and the blotched flab of his belly was sprinkled with sweat. He was panting like a toothless old lion. 'How much more till we can play?'" When Erin replies that he needs to cut at least a ton, Dilbeck scoffs; he is brought up short by Erin's terse comeback: "A migrant . . . cuts eight tons a day" (329). His education on the criminal practices of the sugar industry that owns him, however, is only the beginning; Erin has arranged for the FBI to storm onto the scene and catch Dilbeck in *flagrante delicto* with her, ruining his political career. She thus avenges the murders committed by Dilbeck's aide Moldowsky, effectively destroying a crooked and immoral politician. *Strip Tease* gives us a small blow for justice, rather than an all out round-up of the bad guys; Hiaasen's books illustrate the conviction that corruption cannot be wiped out entirely, but a few of the grey flannel men can meet retribution. Small victories are better than no victories.

Unlike these gray flannel men, the physical deformity of killers like Chemo and Snapper is so outrageously grotesque that they stand out from the usual riffraff. Their amorality is simple, straightforward, and unmasked. This outward manifestation of evil directly contrasts with the other villains who have no physical grotesquery, just inner corruption covered by a mask of hypocrisy. Graveline of *Skin Tight*, Francis X. Kingsbury of *Native Tongue*, the Miami Chamber of Commerce in *Tourist Season*, Congressman Dilbeck in *Strip Tease,* among a host of others, all appear on the surface to be upstanding citizens. Yet each one harbors an amorality that, in Hiaasen's world, may be even more grotesque than the easily recognized killer freaks. They operate in a corrupt society that demands amorality, and they all feel that they are doing nothing more than pursuing the American dream, South Florida-style. That this pursuit endangers other people and destroys the environment is irrelevant, and it is these people with no love for or connection to the land they plunder who drive Skip Wiley over the edge of reason and Skink into the wilderness.

Both Willeford and Hiaasen paint South Florida as a bizarre place that operates under rules different from "normal" society. The alienation of urban life leads to a sociopathic haze in Willeford's books that permeates both villain and hero, and South Florida merely serves as an appropriate place to display the more eccentric manifestations of this spreading disease of American society. Willeford illustrates a sort of numbing survivalist veil that descends over the inhabitants of Miami and prevents them from being too shocked by what they see. Hiaasen invites us to examine the reasons for this acceptance of the grotesque: so few people actually belong there or have any real connection to the area that everything becomes freakish in the end. The natural world becomes a strange and grotesque place to urban dwellers and therefore easier to destroy. Hiaasen laments this phenomenon by showing that the true grotesquery lies not in nature but in man, and that in Miami "sanity, not insanity, is the greater riddle" (*Tourist* 328).

Notes

1. "Lawyers, Guns, and Money" from Warren Zevon's *Excitable Boy* album (1978). An appropriate song for the Miami area, and perhaps Carl Hiaasen thought so, too; he cowrote two songs with Zevon, "Seminole Bingo" and "Rottweiler Blues."

2. *The Way We Die Now* is the final published Mosely novel. But, according to Gehr's review, there exists an unpublished manuscript of a final Hoke Moseley novel called "Grim Haven" (31).

3. For an excellent summary of scholarship on the detective novel as descendant of the frontier novel, see William W. Stowe's "Hard-boiled Virgil: Early Nineteenth-Century Beginnings of a Popular Literary Formula"; also Richard Slotkin, "The Hard-Boiled Detective Story: From the Open Range to the Mean Streets." Both essays can be found in *The Sleuth and the Scholar: Origins, Evolution, and Current Trends in Detective Fiction*, edited by Barbara A. Rader and Howard G. Zettler (New York: Greenwood Press, 1988).

Works Cited

Chandler, Raymond. "The Simple Art of Murder." *The Midnight Raymond Chandler*. Boston: Houghton-Mifflin, 1971.

Gehr, Richard. "The Pope of Psychopulp: Charles Ray Willeford's Unholy Rites." *Village Voice Literary Supplement* Mar. 1989: 30-31.

Hiaasen, Carl. *Tourist Season*. New York: Warner, 1986.

——. *Double Whammy*. New York: Warner, 1987.

——. *Skin Tight*. New York: Warner, 1989.

——. *Native Tongue*. New York: Warner, 1991.

——. *Strip Tease*. New York: Knopf, 1993.

——. *Stormy Weather*. New York: Knopf, 1995.

——. Telephone interview. Apr. 1992.

Jordan, Peter. "Carl Hiaasen's Environmental Thrillers: Crime Fiction in Search of Green Peace." *Studies in Popular Culture* 13.1 (1990): 61-71.

O'Connor, Flannery. "Some Aspects of the Grotesque in Southern Fiction." Paper read by author in the Fall of 1960 at Wesleyan College for Women, Macon, Georgia. Printed in *Mystery & Manners*. Eds. Sally and Robert Fitzgerald. New York: Farrar, Strauss & Giroux: 1969.

Willeford, Charles Ray. *The Burnt Orange Heresy*. New York: Vintage/Random, 1971.

——. *Miami Blues*. New York: St. Martin's, 1984.

——. *New Hope for the Dead*. New York: St. Martin's, 1985.

——. *Sideswipe*. New York: St. Martins, 1987.

5

Miami Noir:
The Woman's Vantage Point

Sarah D. Fogle

As Quin St. James first contemplates working on an investigative team with Michael McCleary, Mac assures her it will be an equitable partnership; she responds with characteristic bluntness: "I have trouble believing that" (*Dark Fields* 53), and he answers with a crack about her lack of subtlety. With this exchange, they form the P.I. team that tries to solve murder cases, as well as the mysteries of male-female behavior, throughout the nine novels in T. J. MacGregor's detective series. Their fictional colleague in investigating crime in South Florida is Edna Buchanan's Britt Montero, whose toughness and crime-busting reporting have folks thinking she's "ten feet tall and green with a tail" (*Contents Under Pressure* 151). Less colorful women who get caught up in criminal investigations are Barbara Parker's Gail Connor, Karen Ann Wilson's Samantha Holt, and Sherryl Woods's Molly DeWitt.

All of these Florida writers feature women in central roles of various subgenres, from the "mean streets" of the hard-boiled private eye to the "cozy village" of the amateur sleuth. Although these writers receive an occasional book review, or a mention in an annotated bibliography, even the most deserving have not been given much critical consideration. This oversight seems odd, given the growing number of recent studies by women about women writers of crime fiction. This chapter will discuss how these novels, all written within the last decade and most within the last few years, fit into their subgenres, with an emphasis on how their women heroes are depicted. In her recent study, *The Woman Detective: Gender and Genre,* Kathleen Gregory Klein observes that most novels featuring women detectives published since the late 1980s "meet what might be called liberal feminist criteria: women doing the same job as men and nobody making too much of a fuss about it" (230). But, in either professional or amateur detecting, a question persists whether these authors' characters simply reinforce longstanding gender stereotypes of women in detective fiction, or whether they really are the "main" characters on their own merits, as both women *and* investigators. As Klein points out, the formulaic elements and inherently male focus of the detective genre are perceived as inevitably limiting to a female hero, even a feminist one. She cannot be entirely successful as a woman or as a detective without subordinating one role to the other (201-02).

All but one of these writers set their novels in Miami, once the homicide capital of the country and a city popularized, perhaps reborn, through the television series *Miami Vice*. In an article on Miami's appeal to a number of writers, R. Z. Sheppard observes, "In writing . . . the operating word is location. Readers like to travel, to escape to a setting, preferably hot, sticky, and glamorous" (65). Accordingly, Miami provides an environment enlivened by pastel colors and bloody violence, Anglo and Latino cultures and conflicts, plus the overall appeal of tropical beauty to attract readers to MacGregor, Buchanan, Parker, and others. In many ways, they draw us into the rich texture of South Florida.

The most prolific of the writers discussed here is South Floridian T. J. MacGregor, who has published nine novels in the Quin St. James –Mike McCleary private eye series: *Dark Fields, Kill Flash, Death Sweet, On Ice, Kin Dread, Death Flats, Spree, Storm Surge,* and *Blue Pearl.* (MacGregor has also published under her maiden name, Trish Janeshutz, and a pseudonym, Alison Drake.) Although, as Klein has noted, "[A]ttempts to categorize mystery fiction are filled with danger" (*Great Women Mystery Writers* 399), MacGregor's series belongs on the continuum of that uniquely American tradition in the genre, the hard-boiled detective novel. The hard-boiled formula has inevitably evolved and been altered with the times and with the emergence of new authors and fictional detectives—especially women—but certain salient characteristics of this formula remain in force, with some differences that reflect the evolution of the subgenre and life in the nineties.

The world in which Mac and Quin live and work is typical of the usual "mean streets" of the hard-boiled novel. The cases they investigate involve serial murderers, experiments with near death experiences, pornography (snuff films with volume discounts), sex cults, hired assassins, burnt-out spies, and faith healers. More often than not, the killers are motivated by bizarre sexual impulses; descriptions of the killings and crime scenes are graphic and viscerally unsettling, and body counts are usually in double digits. In solving their cases, both Quin and Mack hark back to the early days of the hard-boiled novel, when the private eye was also judge, jury, and executioner. Quin and Mac do not confront, capture, and convey criminals to jail; they dispatch them with nine-millimeter gunfire. Both P.I.s share equally in physical danger, getting hit or beaten or shot. Variously, Mac has a near-death experience, gets amnesia, and suffers from aphasia after being beaten or shot. And although Mac-Gregor's plots are fast-paced and engaging if one can stand the brutality, it takes almost no effort to figure out "whodunit."

MacGregor's St. James-McCleary series reflects the changes that have evolved in the hard-boiled style in terms of the traditional isolation, or loner status, of the private eye. Unlike their earlier counterparts, Quin and Mac are not strictly on their own in fighting crime. Neither faces the traditional antagonism of the police, and Quin encounters no resistance as a woman in a what used to be a traditional "man's" role. She is not called Nancy Drew, or asked "What's a nice girl like you doing in a job like this?" To the contrary, both enjoy a positive, ongoing cooperative relationship with law enforcement officials—Metro-Dade homicide chief Tim Benson, police psychiatrist Wayne O'Donald, and coroner Doc Smithers—who willingly support Quin and Mac with manpower, expertise, and other resources. These characters appear with consistency throughout the series but remain primarily within the sphere of Quin's and Mac's work, as opposed to their personal life.

Although both Quin and Mac also have family and friends who figure prominently in the series, with the exception of *Spree,* family is more a reference than a reality and friendships have no continuity from one novel to the next. Unlike many contemporary P.I.s, Mac and Quin in no way have what Maureen Reddy calls a "chosen family" (*Sisters in Crime* 109) to lessen their isolation and provide company and counsel. What does endure, though not without some disruption, is the relationship between Mac and Quin, slightly but significantly augmented by their daughter. This triad circumscribes the extent of their sustained involvement with others. Family members and social friends are present in the novels principally as plot elements to provide a case for Quin and Mac to solve, or otherwise to advance the action.

The setting in MacGregor's novels is in many ways the typical big city cauldron of crime and corruption found in the hard-boiled style, with some additional features. The series is set mainly in Miami, with an occasional relocation (the Everglades, Gainesville) and, eventually, a move to the presumably safer haven of West Palm Beach. Even after the move, they return to Miami for later investigations. Constantly before the reader are the contradictions of Miami: the tropical paradise juxtaposed with the almost routine, constant criminal activity.

Heat, traffic jams, drought, and hurricane threats contrast with pockets of tranquil escape: the pedestrian friendly, trendy promenades of Coconut Grove; the banyan-shaded neighborhoods of Coral Gables; and the pastel beauty of South Beach and Biscayne Bay. The desirable Latin American influences on the city exist along with the "cocaine cowboys" and drive-by shootings. At one point, Mac remembers Miami years ago as "an enchanted, sun-kissed village" (*Dark* 15) with a beautiful skyline; now, however, "it was . . . bad, that was all. Just bad" (*Dark* 171). He describes the downtown area as a sea of desolation where developers continue to build "concrete monsters" with just "enough greenery to have tricked the birds" (*Dark* 215). The ultimate irony in setting, however, is location of the Dade County morgue in a building which is part of an Art Deco preservation program. It is painted in pastel colors—blue, yellow, green, and pink—and the coroner's sign is, of course, neon: "It was the sort of place where you could imagine corpses dancing to old thirties tunes once the rooms had been cleaned out at night" (*Kill Flash* 21-22). Typically in the hard-boiled style, "[T]he presence of the city is always felt. It is a perfect physical counterpart to the chaos, the lack of communal feeling, and the loneliness that seem endemic in the private eye's world" (Gregory 23). The city even assumes a persona in *Kill Flash*, as Mac conducts an ongoing dialog with Miami, which he blames for his frustration with a case. The city "responds" with mockery: "(Looky here. You try my shoes for a day, okay. . . . You think you got problems, McCleary?" (123). Typical of the hard-boiled style, the "city itself becomes almost a character" (Gregory 22). When Quin and Mac later move to Palm Beach, among the other "middle class refugees" (*Death Flats* 18), hope for a safer life is blunted by Mac's getting shot "twice in nearly three years" (*Blue Pearl* 27).

Another hallmark of hard-boiled detectives is the method of investigation and detecting. Those used by Quin and Mac combine rational and intuitive approaches to crime solving. They understand the need for the routine chores of investigation and both perform these tasks thoroughly; but they also rely heavily on other methods less traditional, New Age, or even supernatural (Swanson and James 135). They interview, take notes, and use case boards to list and diagram clues in their search for patterns to help them solve crimes. Unique to the detective is "the ability to see what others cannot see" (Munt 117), and Quin has a way of seeing that she calls a "kill flash." It is a "right brain bridge . . . a way of perceiving. . . . You want to kill the flash and try to discern the pattern in the play of shadows" (*Kill Flash* 38), as opposed to viewing everything brightly lighted, as with a camera flash. Although Mac calls her superstitious, Quin sees herself as an empiricist; however, she attends carefully to her senses and what she calls "portents" to assist her in solving cases.

While Mac sometimes teases Quin about being superstitious, he takes his own sensory impressions seriously. He has a "hunch spot" between his eyes that burns sharply when he gets close to something or someone important in an investigation. The police psychiatrist supports

Mac's intuitive instincts and explains to Mac that his hunches are "a result of the brain combining facts in new ways" (*Death Sweet* 93). In one case Mac feels a psychic connection, beyond a hunch, with the serial killer. He feels he can get inside him and engages in "a kind of sympathetic-magic brainstorming" (*Sweet* 68) by arranging and rearranging items that duplicate those found at the crime scenes. Quin in *Spree* and Mac in *Blue Pearl* also experience paranormal phenomena in what is, to them, the very real presence of Mac's dead sister Cat.

When *Kill Flash*, the second novel in the series, opens, Quin and Mac are partners in both marriage and profession, as assumed coequals in their private-eye firm. Theirs is definitely not a Sam Spade, P.I./Effie Perine, secretary, business arrangement. Their partnership is, however, a logical place to examine Quin's dual roles as a woman and as a detective and to determine whether Quin is permitted to act out the equal billing she gets on the covers of MacGregor's novels as a member of the "team of St. James and McCleary." Since, even in the nineties, equality is not a given characteristic of relationships between men and women in our society, one should not expect equality in a male-female detective partnership; ultimately, one finds "male privilege and power contrasted with female limitations" (Klein, *Woman Detective* 186-87). Throughout the series, Quin and Mac are generally depicted as equals, in terms of narrative point of view and plotting. MacGregor does not narrate through one or the other exclusively but shifts her point of view among Quin, Mac, and, often, the killer. Quin and Mac share investigative duties and responsibilities and usually—but not always—display mutual respect toward each other in both words and actions. As noted earlier, they take about equal turns getting hurt or rescuing one another from being killed by the murderers they are chasing.

A careful reading of the entire series, however, reveals a number of circumstances that relegate Quin to a secondary position in the partnership, whether as an investigator or a woman. Their business relationship is not always equal when decisions are made about whether to take a case. Quin and Mac often communicate through a type of mental and "marital telepathy" (*Kill Flash* 16), to reach a mutual decision about what they want to do, especially when deciding to take a case. At times, though, Mac makes such decisions on his own, without regard for Quin's feelings or opinions. In *Kill Flash*, he agrees to help his longtime friend, filmmaker Gill Kranish, before consulting Quin, who he knows dislikes Kranish. Quin is "miffed at McCleary for having committed them without discussing it privately" (16).

Later, in *Blue Pearl*, Mac takes a case and does not tell Quin at all. He at least feels guilty, as "They rarely kept professional details like this from each other. They couldn't afford to" (11). When Quin finds out, she is surprised and hurt; their usual awareness of each other's cases was "a kind of acknowledgment that they were a team, professional equals, that work was the one area in which they excelled together" (32). She is further angered that he did not leave her any hints about the case so she could follow through when he got hurt: "She would have done it for him. That he hadn't done it for her hinted at many things, both personal and general. But the bonds between men and the inequities of marriage were the two that came most immediately to mind" (35). Occasionally Mac is condescending to Quin during their work. When she suggests revealing her cover identity to someone, he grudgingly agrees. She " 'smiled, but it was thin, restrained. 'I wasn't asking your permission, you know' " (*Kill Flash* 188).

In their personal relationship, inequalities are also apparent. At times these are only the minor annoyances of any marriage—Mac expecting Quin to clean up the kitchen he dirtied, for example. In other instances, however, Mac attempts to dominate her by ordering her around. One of the problems that usually occurs with a female P.I. involved with a man is that he will interfere with her work out of a desire to protect her from harm (Reddy 105). Worried about the danger while Quin is undercover in *Kill Flash*, Mac "demanded—not suggested—that Quin drop out of the case. Their subsequent argument had been one of the most intense . . . of their marriage" (235). Quin refuses, telling him "she was sick to death of his being a bossy cop" (235). Undaunted, Mac assigns one of the firm's investigators to keep an eye on Quin without her knowing about it.

The most disturbing instance of Mac's domination, or use of power, over Quin, however, is a period of lovemaking during which he undergoes a psychic bonding experience with the killer he is pursuing and acts out the killer's sexual aggression with Quin. She recognizes what Mac is doing and tries to dissuade him, but he persists and overpowers her: "Now the hunger swelled inside him, huge and ugly, a ubiquitous hunger that controlled him, drove him, thrust him inside her" (*Death Sweet* 117). Quin feels violated; she had asked him to stop, and he did not even hear her.

In *Storm Surge*, however, the basis for yet another order from Mac to quit a case has much more to do with Quin's role as a wife and mother. Hearing Quin's expression of concern about the amount of time the case is taking away from their time with their child, Mac retorts, "Then quit the case." Her response: " 'No.' Flat. Unequivocal" (125). Clearly, the expectation is that the woman will concede, abdicating the responsibilities of her job for those of the home and family. After such differences, Quin resents being the one who has to make the conciliatory overtures to set the relationship right again, while Mac is often reluctant to apologize at all. Further, Quin's inner conflict makes her doubt her own judgment, and she feels torn between her work and her daughter: "She felt cheated by the choices she had made. She felt incompetent as a mother" (*Storm Surge* 108). The implication here is that to be a competent detective is to be an incompetent mother, and vice versa; Mac never suffers from a similar conflict between work and parenting.

The most striking episode of Quin's dilemma between her roles occurs in *Spree*, shortly after her daughter is born. Mac and Quin are struggling to maintain their morning jogging routine (now in shifts), feed the baby, and get to the office: "It was high-wire tension between her and McCleary over who would do what and when" (25). Quin sees their life now rooted in the traditions of the past: "[P]rimarily it came down to an inequitable division of labor. *She* was the one who usually had to drop whatever she was doing and head home . . . never mind that she and McCleary were professional equals; on the home front, the feminist movement had never happened. Ellie had changed the dynamics of marriage, the balance of power, by conjuring the traditions in which Quin and McCleary had been raised. Dad's business was bringing home the bacon; Mom's was raising the family" (25). When Mac's sister is killed, Quin's choices are clear: to stay home with the baby or figure out how to accompany Mac on the case, take the baby along, *and* make it all work. Swallowing her first impulse to suggest they take turns, she capitulates: "I'll take care of it. . . . I'll figure something out" (50). And without further comment, Mac lets her do just that; the stereotype is clear.

MacGregor's characterization of Mac's and Quin's personal habits also reinforces certain gender stereotypes. Mac embodies such male traits as self-discipline, organization, and neatness in all aspects of his living and working environments. Even in an episode of spontaneous sex, Mac takes time to fold their clothing. His most annoying habit, one frequently associated with women, is his perpetual tardiness and failure to call when he is late. Very much his opposite, Quin is as messy as he is organized and neat; her study, her nightstand, her closet are all in chaos. She is constantly eating and always keeps a stash of snacks in her purse and in her car. Her Toyota is full of litter, in contrast to Mac's sparkling clean series of RX-7s and later, his Miata. Absentminded, she leaves her razor to stain the bathroom tile, and she often forgets where she puts the butter dish. But she is never late; in fact, she is usually earlier than she needs to be.

Even their case boards reflect their differences: "His board was detailed and neat, with photos of the crime scenes pinned across the top.

. . . It was a left-brain diagram that would require right-brain leaps of faith" (*Spree* 49). In contrast, the items on Quin's board look like a wheel with spokes of comments; she uses her board for "brainstorming, a kind of right-brain purging that then required filling in the blanks with good old left-brain detection and synthesis" (*Spree* 49). Again, the contrast is between male neatness and order and female messiness and disorder.

Early on, Mac found most of Quin's behaviors endearing or amusing; later, though, they are the source of genuine irritation and he reacts to Quin's and Ellie's clutter as though it is "the final violation of his sense of order" (*Blue Pearl* 11). Although he loves them, he seems to long for his more solitary days in homicide, when he was unencumbered by a marriage and a family. These yearnings place him in the company of the more traditional hard-boiled P.I.s who shunned relationships and commitments and who saw women as unnecessary complications, at best.

The most personal aspect of the partnership between Quin and Mac is their sex life. The portrayal of their lovemaking before and during their marriage would seem to characterize them as sexually liberated but monogamous. Mac's resumption of an old affair with Sylvia Callahan while working on a case brings considerable torment to both Quin and Mac, but especially to Quin, as she sees the balance of their relationship tilting away from her. Rather than play the role of the wronged spouse, however, it is she who forces the issue with Mac and insists he resolve his feelings and then make a choice: "She had neither the time nor the inclination to be cast as the poor little wifey in all this" (*Death Sweet* 174). At the same time, she wonders what Mac would do if she were the one in his position: Would he grant her the same freedom? Her doubt is implicit in the questions she asks herself. In spite of her own resolve, and her unexpected liking for Sylvia, Quin does not handle the situation as well as she would like to. Seeing them together, she feels "callow and stupid, estranged and betrayed. To approach this intellectually was one thing. To deal with it emotionally was quite another. Yes, indeed, she was certainly a contemporary liberated woman. . . . Now she was waist deep in the consequences of her magnanimity" (*Death Sweet* 198).

Although Sylvia is murdered and Mac works his way through his guilt to reconcile with Quin, this affair haunts their marriage throughout the series. For Quin the memory never goes away, and it undermines her confidence in their relationship; she seems unable to come to grips with her feelings and uses the affair against Mac long after he thinks the matter has been resolved. Quin ends up behaving like the injured wife she was so determined not to be.

Another south Florida writer, Edna Buchanan, widely known as a Pulitzer Prize–winning crime reporter for the Miami *Herald*, has written three novels in her promising Britt Montero series set in Miami: *Contents Under Pressure, Miami, It's Murder*, and *Suitable for Framing*. Drawing on her personal experiences, recounted in her nonfiction works, *The Corpse Had a Familiar Face* and *Never Let Them See You Cry*, Buchanan has created a contemporary feminist heroine, Britt Montero, who is often described as Buchanan's alter ego (Rubins 38). One of her more notable characteristics is her ethnic background—her father was a Cuban who was killed by a Castro firing squad. Her ethnic heritage places Britt in the company of Muller's Sharon McCone and Neeley's Blanche White in that small, distinctive group of non-Caucasian women investigators.

The daughter of a Cuban revolutionary father and an Episcopal mother descended from an old Miami pioneer family, Britt is gutsy, determined, curious, resourceful, physically fit, witty, smart, and good at her profession. She lucks into a job with a Miami paper as a police reporter; the editors' lack of confidence in her ability to withstand the grisly aspects of the job serves only to increase her determination to be successful. Although by usual definition or categorization, Britt is technically not a private investigator. An investigative crime reporter, her job places her very close to the P.I., and Buchanan's characterization and setting are in keeping with the hard-boiled style. Further, Britt stands out as a main character, a woman who makes life decisions by choice rather than by force or default.

The Miami setting again draws us to what Sheppard calls "fatal glamour" (65), contrasting the soft pastels of the revived Art Deco district, the Cuban influences, and the tropical ambiance with the eccentric, the crazy, and the criminal: Miami is a city where "Rod Serling must be the mayor" (*Miami, It's Murder* 156). Rather than merely describe Miami, however, as is often the case in MacGregor's novels, Buchanan has us experience the city. We accompany Britt to crime scenes, ride through the streets of Overtown, visit her Aunt Odalys in Little Havana, go to La Esquina for Cuban food (which the characters actually eat), and have coffee in Howie's parking garage rooftop "home." In a particularly graphic episode in *Contents Under Pressure*, we feel the physical threat as Britt runs a gauntlet of street violence during a riot, while chasing a story. In her novels, Buchanan reveals the "earth tones pinked over by the producers of *Miami Vice*" (Sheppard 66).

Britt Montero may also be associated with notable hard-boiled heroines such as Grafton's Kinsey Millhone and Paretsky's V. I. Warshawski in terms of their separation from their families. After her father's death, Britt's mother, emotionally unable to care for her, sent her to live with relatives. Britt did not rejoin her mother until she was twelve: "By then we didn't know each other well, and had little to talk about. We still don't" (*Contents* 15). It is typical of hard-boiled heroines to be "estranged from their families, who cannot accept or understand the women's choice of careers and life-styles" (Reddy 104). Britt's mother, who works in women's fashion, is concerned primarily about Britt's having the proper accessories, as well as fixing her up with potential husbands. She refuses to try to understand Britt's work and her love for it; Britt's dedication to her job and her desire to be an agent for change are reminders of her father, which her mother deeply resents and interprets as betrayal.

Although she and her mother maintain an uneasy alliance at best, Britt is not a loner. Like Kinsey and V. I., she has important relationships—again, what Reddy terms "chosen families" (109). In spite of her mother's disapproval, Britt maintains ties with her father's family. Britt's landlords, the Goldsteins, watch out for her without being intrusive; they walk the dog for her, bring her food, and take note of her visitors, especially the males. Mr. Goldstein even mounts a mezuzah on her door for protection. Britt's most important friendship, however, is with Lottie Dane, the wisecracking newspaper photographer from Gun Barrel, Texas. They work, share meals, suffer fools, and survive life-threatening experiences together. They are not above ditching their dates at the opera, on the pretense of going to the ladies' room, when they hear sirens and sense a story. Unlike Quin St. James' friendships in MacGregor's novels, Britt's relationship with Lottie is much more than a plot device, and their friendship is an important element in each novel in Buchanan's series.

Like many of her hard-boiled contemporaries, Britt has avoided romantic involvements with men, putting her job first: "My personal life is a battlefield littered with corpses of once-promising relationships, casualties of my job. The two seem unable to peacefully coexist. So right now, I give work priority" (*Contents* 24). When she begins to spend more time with Homicide Sergeant Kendall McDonald while on a story, their chemistry leads to an affair. Britt's resolve to keep business and pleasure separate weakens, even though she senses she will regret it. According to Reddy, few hard-boiled heroines have their "emotional needs being met by their sexual relationships with men" (109), and eventually this is Britt's experience. After a series of "dates" where they do not go out in public, McDonald reveals the pressure he feels from police department gossip and his fear that he will not get a desired promotion if he is seen with her and known to be involved. His priorities prevail over the relationship: "Things change, everything is cyclical. . . . We just have to cool it for a while, Britt. It's not forever" (*Contents* 286). To his credit, he does not ask her to subordinate her work to his; to her credit, she does not get "bummed by a busted romance" (286). The disruption of their relationship by their professions seems to be an equal problem for both of them. He remains a caring friend who provides her with comfort at critical times; he does get his promotion and a new boss, the cycle does seem to swing around, and they resume their involvement in *Suitable for Framing.*

As a woman, Britt feels pressured to remain professional at all times and to refrain from showing what would be deemed feminine emotions. Again, the conflict arises within the female character between job and gender. When Britt first begins her job, the police do not take her seriously, "and the favorite sport of some was trying to gross out the new female police reporter" (*Miami* 11). When invited to view a crime scene, she feels included and excited but quickly realizes that the invitation is not acceptance but a test: "The cops expected weakness. They saw none. I remained coolly professional . . . exhibiting only clinical curiosity. The pretense was not easy" (11). Clearly, to be accepted she has to be more like the male cops than a woman, who is expected to react emotionally to such a scene. Men may pick and choose their battles, but Britt feels she must fight every battle: "[I]t is a matter of principle for a woman in this business. One small sign of weakness or lack of resolve and you are lost" (*Contents* 94). Britt knows there are "[n]o excuses for a woman struggling to make it in a male-dominated profession" (*Miami* 82). Women not only have to be very good at their jobs; others' expectations of them are higher than for men. Britt is tough; she does not want to "acquire a crybaby reputation" (*Miami* 161). Mentoring an aspiring young woman reporter who has just been hired in the newspaper library, Britt gives her this advice: "Whatever you do, don't cry in the newsroom" (*Suitable for Framing* 189). Britt is quite capable of showing her feelings and crying, but she does it privately, away from the work environment.

In *Miami, It's Murder*, the plot line involving the serial rapist brings out the conflict and discomfort that can occur between women and men over things "female." After the attack, the policeman on the scene is embarrassed by having to ask Britt, whom he knows personally, if she has been raped. Above all, Britt does not want to be seen as a weak female, a victim, because that will diminish her: "Their eyes made me uneasy, a feeling that these men were seeing me as a woman somebody tried to rape rather than a professional, a reporter" (189).

In terms of women's roles in Buchanan's novels, the paper's assistant city editor, Gretchen Platt, and new reporter Trish Tierney reinforce the stereotype that women cannot work for, or with, other women. Gretchen is every professional woman's worst nightmare: a female supervisor who does not respect other women, especially those who are strong and competent. Britt observes, "Women striving in this, or any, male-dominated profession should be supportive of one another. But in Gretchen's case, I had seen the enemy and she was us. Ambitious and eager to be one of the boys, she was tougher on women than the men were" (*Contents* 67). Style over substance, Gretchen does not know a news priority from a paper clip. She meddles in Britt's work, tries to keep tabs on her at all times, and thinks up harebrained story ideas like the one that sends a reporter out to sea to replicate the Cuban rafters' experience and nearly gets him killed in the process.

To Britt and Lottie, the most outrageous of Gretchen's brilliant ideas is her insistence that Ryan, a male reporter, go along with them on a potentially dangerous story: "I think a man should go with Britt and Lottie. For their protection" (*Contents* 261). To their objections that Ryan is not streetwise and they will have to look out for *him*, Getchen replies, "None of this silly feminist rhetoric" (261). Veterans of a combat driving course, Britt and Lottie have to deal with Ryan's sterotypically male behavior: " 'I'll take the keys,'" Ryan said manfully. . . . 'I'm the man, I drive' " (262), followed by " 'Where to, girls?' " (261). Ryan's inexperience under the conditions they find themselves in nearly gets them all killed, and Britt and Lottie have to save him after he is injured.

In contrast to Gretchen, Trish Tierney seems to idolize Britt, who takes a lot of her time to mentor her about making contacts, getting stories, writing, and advancing her career in journalism. Trish begins stealing Britt's stories to grab headlines for herself and to make Britt look incompetent and foolish. Trish turns out to be a psychotic killer and is murdered by her lover, who frames Britt for the crime. Before Trish's murder, in a rare concession to public female emotion, Britt had set herself up as a suspect by engaging in a "cat fight" with Trish in the police station parking lot: "Our fight would be the talk of the newsroom. The men would love it, embracing all the stereotypes about women being unable to work together, unable to get along" (*Suitable* 190).

Britt Montero also resembles V. I. Warshawski and Kinsey Millhone in that she has a "unisex" first name (Lehman 177). Although Buchanan does not make an issue of the name or use it to distance Britt from others, the possibility is there. What is interesting, however, is that Buchanan puts a slightly different twist on the name device with a minor character, Lieutenant K. C. (Kathleen Constance) Riley: "Women cops must be tough and ambitious to achieve promotion. She was both. Even to the extent of using both her first initials" (*Miami* 50). When Britt once wrote a story about her, portraying her as professional and heroic, "her anger . . . was wild enough to make my kneecaps tingle. She had warned me never, ever, to use her full name in a story again" (50). K. C. thinks the use of her initials makes her manlike; Britt is put off by her pretense: "I appreciated the obstacles she had overcome but was fed up with her Dirty Harry imitation. Acting *muy macho* doesn't prove you are as good as a man" (50-51).

Another common trait of the hard-boiled heroine is her attitude toward physical violence. The more feminist detectives have conflicting emotions about engaging in the violence the hard-boiled males seem to seek out; they usually do not initiate violence, they are reluctant to carry—much less use—weapons, and they attempt to extricate themselves from danger rather than wait to be rescued (Reddy 113). Britt is resourceful in escaping from a racist police major in *Contents Under Pressure*, as well as in fighting off a rapist. While she does not shy from personal danger in pursuit of a story, she also does not seek physically violent situations. She owns a gun: "Like a hurricane tracking chart, a gun is something you hope you'll never have to use. But if you live in Miami, you can be damn well sure that you will need them both some day. It's a fact of life" (*Contents* 59). But she usually keeps it either in her car's glove compartment or in her bedroom. When he learns of the rapist's interest in Britt, a cop friend sternly advises her to load it, carry it, and shoot to kill. When she actually does need the weapon, the gun is in her purse where she cannot reach it, and she is terrified that the rapist will instead get her gun and kill her with it. Carrying a weapon is no guarantee of invincibility; it may be just the opposite.

While in MacGregor's detective series order is restored by the resolution of crimes on a personal level—that is, the P.I. solves the crime and usually kills the criminal in a final showdown—in Buchanan's novels the administration of justice is both personal and public. MacGregor tells us that justice is corrupt but only one novel, *Dark Fields,* shows this corruption to be a social ill of any magnitude. As a more feminist detective, Britt Montero weaves criminal actions into the fabric of society; such relationships make "neat, complete solutions difficult" (Klein, *Woman Detective* 201). In *Contents Under Pressure* Buchanan broadens the death of a former football hero and family man, African American D. Wayne Hudson, into an indictment of racism and rogue cops in the Miami police department. As a reporter, Britt is able to extend criminal investigations and their resolutions into the public sphere through her job at the paper. In *Miami, It's Murder*, the focus is on a justice system that permits murderers to go free, in large part from a "highly publicized fluke" in Florida law that allowed "Free murders, on the house" (137), and on the exercise of vigilante justice to rectify these inequities in the system. But, as Britt and terminally ill retired cop Dan Flood discover, vigilante justice is as prone to error as the other kind: "The system leaves a lot to be desired, but it's all we've got" (209). Flood defends his actions: "Death is the only known sure rehabilitation. This was preventive: proactive police work instead of reactive. . . . Sometimes life boils down to law and order versus justice" (210-11).

In this same novel, the rape plotline highlights crimes against women, and Britt is relentless in her pursuit of the rapist through her personal actions and her reporting. Demonstrating her concern for other women, she is adamant about warning them of the danger: "The police were trying to keep it quiet, and there were several attacks before word one ever appeared in the newspaper. Women had to be warned, to be made aware, they had to become outraged and aroused enough to help apprehend him" (*Miami* 103). When a rape victim Britt has talked to tells her she intends to sue her employer because she was raped at work, Britt thinks, "Sounded right to me. Too much litigation clogs our courts now, but if this was what it took to keep women safe on the job, I was for it" (152). In *Suitable for Framing*, the plot device of carjacking and chop shops extends to an examination of the lives of young African American males in Overton—neither children nor men—and their limited options, as evidenced by Howie, who aspires to better himself, who has dreams, but who is destroyed by a rule-bound system.

A relative newcomer to Florida crime fiction is Barbara Parker, whose "suspicion" series—*Suspicion of Innocence and Suspicion of Guilt*—joins the growing number of women writing in the legal suspense subgenre. A former prosecutor, Parker knows her way around law firms and courtrooms and delivers realistic scenes in these milieus which add interest and credibility to her writing. Like MacGregor and Buchanan, she sets her novels in Miami. She is more akin to Buchanan in her ability to render the grit and glamour of this diverse, cosmopolitan city. Parker's plots focus on human ambition and the thirst for power which can lead to murder, and she incorporates Latin culture into her plots more successfully than any of the other writers discussed here.

The main character in Parker's new series is Gail Connor, ex-debutante and civil attorney on the partner fast-track at a prestigious, male-dominated Miami law firm. Gail is married to a not very successful businessman and has a ten-year-old daughter, who shows potential in future novels as more than just a complication in her mother's love life following her divorce in *Suspicion of Guilt*. Gail's sometime partner, informally, in crime solving is the affluent, stylish, handsome Cuban, Anthony Quintero, a lawyer in another influential law firm. The chemistry between these two heats up pretty quickly and their affair begins during Gail's separation from her husband in *Suspicion of Innocence*.

The plot of *Suspicion of Innocence* centers around the death of Gail's sister, Renee, an adult wild child who has always been their mother's favorite. Like Britt Montero, Gail has a strained relationship with her family, whose get-togethers "could have been scripted by Tennessee Williams and badly overacted by the cast of a small-town dinner theater" (*Innocence* 13). Rather than use these tensions merely to add to the isolation Gail is feeling in her marriage, Parker instead portrays a woman who struggles with her anger, hurt, and guilt over the family ties that bind them painfully to each other. Gail Connor must not only deal with being accused of her sister's murder, but she must also engage in difficult self-examination, which gives her depth and makes her a sympathetic character. In *Suspicion of Guilt*, Gail takes on as a client a longtime friend who is accused of murdering the wealthy matron of a powerful old Miami family. By the end of the novel, nearly everyone has been considered a suspect, and Gail continues the process of trying to fit together her roles as aspiring law partner, mother to a child who misses her father, and lover to a Latin man who is still tentative about his relationship with both Gail and her daughter.

Parker's novels have been called a "sun-drenched variation on the work of Scott Turow and Patricia Cornwell" (Donovan 176), a status she may attain as the series continues. With her first two novels, however, she seems to be establishing a foundation for what may more realistically follow in the swift disintegration of Gail Connor's marriage, her precipitous affair with Quintero, and her decision to leave the law firm and practice on her own. Gail Connor has the potential to be an even stronger woman in the series than she has been thus far, once she gets a few things sorted out.

The two remaining writers addressed here, Karen Ann Wilson and Sherryl Woods, write what they describe as "romantic mysteries." While these may provide brief interludes of romantic fantasy for readers who enjoy such escape, they do not measure up as detective novels, especially when compared to the work of Buchanan, MacGregor, and Parker. The cover blurbs on Wilson's books announce a "new veterinary series: Dogs, cats . . . and crooks. Samantha Holt can handle them all" (*Eight Dogs Flying*). On the cover of Sherryl Woods's *Hot Property*, the hook alerts the reader to what is in store: "It's hot times in Miami when a single mother and a sexy cop set out to catch a killer." Each of her novels announces that it is "A Molly DeWitt Romantic Mystery." Both Wilson and Woods lead the reader to believe that their main characters are competent women who play an important role in investigating crimes. This is simply not the case. Although both Samantha and Molly have wit and spunk, they are definitely subordinate to their male associates in sleuthing, and, more sadly, they reinforce negative views of women.

Wilson's setting is Brightwater Beach, a fictional Gulf coast town near Tampa, which is apparently inhabited by stereotypical Florida retirees who cannot drive, wear too much polyester, have too much time on their hands, and devote their lives to pampering and overfeeding their pets. Samantha Holt is a trained veterinary nurse who works for Dr. Louis Augustin. The plotting of the crimes is initiated by the vet's attention to a particular animal behavior or ailment—retired greyhounds viciously attacking people, or cats with cleft palates. Samantha is leary of men because her fiancé jilted her at the altar, and Augustin is brooding about a divorce he did not want. Reddy would describe this unlikely pair of sleuths as "freelancing amateurs" who present "problems of logistics and of verisimilitude to the author, and of believability to the reader" (18). When the amateur is a woman, credibility is strained further because of societal expectations and gender stereotypes (Reddy 18-19). These problems are exacerbated in a series because the amateur's involvement in more than one or two murders—infrequent events themselves, especially in a small town—becomes less and less believable.

And believability is indeed a problem where Holt and Augustin are concerned. First of all, detecting is not seen as a serious enterprise but as snooping or an affliction, like a "sleuthing virus" (*Copy Cat Crimes* 74). By her own admission, Samantha (who can handle them all, remember?) is not comfortable as a detective: "I felt stupid and awkward asking a perfect stranger probing questions, like I was some kind of hotshot detective. . . . I just sat there, hoping I didn't sound as foolish as I felt" (*Eight Dogs Flying* 158). She views investigating as interfering, as dirty work, more appropriately the province of the police. Augustin persists in ordering her to check things out, imposing on her personal time to accompany him on breaking and entering expeditions, and behaving in a sexist and condescending manner toward her throughout. She does his bidding, but she occasionally cracks wise or questions him—usually briefly.

Although Augustin is described as sexy, with penetrating eyes and a wealth of masculine charm which he reserves for his female clients, with Samantha and his other staff he behaves like a jerk. He's bossy, demanding, moody, sarcastic, and even cruel to the point of driving an employee to quit. (Why she is the only one who quits is the most puzzling mystery the reader faces.) Even his attempts at genuine humor have an edge, what Klein describes as a technique to "mask a misogynistic sub-text"

(*Woman* 193). This is particularly obvious in his relationship with Samantha. He's "never one to apologize for anything" (*Eight* 30), he feels free to make remarks about Samantha's weight, and he pries into her private life. Yet, at the end of both of Wilson's novels, Samantha falls into the fluttery female role, responding like a puppy to his backhanded invitations to go have a drink or a bite to eat, "something a step or two up from McDonald's" (*Copy Cat* 248). Augustin is a dominating egotist, and Samantha, far from being the main character who takes any kind of charge, is eager and grateful for his personal attention when he deigns to bestow it upon her.

In her "Hot" series—*Hot Property, Hot Secret, Hot Money,* and *Hot Schemes*—Sherryl Woods, a writer of romances and now romantic mysteries, including the Amanda Roberts series, pairs amateur Molly DeWitt with Miami Metro homicide detective Michael O'Hara. Although Woods bills Molly as the central character in her series, she is secondary to the professional, the cop, in investigations. O'Hara, whose mother was Cuban, is a macho, egotistical man who definitely does not appreciate Molly's interest, much less her participation, in his cases. He is a master of the sarcastic put-down, which he uses to discourage her obvious interest in him and her desire to help investigate: "Unless you have a license, you're not an investigator. That puts you in a league with Nancy Drew" (*Hot Property* 16). He warns her that amateur snooping is a quick way to become another victim and tells her he does not have "the manpower to waste on a meddlesome woman who insists on jumping into the path of danger" (126). He talks to her "in the tone of a man instructing the little woman to remain dutifully in the kitchen" (16). There is no end to his sarcasm; he tells her to go bake cookies, and asserts his position as a man and a cop: " 'That's why I'm a policeman and you're a whatever it is you are' " (23). He also imposes himself on her with his physical presence, insisting on sleeping at her apartment to protect her, or in other situations grabbing her elbow or putting his hand on her back to propel her where he wants her to go.

Although Molly bristles at his remarks and implies that she will not stand for this treatment, she always succumbs to her physical attraction for him and tolerates his behavior. She twits him about his assertion that male hormones are what make him tick—a disappointing cliché, she says—but she thinks of him in terms of her own "raging and thoroughly irrational hormones" (*Property* 129). Molly does not even comprehend the contradictions in her own thinking; when she believes Michael is beginning to respect her, she feels that she is stronger and more in charge of her life. Her self-confidence is dependent on his interest in her. Although they eventually gain more parity in their personal relationship during the series, Michael throughout is the competent professional man and Molly the supportive and occasionally helpful girlfriend.

Woods not only fails to deliver the strong heroine implied on her book covers, but she fails to follow through in other areas as well. Her Miami setting is no more than a backdrop, and her characterization lacks depth and credibility. Descriptive detail is ordinary and repetitive: eyes are nut-brown, Latin complexions are olive, bodies are bronzed, and the promised hot action and romance are lukewarm at best. Occasional exchanges of witty repartee are simply not enough to carry these novels.

In response to the question posed earlier—whether these heroes resist gender stereotypes and function on their own merits as both women and investigators—the answer varies with the author. Edna Buchanan's novels are the most promising thus far in depicting an independent, resourceful woman who is human as well. More feminist in her writing than the others, Buchanan does the best job of unifying plot, character, and setting, and Britt Montero is certainly a contemporary, entertaining hero. In fact, one of the things that distinguishes Buchanan's novels from the others is her use of humor, which is largely lacking in the other writers' work. While MacGregor's novels are heavily dependent on plot, her husband and wife P.I. team is uncommon among detective characters, and the challenges of managing their professional and personal lives focus on a contemporary social issue of women trying to balance a career, a marriage, and a family. So far, Quin is "having it all," though not without some concessions along the way. With additional novels in her series, Barbara Parker may well create a character who can easily keep company with Britt Montero and Quin St. James.

Works Cited

Buchanan, Edna. *Contents Under Pressure.* New York: Avon, 1992.

——. *Miami, It's Murder.* New York: Hyperion, 1994.

——. *Suitable for Framing.* New York: Hyperion, 1995.

Donovan, Ann. "Suspicion of Innocence." *Library Journal* Dec. 1993: 176.

Gregory, Sinda. *Private Investigations: The Novels of Dashiell Hammett.* Carbondale: Southern Illinois P, 1985.

Klein, Kathleen Gregory. *The Woman Detective: Gender and Genre.* 2nd. ed. Chicago: U of Illinois P, 1995.

——, ed. *Great Women Mystery Writers: Classic to Contemporary.* Westport: Greenwood, 1994.

Lehman, David. *The Perfect Murder: A Study in Detection.* New York: Free Press, 1989.

MacGregor, T. J. *Blue Pearl*. New York: Hyperion, 1994.

——. *Dark Fields*. New York: Ballantine, l986.

——. *Death Flats*. New York: Ballantine, 1991.

——. *Death Sweet*. New York: Ballantine, 1988.

——. *Kill Flash*. New York: Ballantine, 1987.

——. *Spree*. New York: Ballantine, 1992.

——. *Storm Surge*. New York: Hyperion, 1993.

Munt, Sally R. *Murder by the Book? Feminism and the Crime Novel*. New York: Routledge, 1994.

Parker, Barbara. *Suspicion of Guilt*. New York: Dutton, 1995.

——. *Suspicion of Innocence*. New York: Dutton, 1994.

Reddy, Maureen. *Sisters in Crime: Feminism and the Crime Novel*. New York: Continuum, 1988.

Rubins, Josh. Rev. of *Contents Under Pressure*. *New York Times Review of Books* 18 Oct. 1992: 38.

Sheppard, R. Z. "Urban Razzle, Fatal Glamour." *Time* 28 Sept. 1987: 65-66.

Swanson, Jean, and Dean James. *By a Woman's Hand: A Guide to Mystery Fiction by Women*. New York: Berkley, 1994.

Woods, Sherryl. *Hot Property*. New York: Dell, 1992.

Wilson, Karen Ann. *Copy Cat Crimes*. New York: Berkley, 1995.

——. *Eight Dogs Flying*. New York: Berkley, 1994.

6

Noir: Keys' Style

Harold Nugent and Susan Nugent

I believe if you get the landscape right, the characters will step out of it, and they'll be in the right place.

—E. Annie Proulx
(Skow 83)

Most readers familiar with the environment of the Florida Keys and Key West will agree that they provide a setting conducive to noir novels. The very isolation of the Keys and their many alienated denizens provides ample material for its writers. Passing through the Everglades, U.S. 1 travels over forty-two bridges and across more than a hundred keys. Keys with such exotic and historically burdened names as Key Largo, Islamorada, Lower Matecumbe, Bahia Honda, Cudjoe, and Boca Chica lead to Key West, Cayo Hueso as the Spanish called it, Island of Bones. At the end of the road is Mile Marker Zero. To go any farther by car is to risk a swim with the barracuda and sharks in the ninety miles of water to Havana. Here is the southernmost point of the continental United States, for the many haunted and hunted the last designated resort, the end of the road.

The Florida Keys have a total population of 80,000, with around 25,000 of those in Key West. Violent crimes are high for that population; a sense of a lack of order prevails. First names are plentiful but social security numbers are not. Surrounded by beauty—indescribable water and emerging and disappearing mangrove islands—the Keys appear untamable. Hurricanes are of more concern than the law. John D. MacDonald's and John Lutz's private investigators, Travis McGee and Fred Carver, have traveled down the Keys to solve mysteries, to attempt to establish order. But neither of these characters belongs in this world permanently. They eventually return to the more controlled worlds of Fort Lauderdale and Del Moray. The noir novels of the Keys have characters who either know and understand this world or move here and become part of it. So, too, have their authors.

85

Key Largo has helped shape Thorn, the major character in several of James Hall's novels as well as a minor one in his recent *Gone Wild*. Throughout these novels, readers learn bits and pieces of Thorn's past. His parents died in a car accident ending in Lake Surprise; the woman who raised him is killed in a drug-smuggling incident; his childhood friend, Gaeton, dies fighting drugs; his lover dies diving. In each case, Thorn becomes the one who must solve the mystery. "Thorn, without so much as a Social Security number or a driver's license. Hadn't registered for the draft, hadn't ever paid taxes 'cause he'd never gotten a paycheck. Nothing special about that in the Keys. . . . Revenue men had been as rare as frost" (*Tropical Freeze* 105). But the law has not yet arrived in Key Largo. Thus, Thorn takes charge.

The isolation of Thorn reflects the isolation of the Keys; he is a prime example of the haunted and hunted, haunted by the deaths of his parents and hunted by tilapia farmers. Although his friends (Sugarman, Darcy) help him, Thorn acts as a solitary force against the evil of drug smugglers, drunken drivers, and murderous divers. These crimes are committed and solved in the Keys' isolated areas: the eighteen-mile stretch between the Florida mainland and Key Largo, a patch reef with only one boat in the far distance, and the fringes of the Everglades.

Critics for the most part commend Hall's Thorn novels. They especially note his depiction of the Keys. "Mr. Hall's lyrical passion for the Florida Keys, his spare language and unusual images haunt us long after the story has faded" (Paretsky 38). "*Mean High Tide* is as well written, as violent and as effective in evoking its locale as Hall's earlier novels" (Muste). These critics also note that there is no sense that justice prevails, or that the loner can ever completely restore order to chaos. Instead, as Paretsky comments, "James Hall is too aware of the bitter realities of our day to allow Thorn and Darcy so happy an ending. . . . Thorn gets a respite, but no lasting peace" (31). Such is the angst of noir novels. With Thorn, we travel into the darker side of human nature, feeling fortunate to escape unscathed.

The dark elements of this literature are evident in broad daylight as even Hall's title *Under Cover of Daylight* (and, later on, McGuane's *Ninety-two in the Shade*) suggests. Evil does not act only at night but also in the glare of sunshine. Hall dramatically opens *Mean High Tide* with a snorkeling scene. The day, Keys perfect, finds Thorn fishing, relaxing, while Darcy snorkels, hunting for lobster. Sunshine. Blues and greens. No dark alleys, mangroves or hammocks. But Darcy's hand gets caught in the crevices of coral as she pursues a lobster. Readers gasp for breath as Darcy is murdered in blinding sunshine with Thorn only a few feet away.

Within *Mean High Tide*, the noir conceit of the spider woman presents itself in Sylvie. Truly manic, she half entwines and half seduces Thorn into her web of violence, abuse, and crime. Thorn must fight her as he untangles himself from her world and destroys her web.

Thorn leaves the Keys in *Gone Wild* to help Allison Farleigh fight her daughter's killers and endangered species' poachers. Although, like Crocodile Dundee, Thorn relates to everything that creeps and crawls, he loses his effectiveness outside the Keys. In Miami, caged, facing a diamondback rattler, Thorn is helpless, whereas in the Keys, in nature, he prevails. As with many noir novels, we get the sense that his newfound love of Allison is temporary, at best.

Hall, who has lived in Florida long enough for Floridians to claim him, knows the Keys, and captures them within *Bones of Coral*. Hall takes his readers to the watery environs of Key West, "an outpost for the unstable, maladjusted, the just plain insane" (33). Shaw Chandler, Hall's hero, continues:

If they weren't insane when they came, they turned that way. They became islanders, devolved creatures. . . . A thing with two hearts. One that beat in tune with the rhythms of the nearly forgotten land, one that obeyed only the primitive metronome of the ocean. It was the reason he'd left, part of the reason he so seldom returned. That island made you crazy. (33)

After watching his father die of gun-shot wounds, Shaw, a thirty-eight-year-old paramedic, heads down the Keys. His self-assigned mission is to find the reasons and persons underlying his father's murder, a balm at least for his angst. In Key West, Shaw reunites with his high school sweetheart, Trula, only to find she has contracted multiple sclerosis. Together they seek to solve the murder as well as to get at the source of what is slowly turning into an epidemic disease.

Marilyn Stasio, commenting on *Bones of Coral*, says Hall's "cautionary tale about the Navy's criminally sloppy methods of disposing of its toxic wastes escalates into an overblown horror story" (37). Another reviewer takes a different perspective, "A thoughtful, multifaceted novel that should not be missed" (Kilpatrick 209). In either case, the noir elements of moral decay and concealed horrors are activated by the omnipresence of such emotionalized landscapes as the cemetery and city dump.

Bones of Coral focuses upon "Mount Trashmore," the island dump:

the white hill of garbage that you could see from five miles at sea. The mountain had been growing there since Shaw was a boy. Now beside it was an incineration plant, its two concrete smokestacks soaring a couple of hundred feet. Beside one of the two windowless buildings a line of garbage trucks waited to dump their loads. (54)

Here Shaw finds the source of evil, the perfect noir setting with dead-end hallways, blind stairways, and unknown horrors. For Shaw Chandler, the toxic dump becomes a symbol of violence, disease, and death—its thinly spread soil only a cover for the workings of some of man's worst nature.

Hall's heroes, not detectives, find the strength to seek justice in a chaotic environment. His love stories appear doomed from the start, but the audience still hopes they flourish. His books border on the unbelievable, but we willingly suspend our disbelief because we, like the characters, are psychologically drawn into Hall's world. Writing in the tradition of the noir genre, Hall takes "this high adventure a step beyond the limits of the traditional action novel by introducing clean air issues, wildlife preservation, toxic waste disposal, environmental health, and other topics of current concern" (Kilpatrick 209). Perhaps it is this focus on contemporary issues that will keep Hall from becoming a writer of canon classics. In the meantime, don't plan to put down his novel once you start it.

A contrast in quality to Hall's Thorn novels is the MacMorgan series by Randy Striker. Three of these novels (*Key West Connection, Everglades Assault*, and *The Deep Six*) are set in and around the Keys. Most action takes place on a boat or under the water as MacMorgan used to be a Navy SEAL in Vietnam. More adventure occurs beneath the sheets. The front page of *Everglades Assault* summarizes both the plots and the attitudes within this series: "MacMorgan has blood on his knuckles and a woman in heat on his hands." The plots of these novels are all too predictable: sharks, crooks, and soft pornography fill these pages. Although some readers might find escape in these novels, thought-provoking images or ideas are scarce if not nonexistent.

Joy Williams, probably best known for her history and travel guide to the Florida Keys, has also written a number of novels including *State of Grace* and *Breaking and Entering*. Both novels are deeply disturbing. Not set in the Keys, *State of Grace* pursues the effects of incest on a young woman, showing the trap it creates. In *Breaking and Entering*, a young couple breaks into winter homes in the Panhandle and the Keys, assuming the lives of the owners. The couple's idiosyncratic value system appears at times more rational than that of the displaced inhabitants.

Like Hall and the other Key West writers, Williams exposes the evil that exists in a well-lit world. The manic characters in *Breaking and*

Entering are representative of the consequences of a superabundance of sun. Williams catches the process deftly when she describes the daily occurrence: "The sun was in the exact center of the sky. It was the time of day when things are posed and cast no shadows because they seem so familiar. It was the time of day when the noonlight demons are out" (181). Joy Williams's characters inhabit a demented and paradoxical world—an environment we will see again in other novels where characters are often at the mercy of the Florida Keys' "noonlight demons."

Jim Harrison is equally well known for his five volumes of poetry as he is for his several novels including the trilogy, *The Legends of the Fall,* recently made into a movie. Two novels, *A Good Day to Die* and *Warlock* are examples of what editors of *Contemporary Literary Criticism* call "thrillers, revealing Harrison's admiration for detective fiction in the tradition of John D. MacDonald" ("Jim Harrison" 196). Having spent time in the Florida Keys since the early seventies when he came down to visit and fish with his friends Thomas McGuane and Russ Chatham, he now lives in northern Michigan. He continues to come to Key West to fly fish for permit, bonefish and tarpon.

In *A Good Day to Die* (1973) the unnamed hero and narrator visits the Keys for a month or two each year to do some fishing. The hero, not a Vietnam veteran, is burned out as a result of growing up in the sixties. In the Keys he is in a marathon to pop every pill listed in *The John Hopkins Handbook of Drugs* from Demerol to Valium. All this he washes down with Wild Turkey and beer. A number of reviewers, including Sara Blackburn and William Woods, have criticized Harrison for this noir element of the novel: for preaching a "me-burned-out Tarzan dogma" (Blackburn 4) and for taking the reader on a "facile romp through fields of fashionable despair ending on a crescendo of modish apocalypse" (Woods 4). On the other hand, Harrison has been praised for his bright language and ability to characterize certain rural and urban types "particular and fixed in time." In addition to drugs, violence, and sex is a deprecating attitude toward all the women in the novel, whether they are one night pickups, ex-wives, or current traveling companions.

A Good Day to Die starts off with the narrator double anchored off Cudjoe Key twenty miles northeast of Key West. On board is a young woman he has picked up at a bar the night before. By the time the prologue is over, he has literally dumped her on a pier telling the Hispanic dockhand that she is a "dumbo cunto stupido no fisho" (16). His own lack of self-respect continues throughout the novel and appears to motivate inflicting pain on his companions as one way of relieving his own pain.

Full of Valium and whiskey, he muddles through time indiscriminately until one day, sweating in his room, he realizes the "sun is flow-ing in a sheet through the window" (18) but he can't figure out why he doesn't draw the blind. It seems as if the Key West environment is starting to get to him, the "noonlight demons" that Joy Williams describes are on to him. In the first three chapters set in Key West and environs, Harrison establishes the relationships among this hero and his two conspirators, Tim, a physically and mentally wounded vet, and Sylvia, Tim's high school girl friend. The three leave Key West, to stop the damming of the Grand Canyon.

All the writers discussed in this chapter owe a debt to Ernest Hemingway for style or subject matter or both but it is Harrison, perhaps, who owes the most. For example, here in *A Good Day to Die*, Harrison has the narrator experience some spiritual cleansing, short-termed as it is, in the clear and cold water of the trout streams of Idaho and Montana. There is also the element of hypermachoism in Harrison's novels especially, as mentioned, in his treatment of women. Alison Lurie has a theory about a certain group of male authors associated with Key West. In order that no one might conceive them as gay, they "run around and act foolish and demonstrate their heterosexuality in an exhausting way" (Nadler 48).

The novel leaves Key West after three chapters and goes on the road, Kerouac fashion. The three characters travel west only to change strategy when they find no dam is planned for the Grand Canyon. This noir novel at its best gives us a snapshot of the wandering despair of the seventies but read in the nineties gives us the feeling that "we've been there, done that, and got the T-shirt." The hero represents, perhaps all too well, the particular alienation of that time period. However, Harrison appears to have matured as a writer after he moved away from the Keys to Montana as revealed in more recent novels such as *Sundog and Delva*. The characters seem to be more intelligent and sensitive, and in turn, capable of being identified with by today's readers.

Neither Laurence Shames nor his heroes, Joey Goldman in *Florida Straits* and *Sunburn* and Augie Silver in *Scavenger Reef*, need be considered Floridians. They aren't. But Shames, from New York, spends winters in Key West where his heroes are painfully and comically adjusting to the Keys.

Of *Florida Straits* Marilyn Stasio comments,

Writing as if the cameras were already rolling, Mr. Shames turns out characters flashier than a Key West sunset and dialogue tastier than a conch stew. Keen invention has gone into the culture clash between the big-city gangsters and the laid-back locals. But the most fun is watching Joey go native. (29)

In the novel, Joey heads down to the Keys from New York City with his girl, Sandy, hoping to become a somebody, trying to transplant the only talents he has—that of gangster—to the Keys. After the first night when a falling coconut ominously trashes his windshield, Joey is able to take some time to think about his situation:

> So he parked the car, sat down on the seawall, watched the pelicans move in and out of the glow of lamps on the pier and waited. The air smelled of iodine and wet stone. Joey, to his surprise, became more rather than less patient the longer he sat, and he dimly realized how thin the line could be between waiting for something and waiting for nothing. (42)

Here the weather begins to assuage the incipient maladies of the character.

Joey's compound (a number of Conch houses surrounding a common patio and pool) turns out to be a microcosm of Key West life. Much like the sea, the compound is teeming with inhabitants: Steve, the landlord, ever naked, smoking and reading a newspaper while partially immersed in the swimming pool; Pete and Claude, two gay bartenders; Wendy and Marsha, the lesbian couple who own an antique store; and Luke and Lucy, a reggae musician and a mailperson, respectively.

Joey learns as he goes. When he needs to read a nautical chart, he asks for help. "For some reason this struck Joey funny: a map where all the important stuff was in the water and the nothing part was land. This he'd never heard of in Queens" (167-68). Bert the Shirt has told Joey that the money is in the water. Joey comes to realize the significance of this statement, using this newly acquired knowledge to take charge of his half-brother Gino as well as control his and Sandra's future. When his father commends him, Joey acknowledges how he has changed, "Up in New York, when I lived up there, hey, let's face it, I couldn't get outta my own way, I couldn't do nothin" (266). Key West changes Joey, allowing him to discover his strength.

"Resounding with great Noo Yawk dialogue . . . and packed with bad guys in shiny blue suits and good guys in pink bikini briefs, *Florida Straits* is a wacky caper too wundafull fa woids," says Carol Peace (28). The wackiness keeps this novel from being truly noir, but the New Yorker running aground in Key West makes a good comedy-crime novel. Readers enjoy watching Joey and Sandy grow, becoming a part of this tacky community. In contrast, little empathy is created, or needed, for the characters such as Gino who are truly in danger. Thus, laughter erupts throughout this laid-back suspense novel—laid-back, perhaps only a euphemism in the Keys for a survival mechanism to prevent the mania resulting from too much sunlight and subsequent activity.

Critics continue to praise Shames's work saying he "has a good ear for dialect and an even better sense for using a minimum of description to create real people and believable situations" (Vicarel 139). *Sunburn*, Shames's third novel, continues the saga of Joey's family in Key West, but focuses on the father, Vincente Delgatto, who decides to write his memoirs as godfather with the help of Artie Magnus, reporter for the local paper. However, as with his earlier *Florida Straits*, Shames does not write an unadulterated noir novel. His heroes are not totally isolated or alienated. Instead, a sense of camaraderie exists. In *Sunburn*, Shames writes an entertaining mystery, with a lighthearted side putting evil in perspective.

This feeling of camaraderie does not exist in *Scavenger Reef*, Shames's novel about Augie Silver, an artist killed by a water spout. Or was he? His paintings, owned by many of his comrades, are worth far more if he is dead. So, when he reappears, someone tries to make him disappear permanently. Because few characters lack motivation to kill Augie, he and the reader trust no one, possibly with the exception of Nina, his wife, and their housekeeper, Reuben.

This novel becomes an exploration of motives of the other characters. The reader is led into the seamy parts of Key West, but true iniquity resides in New York. In these three novels, Key West is the place where Shames's characters gain control of their destinies, while New York is the source of moral decay. In these two novels, two of his characters must return to New York to face evil. Bert the Shirt in *Sunburn* returns to face crime lords with much trepidation, while Nina, in *Scavenger Reef* goes to confront the person who has threatened Augie's life. These three crime novels as well as Shames's recently published *Tropical Depression* and *Virgin Heat* reaffirm the therapeutic off-beat value of Key West.

John Leslie, after a journalistic stint in Europe, visited Key West in 1974 and has lived there ever since. After answering an ad in the *Key West Citizen* for a writer to help on a Bermuda Triangle mystery novel, Leslie began to explore the detective novel in his own fashion, with Key West providing settings and characters.

In his *Killing Me Softly*, Gideon Lowry, a Conch, a person born in Key West, plays piano at a hotel bar and solves crimes in his offhours:

I can hear my father's voice: 'They're your people.' It was a favorite expression of his. Meant to insure that I understood my brother and I both understood, that we Conchs stuck together. . . . To be a Conch was to be favored and in some small way protected, perhaps even forgiven. Almost as if my forefathers had recognized that living on an island we were always subject to invasion. (33)

Despite being a Conch, Gideon does not believe that these people are "his people." Rather, fighting alcoholism, he feels alienated from a dominant mentality that wants to develop every square inch of open space.

In this novel, Gideon is working on two, possibly three, or maybe only one (are they related?) cases: Lila's murder in 1955 when he was in Korea, the recent (1990s) death of Virginia, Lila's sister and the one who hired Gideon, and a witness extradition case. All three cases force him to examine the wheelings and dealings of Key West's finest citizens as well as his own family's past. His aggressive style further isolates him from his former wives, his present companion, his family, and other Conchs. His questions tend to be accusative, his probing unwanted.

As Gideon solves these cases, he bikes the streets of Key West, and drives as far as the Bat Tower on Sugarloaf, the site of Lila's murder. His actions and his memories firmly root him in Key West. This P.I. provides a personal investigation into this town, tempting readers to think of real people despite the disclaimer that this is a work of fiction. Leslie has two sequels (with song titles, too) featuring Gideon Lowry: *Night and Day* and *Love for Sale*, released in late 1996 and 1997.

John Leslie's protagonist in *Havana Hustle* is Tony Harwood, a former Miami cop suspended for muscling a suspect. Tony hates the cop image but loves the excitement of the job. Like Jim Hall's Thorn, Tony now is on his own tracking down missing persons, dead or alive. As the novel opens, Tony is living in an Airstream trailer on the Gulf side of Big Pine Key, trying to atone for his suspension through alcohol and sex, only to get shot in the calf by a jealous lesbian lover of his current woman. Through flashback, readers watch Tony, happy to take a job finding the whereabouts of a daughter of a friend of his stepfather. He discovers the body of Nicki Coste, drugged, raped, and buried alive. Leslie spares no detail in describing the skull full of maggots and the tangle of matted hair reaching the skeleton's shoulders. In true noir fashion a newspaper photographer gets a shot of Tony holding the skeleton's hand as he removes a bracelet. This photo makes Tony famous, but all the more anguished and alienated.

Returning to the present and Big Pine Key, Tony finds himself constantly facing the recurring images of the dead Nicki. In an attempt to block these horrors from his mind, he renews an acquaintance with Kay Fulton, now a Key West City Attorney. Tony discovers that she needs him to locate a witness to an attempted murder by one of the gangster lords of Key West. Tony's new case takes place under the "electrified nimbus of Key West . . . the last destination resort where people believe they can get away from it all. Whatever it was" (17).

A ride around Key West with Scott, a taxi driver—a breed whom the narrator considers "the last adventurers on the planet"—gives Tony full exposure to the havens and hells of Key West. In a matter of days he experiences much from the cozy buche cafes (Cuban coffee houses) and sleazy bars to the all-purpose laundromats and the sun-filled beaches. Daily encounters include disemboweled cats, crucified informers, and kidnapped children. He sees key witnesses intimidated and criminals go free, but as Kay tells him, "To think the abyss is to escape it" (68).

While the environment of the Keys furnishes an almost overwhelming amount of violence and injustice, it also provides him with a place to escape it all. On Big Pine Key, thirty miles northeast of Key West, he is calmed as he builds an addition to his Airstream trailer and fishes for snappers in the deep holes near the mangroves. Surrounded by hardwood hammocks filled with raccoons and miniature deer, Tony finds the sustenance to begin to put his life in order. Then he starts to get involved in a mutually restorative relationship with Kate, beginning with another search—helping Kate find her missing daughter.

Less widely read than John Leslie, Richard Lockridge, known for his mysteries, sets *Encounter in Key West* here. However, neither Lockridge nor his characters seem at ease within this setting. The novel, not a mystery or crime novel per se, exploits Key West's gay community in the guise of a search for peace by Janet disoriented by the sexual preferences of men around her. Perhaps the 1966 publication date accounts for the intolerance within this novel.

Alison Lurie, winner of the 1985 Pulitzer Prize for fiction, has owned a house in Key West since 1978. Her early novels include *The War between the Tates* and *Foreign Affairs*. Neither of those novels alludes to Key West. Her eighth novel, *The Truth about Lorin Jones*, published in 1988, has for its dominant setting Old Town Key West. Her central character, Polly Atler, like so many of the other protagonists discussed in this chapter, comes down the Keys searching for information. She is driven to know more about the life of the subject of her biography, Lorin Jones, a young painter who dies much too early in her career.

Polly senses, upon her arrival in Key West, "something loose and overheated." She had started from New York with everything gray and gritty and with such a cold that she was about to cancel her flight. Now, five hours later at a women-only guest house, she climbs out of the shower into a "steamy, glowing tropical afternoon with coconut palm and blue-green ocean . . . a place where the air, blowing from fishing piers and tidal flats, smelled of sex. But as she stood in the cool flood of water, Polly noticed something else: the flu was gone. For some goddam reason, she felt perfectly well" (217).

In her search for the elusive Lorin, Polly interviews numerous people including Jones's ex-husband, gallery owners, lovers, and even a former sister-in-law, all revealing another piece of the mystery. And a piece of the mystery quite evident from the beginning is that Polly's search for Lorin Jones turns out to be a search for her own identity.

Polly is intrigued by the city cemetery and wonders if Lorin Jones could possibly be buried there. In contrast to the cemeteries up north, Polly found "soapy white marble slabs crowned with garish arrangements of plastic flowers." Many of these tombs, she observes, were tilted and shifted, mirroring the homes surrounding the cemetery. She thinks, "You could almost imagine that the dead people inside, Lorin among them, were trying to get out" (254). Alison Lurie is not alone in her concern for the cemetery, the geographical center of Key West where both streets and characters intersect and interact. James Hall, Thomas McGuane, and Thomas Sanchez all have scenes here, providing an active ingredient of the noir.

As a result of her interaction with the Key West environment, Polly undergoes a transformation. Throughout her time in Key West, Polly is bombarded, immersed in sensual stimuli. The result is the numbing of Polly's usually intellectual and moral monitors, allowing her to acknowledge her own identity as well as to be more receptive, more sensitive to relationships with all around her, both nature and people. Polly, as well as the reader, is intrigued by the power of Key West to change her physically and mentally.

Brina Caplan likens *The Truth about Lorin Jones* to other examples of noir literature, "Much of this novel is cinema on the page. Lorin's story has the dramatic pull of those 1940s mysteries like *Rebecca* or *Laura,* in which a somewhat schlumpy protagonist, entranced by a mythically beautiful dead woman, goes about piecing together her less than seemly history" (541). Other critics also commend this novel. Despite her concern about the dated feminism expressed within this novel, Annette Jaffee concludes, "Now this is a good read" (89).

When Thomas Sanchez stopped off in Key West in 1981, en route to the Caribbean, he carried with him over a hundred pages of notes and sketches for a novel to be set in California and Mexico. But Sanchez recalls in a published interview (Strom 7) that a narrative voice suddenly came to him in Key West, a voice that spoke of the cocaine tidal wave building in Latin America and threatening the United States. As a result, his novel, *Mile Zero* is both written in and about Key West. Here is mile zero, the last of the 120-mile markers, stretching from Key Largo to Key West, the literal and symbolic end of the road. George Murphy, editor of *The Key West Reader* calls *Mile Zero* "the definitive novel of Key West."

Erica Abeel, writing in the *New York Times Book Review*, labels the novel's mode a comedy, but "dark and frequently x-rated. . . . Its brilliantly contrived plot uncoils with the suspense of a thriller" (7).

Many facets of Key West are revealed within this novel. "Cayo Hueso, Island of Bones, was the name the Spanish first gave the place, long before it had become a glittering star to the Cubans. Island of Bones, because the Spaniards found it littered with the bleached remains of the hounded, deserted and luckless. It wasn't any star of the sea for the Spaniards" (*Mile Zero* 12). St. Cloud, a disaffected 1960s radical "drifts down to the Keys," taking his "love for granted, looking for nothing and running from everything" (5). St. Cloud recognizes the powerful forces lurking in the setting. He knows, for example, that the ultimate destructive hurricane, what the Cubans call "El Finito" will come from the sea.

St. Cloud's counterpart, Justo Tamarind, a black Cuban policeman becomes an admirable norm to measure other characters against. Justo, a true Conch, "a blessed African black bean amidst all the Spanish yellow rice," has experienced the full impact of the Key West environment. The formation of Justo's character has been achieved over generations and has left him as "that rare creature on the island, a man going some place who knows where he is from. He was an old fashioned man, an island of integrity on an island of shifting morality. Long before the town tricked itself out for tourists, and rolled over for frigid northerners" (13). As this novel unfolds, Justo's poignant isolation is clearly revealed. St. Cloud soon gets drawn into Justo's hunt for a mysterious killer, called Zobop, who is terrorizing the island. The noir landscaping breaks out in full bloom in the city cemetery. Through Justo's sensitivities, we read that the cemetery:

possessed an odd calm at the island's crowded heart. It was corralled on all four sides by narrow streets of cigar makers' cottages and steep-roofed Conch houses, nudging for a better view of this high point on the island, was reserved not for the living, but for the dead. An unnatural peace prevailed . . . where one path bisected another, a short cement monument had been erected, stenciled with avenue destination, First Avenue, Second Avenue, Third Avenue, avenues not intended for cars, but a grid laid out for ghosts in a city of the dead. Over the years the cemetery was the scene of many such [Santeria] rituals. At dawn tombstones were discovered with chicken blood smeared across them to drain evil from the graves. (81)

And it is here in the ambivalence of the cemetery, that Justo discovers much about himself. The gravestones of his ancestors remind him of his heritage. It is, however, in the midst of Voodoo and Santeria rituals as well as the bizarre history of a count who kept a teenage girl embalmed, making her his lover over the years, that Justo finds the answers to the mystery of Zobop and reclaims his own "formidale."

While Sanchez has only one novel with Key West as a dominant setting, Thomas McGuane has a number: *The Bushwhacked Piano, Ninety-two in the Shade*, and *Panama*. First visiting Key West in the late sixties and owning a house there until recently, McGuane has an intimate knowledge and relationship with Key West. He states that while he can work anywhere, "It is nice to arise from the latest effort, go out the door, and find that life reinforces one's worst suspicions. There's nowhere like Key West for guaranteeing this satisfaction" (qtd. in Kaufelt 81). These novels, Jonathan Yardley says, are works of a writer with a "vivid, idiosyncratic style and outlook," a writer possessing "a talent of Faulknerian potential" (3).

All three novels focus on young men who have rejected materialism in favor of a closer relationship with the natural world. From the start McGuane's respect for the beauty and power of the natural world contrasts with the depravity he believes undermines American culture. In *The Bushwhacked Piano* we are exposed to the picaresque story of Nicholas Pain, an eccentric young man who travels through Michigan and Montana only to end up in the Keys. His travels reveal his restless aspiration for change and his feelings of alienation. From shooting his neighbor's piano full of holes, to ridding the Keys of mosquitoes in the great Bat Tower scheme, to taking, without consecration, the Eucharist of crusty bread and peanut butter on a lonely beach, Nicholas fails to cope. In this process, McGuane exposes the reader to a bizarre array of American characters and noir experiences.

In *Panama* McGuane uses the environs of Key West as a background for the most autobiographical of his novels. It is an understatement to say that the novel received less than accolades as critics responded with such comments as "a drearily self-indulged little book" (Yardley 14) and a "sadly bitter book about what became of the alternative American dream" (Katz 38). *Panama* tells the story of another isolated protagonist. Like Nicholas in *The Bushwhacked Piano* and Thomas Skeleton in *Ninety-two in the Shade*, Chester Hunnicutt Pomeroy is trying to solve the mystery of the meaning of contemporary life. Chet has a major problem: his overnight fame has made connecting to his former friends and estranged wife, Catherine, very difficult for him, if not impossible. While exploring the limits of cocaine in the sensually laden atmosphere of Key West, he contemplates such scenarios as throwing himself under a passing car. All this is motivated by his desire to renew his relationship with Catherine. Finally he ends up at her house and comes, in noir fashion, to the conclusion that the only way he can gain Catherine's undivided attention is to nail his left hand to her front door. This he does, but with only short-lived success. His only option left, it appears to him, is to make friends with Catherine's lesbian lover.

Chet's total experience, some of it mirroring McGuane's own travails, results in a character change, but not much of one. Chet finds that he is able at the end of the novel "to tolerate every creep on earth" and perhaps even himself. All the elements of the noir novel are present in *Panama*. Most readers would be hard pressed not to agree with the editors of *Contemporary Literary Criticism* when they describe Panama as a "hallucinatory and macabre story set amidst a squalid world of drugs, insanity, moral indifference, escapism and despair" ("McGuane" 257).

The novel that exemplifies most thoroughly the influence of the Florida Keys on McGuane is *Ninety-two in the Shade*. Tom Skeleton is a former marine biology student and an angry dropout from materialism. Like the other McGuane central characters, an emotional casualty, Thomas Skeleton also has much in common with Lurie's Polly Atler and Hall's Shaw Chandler in that he, too, comes down the Keys looking for something. In Tom Skeleton's case he is looking for some control and meaning in his life, an existential quest in theory, a bonefish guide in reality. Jonathan Yardley, in *Washington Post Review*, finds McGuane much more compassionate and understanding toward his characters in *Ninety-two in the Shade* than in his previous novels (3).

Skeleton's trip down the Keys just brings out all the more angst, wiring him to the point of planning to respond violently if anyone suggests he is insane. No one does. Along with these paranoid thoughts, Skeleton makes plans to get a six-pack and take his skiff out to the reef the moment he hits Key West. This he eventually does and drifts "over a million fold expansion of the bait school," and as a result finds himself "calming down and finishing his six beers" (5). Skeleton's existential search takes place much of the time surrounded by the recuperative sea. His quest is often filtered through his marine biology background as he contemplates his relationship to these "radiant sea creatures" in terms of "indecipherable links of change" (15).

Skeleton, now living in a fuselage of a junked plane, is, as with other central characters of these search-for-self novels, influenced by the adjacent Key West cemetery. Like the water, which offers both life and death, the cemetery is also ambivalent in that at the same time it reminds Skeleton of the inevitability of death, its statues of sailors and Cuban heroes provide him "some irrational desire to be a liberty apostle and horseman of the light, a shy delivery boy of eternity's loops" (25-26).

Skeleton is fatefully forced to a deadly confrontation with Nichol Dance, the supreme bonefish guide of the Keys. Driven by his need for mortality and control, Skeleton gets both in the end as he points to his heart when Dance asks where he wants the bullet. In this final day of his life, McGuane's existential hero exits less a victim of his circumstances and environment than a man who discovers the requisite conviction and courage needed to achieve his quest. Many readers will readily agree with Bill Ott's claim that *Ninety-two in the Shade* is "the definitive noir fishing novel" (608).

Keys' characters, from McGuane's Tom Skeleton to Hall's Thorn, are as strung out as are the 120 miles of semitropical islands. These representative novels contain various elements of the noir genre: the alienation of an isolated and burned out character; a search for information and evidence; a pursuit of his or her own identity; a confrontation with evil; an exploration of the darker side of human nature. Despite its much lighter and laid back Margarittaville tone, even popular singer Jimmy Buffett's *Where Is Joe Merchant?*, only partly set in the state, reflects many of these characteristics. As with film versions of noir, these characters are shown within their environment, a world where characters are both pursued and pursuing. The Florida Keys manifest a lack of order, raw, violent, at times both too dark and too bright, a mysterious world, literally on the edge, terminal, both geographically and emotionally, the last resort of the hunted and haunted.

But what makes these noir novels different from other detective works of fiction written in the South, or even the Florida mainland? The answer, we think, lies in the interaction of the alienated characters with the semitropical weather, the omnipresent ocean and bay, the geographically centered cemetery, and the solid waste dump on Stock Island, "Mount Trashmore." This environment plays a significant role in both the lives of the authors and the lives of their characters. After experiencing the Florida Keys themselves, these representative writers expose their characters to the unique combination of forces and elements found in the Keys—the only place in the world where tropical sun and flora meet with people and fauna escaping from the mainland. Here the environment with its sights, sounds, smells, tastes, and feelings assuages and massages both the physical and psychological states of the author, the characters, and even the readers. This interactive process between such a tactile setting and such hunted and haunted characters results in a final product: the noir novel, Keys' style.

Works Cited

Abeel, Erica. "Mile Zero." *New York Times Book Review* 1 Oct. 1989: 7.

Blackburn, Sara. Rev. of *A Good Day to Die. New York Times Book Review* 9 Sept. 1973, sec. 7: 4.

Bogey, D. "Book Reviews: Fiction." *Library Journal* 1 Sept. 1991: 230.

Buffet, Jimmy. *Where Is Joe Merchant?* New York: Harcourt, 1992.

Callendar, Newgate. "Book Reviews: Spies and Thrillers." *New York Times Book Review* 26 Mar. 1995: 27.

Caplan, Brina. "Unreal Women, Foolish Choices." *Nation* 21 Nov. 1988: 540-42.

Hall, James W. *Bones of Coral*. New York: Knopf, 1991.

——. *Gone Wild*. New York: Delacorte, 1995.

——. *Hard Aground*. New York: Delacorte,1993.

——. *Mean High Tide*. New York: Delacorte, 1994.

——. *Tropical Freeze*. New York: Warner, 1989.

——. *Under Cover of Daylight*. New York: Norton, 1987.

Harrison, Jim. *A Good Day to Die*. New York: Delta, 1973.

"Harrison, Jim." *Contemporary Literary Criticism*. Vol. 6. Detroit: Gale, 1985. 196.

Jaffee, Annette Williams. "Redress for Success." *Ms*. Oct. 1988: 88-89.

Katz, Donald R. "Thomas McGuane: Heroes in 'Hotcakesland.'" *New Republic* 181.7 (1979): 38-39.

Kaufelt, Lynn Mitsuko. *Key West Writers and Their Houses*. Sarasota: Pineapple, 1986.

Kilpatrick, Thomas L. "Book Reviews: Fiction." *Library Journal* Aug. 1991: 209.

Leslie, John. *Havana Hustle*. New York: Pocket, 1994.

——. *Killing Me Softly*. New York: Pocket, 1994.

——. *Love for Sale*. New York: Pocket, 1997.

——. *Night and Day*. New York: Pocket, 1995.

Lockridge, Richard. *Encounter in Key West*. Philadelphia: Lippincott, 1966.

Lurie, Alison. *The Truth about Lorin Jones*. New York: Avon, 1988.

Lutz, John. *Hot*. New York: Holt, 1992.

McGuane, Thomas. *The Bushwhacked Piano*. New York: Vintage, 1971.

——. *Ninety-two in the Shade*. New York: Penguin, 1972.

——. *Panama*. New York: Farrar, 1978.

"McGuane, Thomas (Francis) III." *Contemporary Literary Criticism*. Vol. 45. Detroit: Gale, 1987. 257.

Murphy, George, ed. *The Key West Reader: The Best of Key West's Writers 1830-1990*. Key West: Tortugas, 1989.

Muste, John M. Review of *Mean High Tide*. *Magill Book Reviews 1995: Magazine Article Summaries*. CD-ROM Ebsco. Sept. 1995. 9503097014.

Nadler, Susan. "Skullduggery under the Palm Trees." *Florida Keys Magazine* May 1986: 44-50.

Ott, Bill. "Literary Florida." *American Libraries* 25.6 (1994): 608.

Paretsky, Sara. "The Wolves of Key Largo." *New York Times Book Review* 15 Oct. 1989: 38.

Peace, Carol. "Picks & Pans: Pages." *People* 29 June 1992: 28.

Plummer, William. "Gone Wild." *People* 17 Apr. 1995: 40.

Sanchez, Thomas. *Mile Zero*. New York: Knopf, 1989.

Schindehette, S. "Tree Hugger from Hell." *People* 21 Oct. 1991: 95-96.

Shames. Laurence. *Florida Straits*. New York: Simon and Schuster, 1992.

——. *Scavenger Reef*. New York: Dell, 1994.

——. *Sunburn*. New York: Little, Brown, 1995.

——. *Tropical Depression*. New York: Hyperion, 1996.

——. *Virgin Heat*. New York: Hyperion, 1997.

Skow, John. "True (as in Proulx) Grit Wins." *Time* 29 Nov. 1993: 83.

Stasio, Marilyn. Rev. of *Bones of Coral*. *New York Times Book Review* 24 Mar. 1991: 37.

——. Rev. of *Florida Straits*. *New York Times Book Review* 16 Apr. 1995: 29.

Striker, Randy. *The Deep Six*. New York: New American Library, 1981.

——. *Everglades Assault*. New York: New American Library, 1982.

——. *Key West Connection*. New York: New American Library, 1981.

Strom, Stephanie. "Key West Was the Key." *New York Times Book Review* 1 Oct. 1989: 7.

Vicarel, JoAnn. "Book Reviews: Fiction." *Library Journal* 1 Jan. 1995: 139.

Williams, Joy. *Breaking and Entering*. New York: Vintage, 1981.

——. *The Florida Keys: A History and Guide*. New York: Random, 1987.

——. *State of Grace*. New York: Scribner, 1986.

Woods, William Crawford. "What a Strange Accomplishment!" *Washington Post* 9 Sept. 1973: 4.

Yardley, Jonathan. "Thomas McGuane Reaches for the Big Sky." *Washington Post* 28 Feb. 1982: 3, 14.

7

Paradise Noir:
Land of Gold, Moon, and Pixie Dust

Anna Lillios

In John Lutz's *Torch*, a police detective recounts his morning's activities: "a woman's mutilated body had been found in Lake Eola [in downtown Orlando], floating out by the fountain near the center of the lake. Some tourists in one of the boats built to resemble swans had discovered it. The experience was nothing like Disney World" (249). "Nothing like Disney World" summarizes the worldview of detective novelists whose locale is Central Florida. Far from the mean streets of Raymond Chandler's fictional world, these novelists find Florida noir in the least likely places: the Magic Kingdom, the space shuttle, and the mansions of Palm Beach millionaires.

Central Florida—or Area Code 407—which until recently stretched from Sanford and Orlando in the north to Palm Beach to the south; as the most popular tourist destination in the world, it is the home to Disney World, Epcot Center, MGM and Universal Movie Studios, the Space Center at Cape Kennedy, and the spectacular residences along the Gold Coast of Palm Beach.

These attractions at first glance have nothing in common, yet all are monuments to the human desire to create ideal worlds. NASA's space station and the Disney Company's planned community Celebration are good examples of this utopian impulse, which does not tolerate any imperfection, from a millimeter burn on an O-ring to an earring on a male employee.

It is interesting to speculate what it is about this Central Florida locale that inspired Walt Disney to turn swampland into a magic kingdom, scientists to launch rockets to the moon, and Addison Mizner to build American palaces. Perhaps, a change occurs in people as they step over the frostline, which crosses Florida north of Orlando at around the twenty-ninth parallel. The frostline signifies a boundary between the exigencies of life in icy northern climes and mid-Florida basking in the paradisaical and humid subtropical zones. It is a symbolic line that frees the

103

imagination to play and take risks. From the records and chronicles of the first historic explorers to the present day, this area has inspired bizarre fantasies, schemes, attractions, and superhuman exploits. The search for the fountain of youth and the journey into outer space originated here.

This area, between the materialism and obligations of mainstream America and the "anything-goes" mentality of tropical American margaritaville, is the mid-Florida setting of detective novelists, such as Kevin Robinson, John Lutz, Lawrence Sanders, and Elmore Leonard. These writers take the everyday elements common to the upper forty-seven states and bake them in the Florida sun. This is the recipe that Sue Grafton uses in *"B" Is for Burglar*, as the private investigator heroine, Kinsey Millhone, stumbles into the lair of the murderess, Marty Grice, who has just been evicted from her apartment:

The stench came at us like a wall the minute the door was opened. The destruction was systematic and complete. What she'd done . . . was to open all the canned goods and pour the contents on the carpeting. She'd ground in crackers and dried pasta, jams, spices, coffee, vinegar, soups, moldering fruit, adding contributions from her own intestinal tract. The whole sick stew had been sitting there for days and the Florida heat and humidity had cooked the mess to a boiling foment of fungus and rot. (179)

The rotten chaos that Millhone finds typifies borderlands. Central and South Florida, as the symbolic limits of American civilization, are such marginal regions between order and chaos. Like other frontiers in general this region is "neither inside nor outside, neither known nor unknown" (Moi 167). The classic American detective hero has always resided in this marginal state of being, caught between conventional American life and outlaw society. Furthermore, he or she is not averse to crossing the line if the case warrants a transgression. These heroes recognize a different America, as Frederic Svoboda points out in "The Snub-Nosed Mystique: Observations on the American Detective Hero": "[T]he detective hero must acknowledge with the cynicism of a disappointed romantic that established civilization is no more than a veneer, that an unwinnable frontier still divides the civilized and savage elements of modern life" (558).

Svoboda also speaks of a second, deeper "moral" frontier that these heroes must navigate, similar to the "nightmare forest" that the hero confronts in Hawthorne's "Young Goodman Brown." Although Florida's fictional detectives reside mainly on "civilization's side of the line," they also make "forays across the frontier in pursuit of those just on the other side" (559). Their movements back and forth across the line fit America's "ambiguous moral frontier."

All of the Central Florida detective heroes discussed below are familiar with this frontier. They are outsiders who sometimes break the rules of society in order to save society. As Gary Hoppenstand explains in *In Search of the Paper Tiger,* such a hero is "neither crook nor cop; but instead observes his own moral code" (119). Ironically, these Central Florida detectives, who live in a milieu that seeks perfection, are themselves physically or psychically flawed, further marginalizing them. Thus, Kevin Robinson's Stick Foster is a paraplegic, John Lutz's Fred Carver is crippled, and Lawrence Sanders's Archy McNally is a soft-boiled aesthete. These unlikely private investigators do not hesitate to cross lines, which is the secret of their appeal (Slotkin 99).

Kevin Robinson, born in 1951 in Kingston, New York, and a current resident of Shawnee Mission, Kansas, is the author of three novels in the Stick Foster series: *Split Seconds* (1991); *Mall Rats* (1992); and *A Matter of Perspective* (1993). Like his fictional prototype, Stick Foster, Robinson is also confined to a wheelchair as a result of a spinal cord injury in 1975 that left him a quadriplegic.

Despite his injury, Kevin Robinson's paraplegic Stick Foster fits the hard-boiled stereotype, which Raymond Chandler defines in *The Simple Art of Murder*:

Down these mean streets a man must go who is not himself mean, who is neither tarnished nor afraid. The detective in this story must be such a man. He's the hero. He's everything. He must be a complete man and a common man, yet an unusual man. He must be, to use a really weathered phrase, a man of honor. . . . He has a sense of character or he would not know his job. He will take no man's money dishonestly, and no man's insolence without due and dispassionate revenge. He is a lonely man, and his pride is that you will treat him as a proud man or be very sorry you ever saw him. (20-21)

Frederic Svoboda summarizes the qualities of the hard-boiled detective by pointing out that he is a "self-reliant, strong, and potentially violent man, well-equipped to endure suffering" (560). In John D. MacDonald's *Dress Her in Indigo*, the detective's strength and capability is contrasted with his employer's paralysis, which stands for "a moral paralysis the detective does not share" (Svoboda 562). In other words, the detective is the man always "able to move and act" (562).

In Robinson's fiction, however, the detective is the one who is paralyzed. His paralysis, though, is not a reflection of his moral corruption.

Stick Foster became paraplegic when he fell off a garage roof as he was helping his father repair shingles. His mishap differs from the injury of John Lutz's Fred Carver, who was wounded by a mad criminal in the line of duty. Foster's wound is also psychological, because he must deal with the randomness of fate. In this sense, his injury heightens his heroism. He must try harder and overcome more physical and mental barriers in order to solve the mysteries that surround him. He doesn't always succeed. When a fire is set in his house and the doors are locked by the villain in *A Matter of Perspective*, Foster passes out before he can find a way to escape. His paraplegic wife, Sam, is the one who recalls that he has a pistol in the house and shoots their way out.

The narrow escapes of a disabled detective increase the tension in the story, but they also return the detective novel to its roots as formulated by Edgar Allan Poe. In "Murders in the Rue Morgue," Auguste Dupin, as the emblem of "pure reason," is "the most intelligent person in the story." By assembling all the pieces of the puzzle, he controls the environment by intellectual means, thus suggesting a "fictional world where the individual controls Fate, possesses free will and conquers his environment" (Hoppenstand 111). This is the lesson that Foster hopes to teach the young adolescents whom he befriends in *Mall Rats*.

Finally, Foster's injury forces him to take a different perspective on reality; from his angle of vision, he can see clues that other people overlook. In *A Matter of Perspective*, a photograph that he shoots captures an image that helps unlock the mystery of the murder. He even proposes to write a newspaper photo-column entitled "Take This Sitting Down," in which he would "humorously portray Orlando as it might be seen from the eye level of someone in a wheelchair" (4).

Stick's eye-level perspective shows him that Central Florida is not the innocent fantasy land that most tourists pay money to see. In Robinson's first novel, *Split Seconds*, Disney World and the Space Center are both threatened by a mad antispace terrorist—who also happens to be a lesbian, Palm Beach heiress, the daughter of an astronaut killed in a test flight. She plots to subvert the space program by reprogramming the flight of a rocket to explode over Orlando. Stick figures out her nefarious plan in time and is able to avert the catastrophe. One terrified observer remarks, before the wayward rocket is brought under control, "it just might land on Cinderella's Castle" (206). Instead, the rocket explodes harmlessly above Disney World:

The debris from the trashed *Excaliber* came down all over central Florida. It broke windows, dented cars, and cut up the flora and fauna, here and there, like a Vegomatic from outer space. Disney World's 27,000 acres did, in fact take the heaviest shower of space junk; but, of course, the famous theme park was not yet open for business at that time of the morning. . . . Then, in a bizarre bit of reflection, it occurred to me that the world famous efficiency of Disney's maintenance personnel had surely been put to the test. (211)

Robinson gives the reader a surreal Disney World not pictured in the tourist brochures, while satirizing its legendary perfectionism.

Robinson's worldview grows darker by his third novel, *A Matter of Perspective*. He vehemently attacks the legal profession, just as Dickens does in *Bleak House*. Whereas Dickens uses fog imagery to portray the deadening effects of a legal system that is drowning in its own bureaucracy, Robinson uses shark imagery to show how cut-throat Sam's colleagues are. Foster calls them Sam's "befinned predator friends" and wants to "stir up the shark tank to see which dorsal fins broke water first" (87). The danger in the novel comes not particularly from the fear that Sam or Stick will be murdered next or their house destroyed, but from the fact that Sam is flirting with crossing the line to become like the other lawyers around her. Stick is deeply troubled by Sam's view: "It doesn't matter what's right or wrong so much as what you can convince a jury they *must* do under the circumstances" (131). He begins to wonder: "What would it take for Sam to cross the kind of lines" that the corrupt lawyers with whom she is associated have been "crossing freely": "I didn't like thinking about that. First, of course, because when I looked hard into the stern face of reality, I suspected that I knew the answer. Sam hates to lose. Period. More to the point, I realized to my own amazement, I was really wondering about myself. How far would I go" (156).

Later in the narrative, Stick does, in fact, cross the line between legal and illegal behavior, by sending Butch Grady, dressed as an exterminator, to spy in Lester Brown's house. His retort to Detective Henderson's query about his activities is a refusal to tell what he has been up to, "just in case it's illegal."

Stick's existence between the margins of the legal and the illegal often causes him to feel alienated from other people:

I have a wife I adore, friends I cherish, and acquaintances who fill my life with warmth and fellowship . . . most of the time. It's those shaky in-betweens that get me, those dark moments when the edges of life's security blanket start to come unraveled. Oh, there's enough of the soft comforting material to last for months yet, maybe years, but to notice the dangling threads is to know that nothing lasts forever. (51)

During such moments, Stick retreats into his own fantasy land, that is, a novel that he is writing: "It began as a fanciful idea about lost books, a dying culture, and the old magic that once gave it life" (19). Writing circumvents his feeling of marginality by allowing him to escape the issue altogether: "It was as if we lived on the edge of civilization . . . in the middle of America's fastest-growing metropolitan area. Central Florida had the Magic Kingdom. I was creating the 'Land of Life.' Fantasy is, after all, the highest literary form of escapism" (48).

John Lutz has been writing novels since his first, *The Truth of the Matter* was published in 1971, when he was thirty-two. In 1986, he started the Fred Carver series, which includes *Tropical Heat, Scorcher, Kiss, Flame, Bloodfire, Hot, Spark*, and *Torch*. In an interview with *Contemporary Authors*, Lutz claims that he writes because he loves it: "It would be difficult for me to say exactly what motivated me to begin writing; it's possible that the original motivation is gone, much as a match that starts a forest fire is consumed in the early moments of the fire. I continue writing for selfish reasons. I thoroughly enjoy it" ("Lutz, John" 290).

A *New York Times* reviewer describes Lutz's latest novel, *Torch*, as "[a]nother savage entertainment set in that surreal hell Lutz calls Florida." To create a sense of surreality, Lutz juxtaposes the "Ku Klux Klan and Mickey Mouse and drugs and the Bible and sunshine and murder and palm trees" (*Tropical Heat* 161). He makes even sunshine and palm trees look dark and menacing as this description of a Florida morning in *Scorcher* shows: "After about 10:00 A.M. it gets too hot to sit outside during July in central Florida. It was nine o'clock now, and already bright, baking, and humid. Everything warm-blooded and not working on a tan sought the shade" (1).

Lutz's "Disney-dominated, enchanted central Florida" (*Tropical Heat* 30) is not what it seems. A child's paradise like Disney World is transformed into "a startling example of lockstep efficiency and the reach of technology" (*Tropical Heat* 192-93) that disturbs the adult visitor. Miles of coastline and beautiful, sandy beaches are the setting of families enjoying the ocean, but they also harbor drug-dealing Marielitos. Even Lutz's hero, Fred Carver, is not what he seems. Although he is a cripple, his superhuman upper body strength compensates for the limitations of his legs.

Not only with setting but also with characterization, does Lutz's fiction play with boundaries and alternative states of being. Carver himself is crossing a boundary in his life when the series begins with *Tropical Heat*. Six months earlier, he had been a detective sergeant in the Orlando Police Department. During a routine grocery store robbery as he held a gun on a suspect, a second gunman emerged from a back room and cold-bloodedly "blasted away" his left knee cap. His career ended, Carver retires with $80,000 in insurance money and a knee "locked at a thirty-degree angle." At the start of *Tropical Heat*, Carver hasn't accepted his new reality and is spending "too much time alone. . . . Planted in the past" (21).

Carver knows from his failed marriage that work, "Business, keeping ceaselessly busy, could fill the void, absorb the wild energy of volatile depression" (85). He recognizes that he is a survivor—and not "the suicidal type"; therefore, he attempts to transform his weaknesses into strengths. He swims in the ocean to build up his body and meditates to heal his mind: "The past few months had toughened him in and out, created a man not only stronger where he had been broken, but stronger everywhere" (42). When danger threatens, Carver is now able to draw on new inner resources. A fire set in his hotel room in Solarville forces him to rely on his sense of smell to escape; Jorge Lujan who attacks him with a knife is overwhelmed by Carver's skillful use of his cane; Lujan, who then chases Carver into the sea, is "surprised by the awesome strength in Carver's arms and torso," which is the "physical compensation and unnatural upper-body strength of the lame" (181). Carver dives below Lujan, pulling him down, and forces him to drown: "His hours in the ocean had altered his being, saved his life" (186). Finally, drawing on a new understanding of, and empathy with, women since his divorce, Carver shatters Verna Blaney's illusions about Willis Davis and causes her to realize a necessary truth: "Life was like that: illusion, delusion, deception, self-deception, worlds and castles constructed of our personal perceptions, masquerading as reality until something interfered. Verna's magic kingdom had been built here before Disney's, and now Carver was tugging at the cornerstone of her castle" (241).

The theme of Lutz's first book and his subsequent novels is the magic kingdoms we create in our minds and then project onto our surroundings. As Carver points out, "Disney didn't have a monopoly on magic kingdoms in Florida; they were dotted up and down the coasts" (71). Each magic kingdom represents one person's obsession. Lutz shows how KKK members, drug smugglers, and real estate developers take this tropical paradise and corrupt it for their own ends. Untouched nature is beautiful but neutral; people's activities change it to reflect their preoccupations. The description of the swamp in *Tropical Heat* illustrates how easily this transformation occurs.

When Carver suspects that Willis Davis is a drug dealer, the swamp takes on an evil, menacing character: "The swamp seemed to loom around him, dank and threatening, full of life, full of death. None of it subject to reason. There were eyes watching from the black shade beneath the moss-draped trees" (125). Or, "Racketing with the screams of cicadas, the swamp bent green and malevolent" (214).

The dark qualities of the swamp have the power to invade Carver's mind as he searches for Davis within its interior: The search for Willis Davis had about it a dreamlike quality of quiet madness. Carver felt at times as if he were trying to feel his way through the miasma of nightmares. Then there were times when he seemed to see clearly, but objects on his mind's horizon simply receded further out of reach as he advanced, eluding him. (202)

The mysterious, threatening qualities of the swamp completely evaporate when the truth about Davis emerges and Carver learns that he is a real estate con artist who marries Verna Blaney in order to grab her property before the Disney company can purchase it. The same swamp that had been primordial, horror-filled, and wild will now become another controlled Disneyesque attraction, Everglades Kingdom: "Disney plans to drain some of the land here, build up roads, create a scenic waterway and a monorail system serving luxury hotels and tourist attractions" (239).

Carver's strong moral character allows him to escape the gravitational pull of this surreal landscape. He is a private eye in the hard-boiled mold, because he can successfully undergo the physical trials of the detective hero in the course of his odyssey toward a more ordered world and because he has the ability to "think like a criminal"; but, Carver also has compassion. He is a man "who is not himself mean," as his former colleague Desoto realizes: "You were tough, skeptical, had principles, and would surprise me, and you, with your compassion" (15).

Along with the compassion, Carver can see this world and its ambiguities clearly. Much like Stick Foster, Carver tells how he solves crimes: "It didn't take Sherlock Holmes, just someone with the proper slant" (239). He needs all his skills for the next event that will transform him; at the start of *Scorcher*, his life will shift again as he confronts the reality of his only son's murder.

Lawrence Sanders, born in 1920 and a resident of Pompano Beach, Florida, has written twenty-seven major novels—nineteen of them best-sellers. These books include four in the Commandments series; four in the Deadly Sins series; and six, thus far, in the Archie McNally series. Since 1991, Sanders has published *McNally's Secret, McNally's Luck, McNally's Risk, McNally's Caper, McNally's Trial,* and *McNally's Gamble.* Sanders began writing novels when he was fifty years old; before then he had been an editor of various men's magazines.

Sanders's McNally cycle, set in Palm Beach, is a world away from the dark-edged Florida of Lutz and Robinson. Archy McNally, the thirty-seven-year-old son of a rich lawyer, lives in sybaritic splendor on the third floor of his parents' mansion on Florida's Gold Coast. He leisurely spends his days as the Chief of Discreet Inquiries for his father's law firm: "My investigations are mainly concerned with solving the personal problems of our prestigious clients before they come to the attention of the police or those supermarket tabloids that might feature the client's tribulations between a truss ad and a story about twins borne by a ninety-eight-year-old Samoan transvestite" (*McNally's Trial* 1).

At first glance, McNally seems to fall into the hard-boiled role; but, after reading a few pages, the reader realizes that Sanders is parodying the hard-boiled stereotype rather than imitating it. McNally is what Larry Grimes in an article refers to as a "stepson of Sam," that is, a character who at first appears to be similar to Sam Spade, but then deviates from the ideal. Grimes describes how a few contemporary novelists, such as Richard Brautigan and Thomas Berger, depart from the hard-boiled model, to create characters that have more in common with Kafka, Joyce, or Nabokov than Dashiell Hammett or Raymond Chandler.

The hard-boiled paradigm, as defined by John Cawelti in his book *Adventure, Mystery, and Romance: Formula Stories as Art and Popular Culture*, includes the following characteristics: 1) the story "moves from the introduction of the detective to the presentation of the crime, through the investigation, to a solution and apprehension of the criminal" (141); 2) the urban jungle is the setting and it symbolizes "empty modernity, corruption and death" (146); and 3) the hard-boiled detective not only solves the crime but also defines "his own moral position, which often puts him in the margins of society." As a marginal professional, he "must reject the public ideals and values of society to seek to create his own personal code of ethics and his own set of values" (161).

Sanders, in the McNally series, has softly poached the detective hero; he has made him into what Grimes labels as "the unembroiled hero," who is narcissistic and "detached from the world" (541). McNally is self-centered, someone who creates his own peculiar set of values: "I am a lad devoted to the frivolous and the trivial. I simply refuse to take anything seriously. I have absolutely no absolute beliefs—other than grated ginger is wonderful on fresh oysters" (*McNally's Trial* 269). His attitude is a parody of the typical detective hero who takes his values seriously; thus, McNally is more of a character out of slapstick than the mean streets. At times, Sanders makes the character too precious, as this dialog from *McNally's Trial* shows: "Momentous events have been set in motion, and I fear the Whitcombs, Gorton, and their coterie are quite likely to have their hilarity squelched and their lifestyle dampened by stalwarts of the law. Why, they may even be shackled and dragged off to durance vile" (272).

By parodying the serious tone that is typical of the detective novel, Sanders undercuts the moral and ethical concerns that are the bases of the genre. Sanders does not fully develop the theme that would lead to deeper issues, that is, the discrepancy between the glittering surface of Palm Beach society and the rotten reality underneath. The closest Sanders comes to discussing it, occurs in a comment made by one of McNally's friends: "Now I find upper-drawer citizens with big bucks and mansions can be just as slimy as your average mugger. It comes as a bit of a shock" (*McNally's Trial* 273). McNally retorts: "Net worth and beluga for breakfast do not prevent ignobility" (273).

McNally would have plenty of background material on which to draw if he were to elucidate ethical or moral concerns. He could look as far as his own father for an example. Initially, McNally presents his father as a man of honor and propriety. Archibald, Senior, appears to be a strait-laced, morally righteous man, whose approval his son seeks. Archy describes his father: "Yes, he can be an intimidating man, but he is also an extremely upright man. Never in a million years would he order me to end a criminal investigation" (*Trial* 224).

On the other hand, his father is not averse to overlooking the moments when his son crosses the line and uses illegal means to get the job done, as Archy reports:

Ordinarily I do not give the boss progress reports during the course of my discreet inquiries. He is only interested in the final results. Also, I suspect he would rather not know the details of my modi operandi, fearing they might be an affront to his hidebound code of ethics—which, of course, they would be. (*McNally's Trial* 248)

His father is also not averse to carrying on a clandestine affair with the richest woman in town, Lady Cynthia Horowitz. In fact, Archibald, Senior, has simply concocted his whole life as a fantasy:

The world my father envisioned—and this was years before Ralph Lauren created a fashion empire from the same dream—was one of manor homes, croquet, polo, neatly trimmed gardens, a wine cellar, lots of chintz, worn leather and brass everywhere, silver-framed photographs of family members, and cucumber sandwiches at tea. (*McNally's Secret* 13)

In reality, Archibald, Senior, is the son of Ready Freddy McNally, who was a "gapping-trousered, bulb-nosed burlesque comic"—and not a "wealthy member of the British landed gentry" (*McNally's Secret* 12).

Since the apple does not fall far from the tree, McNally is in danger of the same fate. At the end of *McNally's Trial*, after he has solved the Whitcomb case, McNally abandons himself to his favorite fantasy. He is strolling along a moonlit beach with his girlfriend, to whom he is often unfaithful, drinking champagne, and dreaming:

It was a fantasy and I was aware of it. After experiencing the crudity of the Whitcomb case I wanted to recapture the laughing elegance of a world I never knew and perhaps never existed; the clever, self-mocking era of Noel Coward songs, Fitzgerald novels, Broadway musicals, and William Powell movies. I was trying to re-create a madly joyous time I imagined. (*McNally's Trial* 308)

The book ends with Archy's reflection on dreams and "how they shape our lives." The McNally series, underneath the effervescence of champagne bubbles, warns of the evil that befalls those people who allow dreams to override reality and demand them at all costs. Archy's propensity to escape reality, as his father has done, is just as much a handicap as a lame leg. He is a thirty-seven-year-old man who still lives in his parents' home, is "a klutz with women," and obsessed with the right way to eat, drink, and dress. As Grimes points out, "a distinguishing trait" of the stepsons of Sam is the "substitution of style for morals." Sanders continually emphasizes McNally's style rather than his deeper values; therefore, the character never rises above a caricature. The cyclical nature of novels that fall into a series suggests that McNally will simply repeat the same pattern of behavior over and over again, thus never changing.

Elmore Leonard's detective heroes are also the stepsons of Sam. Instead of parodying the serious detective hero, as Sanders does, Leonard creates characters who are simply reflections of contemporary American life in all of its random, violent, and bizarre facets. Leonard's characters are permeated with the evil of our times, because they are situated at the nexus at which the breakdown of order occurs. They are rarely men and women of honor, as Chandler describes in *The Simple Art of Murder*. They are, instead, "chronics—small-time, small-minded losers," as Andrew Vachss labels them in a review (1). Walker Percy calls Leonard's characters: "the usual diverting cast of grifters and creeps" that Leonard "keeps up his sleeve" and points out that Leonard never sticks "to the same guy or the same place" (Percy 7).

For his Florida detective novels, Leonard, in fact, shuns the series narratives that his other colleagues, Lawrence Sanders, Kevin Robinson, and John Lutz, have popularized. The series books build up a following among readers who demand "continuing interaction with one hero," according to Frederic Svoboda: "symbolically, the series reflects the nature of the detective's task; he works again and again to cleanse his city, yet it can never quite be cleansed" (561). The detective's work is futile but predictable. By the end of the book, good will prevail and a resolution of the case be reached. Such hallmarks of the detective genre are absent in Leonard's novels. Good may not emerge victorious and the hero may not resist evil. *Rum Punch* is a good example. Throughout the course of the novel, Max Cherry, a bail bondsman, has resisted all the enticements to turn dishonest. He has spent his life "dealing with scum and trying to act respectable." He has succeeded without too much mental turmoil, until he meets Jackie Burke, a flight attendant who has been smuggling money in and out of the United States for gun dealer Ordell Robbie. Jackie is accustomed to crossing borders illegally, but Max is not. Nevertheless, he apparently follows her at the end of the novel. Their final conversation—"Where would we go?" "I don't know. Does it matter?" (297)—indicates that their destination is the limbo in which most of Leonard's men and women reside. David Geherin explains how Leonard blurs the lines:

Leonard's good guys and bad guys are just ordinary people. His antagonists sometimes have good qualities; his protagonists, who are no storybook heroes, are sometimes even criminals themselves. By alternating point of view, between the hero and the villain as he often does, Leonard further narrows the distinction between the two. Because there is no controlling authorial voice in the novel, both points of view are given equal time, so to speak. This has the effect of forcing the reader to relate to both on a common human level. (129-30)

Not only does the reader relate to both points of view "on a common human level, but he or she also is morally disturbed by the irony of this technique," according to Glenn Most in his article, "Elmore Leonard: Splitting Images." Most points out that other authors, such as Patricia Highsmith, have narrated detective novels from the point of view of the villain; and the reader usually can reject this perspective en masse, because "we have long since concluded that the restrictiveness of the point of view from which the story is being told is part of the very sickness of the schizophrenic who is telling it." But in Leonard's fiction: "Both evil and good have become equally respectable alternative points of view from which a story can be told. How can we bestow our sympathy upon the hero from whose perspective one chapter is narrated and then withhold our sympathy from the psychopath whose viewpoint shapes the next one?" (Most 106). Most concludes that "there is something profoundly disturbing here."

The novel that best demonstrates Leonard's perspective of splitting images, which, in turn, creates settings that take place in the boundaries between states of being, is *Maximum Bob*. This novel also demonstrates Leonard's affinity with his Florida detective-novelist colleagues and their subject, the limbo-land of Central Florida.

The story takes place in the space in which the Everglades and Palm Beach intersect: "Cross Lake Worth east and you were in a different country, the top end of the Gold Coast where the rich and famous lived. But you know what? Go the other way, drive west beyond Twenty Mile Bend and, man, you were in a different *world*, the Glades, bottomland America with a smell of muck and fish" (85). In *Maximum Bob*, Judge Bob Gibbs has made a national reputation of throwing the book at the criminals who appear before him in court. He adheres to the rigid letter of the law not out of principle but out of meanness. When a defendant protests that a sentence isn't fair, the judge retorts: "Fair? What's fair got to do with it?" (103).

In the beginning of the novel, the characters appear one way; by the end, they have transformed themselves into their dark alter egos. Judge Gibbs, for example, initially is known for his honest court decisions. His face even graces a *Newsweek* cover dealing with a story entitled, "In Florida Maximum Bob Throws the Book." Slowly, though, the reader learns that he is a man of the flesh, whose physical lusts rule his principles. He bends the law in the case of Dicky Campau, a frog gigger, when he wants a favor done. He warns Dicky, "You can be let off with a warning, or draw a five-hundred-dollar fine and a year in the stockade. Take your pick" (45).

The judge's wife, Leanne Lancaster, provides an even better example of a Leonard character lost in space. She enters the judge's life as a lovely, innocent girl from Sandusky, Ohio: "The first time Bob Gibbs saw his wife she was performing sixteen feet beneath the surface of Weeki Wachee Spring, in a mermaid outfit" (24). Gibbs proposes to take her home and make her the mermaid of his backyard pool. Before he can realize this dream in his Garden of Eden, a serpent, in the form of an alligator; pushes Leanne over the brink from sanity to madness. In one of her shows as she is eating a banana underwater, she notices a shadow above her:

Then looking up and seeing the alligator, its pale belly, its snout, its stubby legs moving in the water almost on top of her as she was swallowing the bite of banana, in that exact same moment, . . . [s]he saw the alligator's tail fanning in the water as it turned and came back. . . . She remembered twisting frantically in that sheath of lamé binding her legs. (33)

The "Experience," as she calls it, changes her life. During the middle of it, an imaginary slave-girl, Wanda, tells her to return to life. Leanne does survive to marry Gibbs, but she is left with a "serene, netherworld, airy-fairy expression" on her face and Wanda's 135-year-old personality inside her. After seven years, she has riled her husband to the point that he plots to reintroduce an alligator in her life, hoping this horror will force her to leave him.

Dale Crowe is another character who exists neither here nor there in the story's reality. Maximum Bob has sentenced him to five years in prison for violating his parole and then given him seven days in the outside world to put his affairs in order. Dale promptly drives under the influence and then worries that he'll be arrested. His uncle, Elvin retorts: "What're you worried about . . . they might put you in jail? Tell them you're about to do five years, have to catch you later" (47).

Elvin Crowe, too, carries on a precarious existence between prison terms. At the moment, he's been "out of circulation" for ten years and is re-adjusting to life outside prison. It's only a matter of time, though, before he breaks the law and returns to Florida State Prison. In the meantime, he is teaching young Dale how "to jail." Most of the lessons revolve around how to survive sexually within prison walls: " 'Listen to me,' Elvin said. 'I'm a person was never married on the outside. But you get in there, something happens to you. Soon as I was put in with the population I started looking for a wife' " (50).

Even the good character of the story, Kathy Baker, appears to be ready to cross lines at the end of the narrative. After she shoots Elvin, Gibbs suggests that he "work it" so that he can get her a job in law enforcement. He then asks her for a date. The reader does not know what Baker's response will be; the nagging thought lingers that even she will move into Gibbs's sphere of influence.

These characters, like the alligator which is transported out of the Everglades by Dicky Campau as a present for Leanne Gibbs, are all confused by the landscape in which they find themselves. The poor animal, "disoriented, not knowing where she was, not catching the scent of anything familiar," is doomed. She moves to her eventual death, because she smells a dog: "she began to move in a sluggish sort of way as though half asleep, not entirely upright on her legs, brushing the grass with her tail. The scent she liked became stronger as she moved" (69).

There is not much hope for the characters who live in this world; Leonard does not allow them to transcend their surroundings and gain insights into their predicaments. Yet the reader, by traveling along with them on their journeys, discovers what it's like to be a frog gigger, or an bail bondsman, or a gun runner—or even a corrupt judge. Glenn Most poses the questions: "Why do we read Leonard's novels? What are the possibilities for evil within ourselves that respond to Leonard's narratives, and what forms might our response one day take?" (109). Reading a Leonard novel, the reader lands in the same limbo as the characters, without a map or moral compass for guidance. The most the reader can do is sit back and enjoy the thrill of crossing boundaries—at least in the imagination, if not the reality.

Works Cited

Cawelti, John G. *Adventure, Mystery, and Romance: Formula Stories As Art and Popular Culture*. Chicago: U of Chicago P, 1976.

Chandler, Raymond. *The Simple Art of Murder*. New York: Ballantine, 1972.

Geherin, David. *Elmore Leonard*. New York: Continuum, 1989.

Grafton, Sue. *"B" Is for Burglar*. New York: Bantam, 1986.

Grimes, Larry E. "Stepsons of Sam: Re-Visions of the Hard-Boiled Detective Formula in Recent American Fiction." *Modern Fiction Studies* 29.3 (1983): 535-44.

Hoppenstand, Gary C. *In Search of the Paper Tiger*. Bowling Green, OH: Bowling Green State University Press, 1987.

Hynes, Joseph. " 'High Noon in Detroit': Elmore Leonard's Career." *Journal of Popular Culture* 25.3 (1991): 181-87.

Leonard, Elmore. *Glitz*. New York: Warner, 1985.

——. *Gold Coast*. New York: Bantam, 1985.

——. *Maximum Bob*. New York: Dell, 1992.

——. *Rum Punch*. New York: Delacorte, 1992.

——. *Split Images*. New York: Avon, 1983.

——. *Stick*. New York: Avon, 1984.

Lutz, John. *Kiss*. New York: Holt, 1988.

——. *Scorcher*. New York: Holt, 1987.

——. *Torch*. New York: Holt, 1994.

——. *Tropical Heat*. New York: Holt, 1986.

"Lutz, John." *Contemporary Authors. New Revision Series*. Vol. 24. Detroit: Gale, 1988. 289-90.

Margolies, Edward. *Which Way Did He Go?* New York: Holmes and Meier, 1982.

Moi, Toril. *Sexual/Textual Politics*. London: Routledge, 1990.

Most, Glenn W. "Elmore Leonard: Splitting Images." *The Sleuth and the Scholar*. Ed. Barbara A. Rader and Howard C. Zettler. Westport: Greenwood, 1988. 101-10.

Nelson, William, and Nancy Avery. "Art Where You Least Expect It: Myth and Ritual in the Detective Series." *Modern Fiction Studies* 29.3 (1983): 463-74.

Percy, Walker. "There's a Contra in My Gumbo." Rev. of *Bandits*. *New York Times Book Review* 1 Apr. 1987: 7.

Poe, Edgar Allan. *Poetry and Tales*. Ed. Patrick Quinn. New York: Library of America, 1984.

Robinson, Kevin. *Mall Rats*. New York: Walker, 1992.

——. *A Matter of Perspective*. New York: Walker, 1993.

——. *Split Seconds*. New York: Walker, 1991.

Sanders, Lawrence. *McNally's Caper*. New York: Berkley, 1995.

——. *McNally's Luck*. New York: Berkley, 1993.

——. *McNally's Risk*. New York: Berkley, 1994.

——. *McNally's Secret*. New York: Berkley, 1993.

——. *McNally's Trial*. New York: Putnam, 1995.

Slotkin, Richard. *The Hard-Boiled Detective Story: From the Open Range to the Mean Streets*. New York: Greenwood, 1988.

Svoboda, Frederic. "The Snub-Nosed Mystique: Observations on the American Detective Hero." *Modern Fiction Studies* 29.3 (1983).

Vachss, Andrew. "Back in Top Form: Tough Honest Elmore Leonard." Rev. of *Killshot*. *Chicago Tribune-Books* 9 Apr. 1989: 1.

8

Ecological Noir

Maurice O'Sullivan

As the godfathers of American noir, Dashiell Hammett and Raymond Chandler did more than remove murder mysteries from the harmoniously hierarchical world of quaintly placid British villages to the mean streets, sterile architecture, and dysfunctional families of urban America. They also created a ravaged social and physical environment as the perfect elegiac background for their tales of the bleakness enveloping the postindustrial world. Building on their work, John D. MacDonald found in humanity's war upon nature the source of that bleakness. In his Travis McGee series and two novels set along Florida's southwest coast *A Flash of Green* and *Condominium* he dissects the voracious developers, relentless consumers, and thoughtless intruders spoiling Eden.

MacDonald's most fully realized character, the curiously innocent knight errant Travis McGee, often rails about the result: "instant Florida, tacky and stifling and full of spurious energies" (*Dreadful Lemon Sky* 49). Those distorted and distorting energies not only pervert the physical environment, they also infect every family and community structure in MacDonald's technicolored world. Relentlessly romantic, McGee can only remain untouched by removing himself from his fading paradise to a houseboat just off its coast.

Although many of Florida's mystery writers have continued MacDonald's legacy by exploring the human capacity to corrupt both society and nature, no one has succeeded with the ecomystery in as sustained and sophisticated a way as Randy Wayne White, a Sanibel fishing guide who developed a cult following while writing essays for *Outside Magazine*. Like MacDonald's McGee, White's hero, Marion "Doc" Ford, an ex-National Security Agency operative with a Ph.D. in marine biology, retains his innocence by physically separating himself from his corrupted Eden. While McGee regularly retreats to his luxurious houseboat moored at the Bahia Mar marina in Fort Lauderdale, however, White has moved his hero across Alligator Alley and into a stilt house off Dinkin's Bay Marina in Sanibel, a key off Fort Myers. Unlike

119

McGee, who attempts to recreate a prelapsarian state by devoting his life to an endless spring break without long-term responsibilities and relationships, Ford commits himself to a business career by founding a biological supply company, engages in sustained scientific research into the ecology of Dinkin's Bay, and attempts to develop lasting relationships with both his neighbors and a series of mature, career-oriented women.

With an educational background and scholarly, introverted temperament that allow him to offer detailed scientific evidence of the effect Floridians' lives and lifestyles have had on the state's ecology, Ford finds in the decaying of Florida's marine ecosystems a clear parallel to the corruption of the state's moral, social, and political systems. In the first two of these ecomysteries (*Sanibel Flats* and *The Heat Islands*), Ford combines a scientific, methodological, analytical approach to problem solving with a good dash of traditional action. While his third, *The Man Who Invented Florida*, substitutes irony and history for action and detection, his fourth, *Captiva*, returns to the pattern of his first novels.

In the Chandler tradition of loyalty to old friends, Ford's primary goal involves helping friends, especially friends with whom he has an ambivalent relationship. Whether rescuing the seven-year-old son of an old high school teammate, saving a fishing guide neighbor from a murder charge, or helping out his scheming uncle, Ford finds his loyalties tested in a human society far less reliable than the world of his aquarium.

In many ways, Ford is a conventional hero. He left the NSA after realizing that his sympathies lay with Latin America's Marxist rebels rather than its privileged ruling class. His protests—sleeping with the wife of a Central American tyrant and providing baseball uniforms emblazoned with the legend "Masaguan People's Army" for an insurgent group whose leader envisioned a utopia modeled after American professional baseball—make him safely suspect to his former employer. His baggy clothes, bookish manner, and wire-rim glasses convince most people that he is a harmless scholar, an image that he overthrows whenever forced into physical confrontation.

A product of the nineties, Ford first appears fleeing an interrupted sexual encounter, naked except for his Nikes. In much the same spirit, near the end of the novel he leaves a lover by riding off into the moonlight on his ten-speed bike. Ford's frequently frustrated romances allow him to remain the isolated hero, reflect his limited understanding of women, and suggest the fragility of the human ecosystem. His involvement in his work often blinds him to the niceties of social interactions and leads him to project his responses onto others. With the photographer Sally Carmel, for example, he recognizes the need for caution in an early encounter that foreshadows the end of their relationship.

It had almost happened that night, but not quite. Sally had said she wasn't ready yet, because of the marriage. The divorce, she meant. But then they were holding and kissing again, touching, yet it still didn't happen because of something she said they had to talk about.

"I don't know how to . . . what I'm trying to say is . . . we should talk about our backgrounds. It's so terrible even to have to worry about it. . . . Do you understand what I mean?"

Ford had understood. He and Tomlinson had spent enough time talking about it. "The Modern Specter," Tomlinson had called it. "The Dark Gift. Because of it," Tomlinson had said, "the human race will never again know total spontaneity. Never again will we know a moment free of the knowledge of our own vulnerability. Or our own mortality. The last retreat has been taken from us."

Which, Ford had thought at the time, was just more spiritual wailing in the face of a serious biological anomaly: a fatal virus, sexually transmitted. But in that instant, in Sally's arms, Ford realized that Tomlinson was close to being right. (*The Man Who Invented Florida* 191)

As this passage suggests, the language and principles of science are never far from Ford's mind or White's prose. In fact, White's major achievement involves integrating the imagery of science into the detective genre. Physics, biology, chemistry, and mathematics have traditionally been the province of hard-core science fiction. Although a number of best-selling action/adventure writers like Tom Clancy and Dale Brown have built their plots around themes and imagery from technology, only Michael Crichton has consistently attracted readers to popular fiction that explores such ideas as molecular biology, evolution, and chaos theory. For White, the biological organism becomes the essential model for human life and behavior. When Ford attempts to justify to himself manipulating a recalcitrant judicial system so that it will recognize a friend's death as a murder rather than a suicide, for example, he expresses his frustration in typically biological imagery:

What he was trying to do was get the right organizations in line; to nudge them in the right direction. It was the one hope he had of securing justice for Rafe Hollins. . . . People didn't deal with people anymore, they dealt with beings Ford thought of as Bionts. In the literature of natural history, a biont was a discrete unit of living matter that had a specific mode of life. In modern America, to Ford's way of thinking, a Biont was a worker or minor official who, joined with other Bionts, established a separate and dominant entity: the Organization. A Biont was different from an employee. Ford was seeing fewer and fewer employees around. The Biont looked to the Organization as a sort of surrogate family; depended on the Organization to care for him in sickness and in health, to provide for his recreational, spiritual, and social needs. The Organization was an organism, much as a coral reef or a beehive could be considered an organism, made up of individual creatures working for the good of the whole. When the Organization prospered, so did the Biont—a sort of professional symbiosis, with loyalty built in. A Biont might grumble about his host in private, but just let an outsider try to sneak in, ask for information, arouse suspicion, or endanger the Organization, and all the unit members would unite like a shield to rebuff the intruder. Ford thought of the way Aztec ants rushed to attack anything that happened to touch their hosting Cocoloba tree. He thought of killer bees. (*Sanibel Flats* 105-06)

Even Ford's sidekick Tomlinson, a gently aging hippie with a Ph.D. in religion from Harvard, translates his own mystical vision of the world into scientific imagery:

"See what happens when you think about killing border guards?" Tomlinson said kindly. "It sets all the negative ions in motion. Really destructive stuff, man. I've got some books you should read."
"Okay," he said. "All right. I believe you."
"See, we all got auras, man—these sort of electrical fields around us, only you can't see them—" (*Sanibel Flats* 179)

At one of the novel's critical moments, when the hero must steel himself to continue his quest despite its dangers, Ford's reasoning moves back to his overarching theme: our roles in the complex nexus of organisms that we constitute:

Ford stood in the darkness beneath a huge guanacaste tree. . . . Touched by the flashlight's beam, each big leaf became a separate and living entity, each leaf the possible host or habitat of a variety of insects and animals, and Ford studied the leaves, trying to relax.
By crouching he could see . . . a colony of small bats roosting: disk-winged bats, their leathery wings pulsing with the regularity of lungs.
The sudden light stunned them for a long instant and then they were gone in a panic, their eerie shapes silhouetting against the moon. There were beetles feeding on striations of the leaf, some kind of heliconia-feeder, but Ford didn't know which kind. Nearby, frogs began to trill again, and Ford used the flashlight to find them: red-eyed and brown tree frogs. It was the mating season, and several of the females had smaller males clinging to their backsides. That made Ford search for something else, and it didn't take him long to find the glutinous deposits of frog's eggs stuck to the undersides of the leaves. Some of the eggs

had already matured into tadpoles, and the viscid masses hung in the light like icicles, dripping life into the water below . . . where two—no, four—cat-eyed snakes waited, feeding on the globs of tadpoles in a frenzy.

Ford watched the snakes feeding, taking an odd pleasure in knowing that this same drama was going on all around him; the same cycle of copulation, birth, and death; the same earnest theater being played out by jaguars, dung flies, tapirs, leaf-cutter ants, crocodiles, boas, and men throughout the millions of acres of jungle darkness. (*Sanibel Flats* 196-97)

This pattern works its way through all of his novels. In *The Heat Islands*, for example, the connection between biological phenomena and the social and criminal behaviors of humans dominates Ford's attempt to explain to Tomlinson how a dinoflagellate, *Gymnodium breve,* causes a red tide.

The complexity of the biological universe offers an effective metaphor for the intricacies of White's plots. In *Sanibel Flats*, for example, he juggles Mayan theology, Central and South American history, shark anatomy, American foreign policy, Shining Path guerrillas, the development of barrier islands, the culture of fishing guides, and smuggling pre-Columbian artifacts, while allowing Ford to come to grips with his past. And in *Captiva* Florida's ban on netting fish incites a war between commercial and sports fishermen: "When disturbed, water oscillates far beyond the point of contact. The same dynamics apply to the environment—and to society." (26) Ford eventually resolves the disturbance's effects on his community and his own life with the help of Burmese junks, Gurkha warriors, historical artifacts, and, perhaps, divine intervention.

White's style offers the pleasures of humor as well as intricate plotting as when he describes US 41 as "a six lane Cuisinart" (*Sanibel Flats* 121) or survey stakes as "Florida's state flag" (*The Man Who Invented Florida* 53). As befits a writer who often reflects on the parallels among species, much of this humor occurs in Ford's monologues with the creatures in his aquarium about his romantic life. He can complain, "Here it is, Friday night, and I'm talking to cephalopods" (*Sanibel Flats* 42) or quizzically reflect, " 'It's not that I don't like women,' he told the squid. 'It's just that I find biology less complicated' " (*The Heat Islands* 197). At other times the comedy stems from ironic human interactions as in the apparently uninterested Native American Joseph Egret who finds himself the object of unbridled sexual appetites as the mature wives of Florida's newest pioneers take him under their wings.

At the heart of White's fictions lies his recognition of humanity's and nature's capacity for rebirth and regeneration. Nature's capacity for renewal is reflected in the biofouling assemblies that Ford develops to filter the turbidity from Dinkin's Bay at the end of *The Man Who Invented Florida*. The headnote to White's first novel—Edna St. Vincent Millay's lines "Whether or not we find what we are seeking/Is idle, biologically speaking"—begins his work by asserting a world of natural imperatives separate from human concerns. As humans, we must, therefore, accept responsibility for our own activities. Among those responsibilities are our conflicting needs to understand ourselves, to uncover the truth, and to continue our species. From Ford's first appearance arising out of the ground in a park like the Mayan god Quetzalcoatl, he attempts to combine all three of these drives while recognizing nature's essential indifference to us. It is our destiny to deal with our history, a history, which Tomlinson points out, invariably recycles itself: "It hit me yesterday when I was out on my boat meditating. . . . These people are acting out the whole conquest scene over and over again. Like punishing themselves in utter damn humiliation. The fighting, the revolutions, killing their own kind—just like when Alvarado came. And they're still following the white god, Quetzalcoatl, only now Quetzalcoatl goes under a couple of names, like the Soviet Union and the good old U. S. of A" (*Sanibel Flats* 118).

Our hope lies in our capacity to adapt, evolve, and survive. That hope manifests itself in the novels' emphasis on birth from Ford's admission, "I would like to have a child" (*Sanibel Flats* 198), and the apparent fulfillment of that wish, to Tomlinson's fathering a child in *The Heat Islands*. When Sally Carmel becomes midwife to a dolphin in *The Man Who Invented Florida*, her action sparks her desire for maternity. Despite Ford's knowledge of marine biology, however, the empathy between Sally and the dolphin during the birth symbolizes a fundamentally female experience in which men are, at best, tangential. In fact, the two women who bear children in these novels choose not to maintain close ties with the biological fathers.

The occasional jibes at Florida's history that appear in *Sanibel Flats* become sharper and more explicit in *The Heat Islands*:

Florida's history is a chaotic thing built upon thin layers of human endeavor that are covered or quickly absorbed by more thin layers, then forgotten entirely. Because Florida has always appealed to the provisional and the transitory, what has gone before and what inevitably must come have never been of much interest. Which explains many of Florida's ills, and is also why Florida has always been the nation's tackiest, glitziest state. (208)

White's third novel devotes itself to this theme. The very title of *The Man Who Invented Florida* recognizes that Florida is as much a state of mind as a physical reality, as much a cultural construct as a geographical location. Tuck Gattrell, Doc's uncle, loosely and unkindly alluded to in *Sanibel Flats* as "an ex-triple-A pitcher who picked up the bottle the day his contract was dropped" (17), works a sophisticated scam as he rides his ancient horse along the coastline with Joseph Egret, who claims to be the last Calusa Indian. In Tuck, White creates one of his finest characters, a man torn between ego and nostalgia, a visionary willing to sell cheap.

While Tuck sees himself as the last Florida cowboy, a Cooperesque Natty Bumppo outwitting the bureaucrats and bumpkins invading his terrain, he acts more like P. T. Barnum with his schemes for developing land and attracting tourists. Tuck counts among his achievements inventing stone crabbing and night shrimping, running rum for the syndicate and guns for Castro, inventing floating dredges for the Tamiami Trail and other roads bisecting the state, and suggesting the first theme park to Dick Pope, founder of Cypress Gardens. What he fails to realize until very late in the novel is how each of these discoveries and ideas attracted a broader and broader array of tourists and residents, an invasion which would inevitably destroy the very things Tuck wanted to preserve.

Ford views Gattrell as far from harmless. As he tells Tomlinson: "He likes to steer people. Like his cows. Turn them this way and that. A Florida cowboy, that's what he was. A fisherman and a cow hunter. Tuck never comes right out and says what's really on his mind. He wants to use me somehow. It was bad enough when he wasn't crazy. I mean, senile" (13).

But even deeper than that, Ford sees Tuck as a principle of confusion: "But Tuck is different . . . on purpose. He sees himself as an inventor, smarter than everybody else, but in fact he's just contrary. Give him the simplest problem and he'll take the most absurd route to solve it. The stranger the better. Tuck confuses convolution with brilliance. He always has. He likes being different because that's the only thing he's ever been successful at" (149). Like most detectives, Ford represents both moral clarity and the preservation of order. Tuck's failure to anticipate the often tragic consequences of his schemes infuriates his nephew. In addition to the environmental impact of his various inventions, Tuck's plans lead indirectly to the deaths of Ford's parents and Joseph Egret, who may, in fact, be the true source of many of these ideas.

By linking Florida's human and aquatic ecologies, Randy Wayne White has revealed not only the connections between the two but the complex vitality of each. Above all, he has captured the glory, folly, and frailty of both our environment and our selves. As Doc Ford painstakingly collects his marine specimens and relentlessly dissects his friends' crises, he invariably exposes the wide range of physical and social threats to life in contemporary Florida. But even in the midst of his elegiac evocations of the state's lost treasures and his sharply etched sketches of its modern predators, he never loses hope in our ability to adapt, evolve, and survive. With his graceful prose, elegant plots, beautifully integrated science, and ironic humor, Randy Wayne White has become a richly rewarding guide to the distinctive culture of Florida's southwestern islands.

Note

Along with all John D. MacDonald fans, my view of both the author and his hero has been shaped by the work of Edgar Hirshberg. I am also indebted to a highly perceptive senior honors thesis by one of my students at Rollins, Richard B. Troutman's "Adam Unparadised" (1978), which examined Travis McGee's relationship to the tradition of the American Adam.

Works Cited

MacDonald, John D. *Condominium*. Philadelphia: Lippincott, 1977.
——. *The Dreadful Lemon Sky*. Philadelphia: Lippincott, 1975.
——. *A Flash of Green*. New York: Simon and Schuster, 1962.
White, Randy Wayne. *Captiva*. New York: Putnam, 1996.
——. *The Heat Islands* New York: St. Martin's, 1992.
——. *The Man Who Invented Florida*. New York: St. Martin's, 1993.
——. *Sanibel Flats*. New York: St. Martin's, 1990.

9

Fairy Tale Noir

Maurice O'Sullivan

While Sanibel's Randy Wayne White finds in the delicate designs of biology images to explore human ecosystems, his Sarasota neighbor Ed McBain uses fairy tales to map the dangerous intersections of family conflicts. McBain's titles, which range from *Goldilocks* and *Cinderella* to *Three Blind Mice* and *Puss in Boots,* not only provide essential clues to the mystery at the heart of each book, they also offer ironic introductions to the violent eroticism and graphically realistic details in his deconstructions of these classic fairy tales. His novels offer concrete examples of Leslie Fiedler's reflection on the contemporary heart of darkness: "The final horrors, as modern society has come to realize, are neither gods nor demons, but intimate aspects of our own minds" (446).

Born Salvatore A. Lombino in New York City, Ed McBain first adopted the pseudonym Evan Hunter as a tribute to his education at Evander Childs High School in the Bronx and Hunter College. Soon after the success of *The Blackboard Jungle* in 1954 allowed him to give up substitute teaching and become a full-time writer, he adopted a second pseudonym and began to explore the relationships between character and crime in his carefully and realistically detailed 87th Precinct police procedurals. In establishing his position as the dominant force in this genre, the Americanized version of the French *roman policier* most often identified with the works of George Simenon, McBain presents a squad of fairly unimaginative detectives methodically puzzling through increasingly violent urban crimes, relying as much on accident and luck as training and procedure to preserve and protect the citizens of Isola, the fictional city that closely parallels McBain's native New York City. In 1978 McBain shifted his focus from the institutionalized, collective effort to achieve order in a coldly isolated traditional American megalopolis to an individual's quest for understanding in a postmodernist, mobile paradise on the southern fringe of the United States.

Although he traded ghetto tenements for gulf-side condos and the shift workers of the 87th struggling to make mortgages for Matthew

Hope, an affluent Midwestern-reared lawyer racing to make gallery openings, McBain preserves the essential stylistic components of the 87th Precinct works: the relentlessly metronomic prose of his interrogations, the telegraphic presentation of detail, the methodical accumulation of evidence, and the severely mechanical visual representation of forms and printed material. Rather than moving from police procedurals to legal procedurals—the courtroom plays a very small role in his novels, with the single exception of *Mary, Mary* (1990), the series' tenth book—he seems far more interested in interviewing people in their private spaces than on the witness stand. As a more educated and sophisticated hero unrestrained by the rules of police procedure and their codes of conduct, Matthew Hope can become more personally involved in his cases and can explore more fully the psychology of both criminal and victim.

McBain suggests his goal in *Goldilocks*, the first novel of this new series. During a cocktail party, a casual acquaintance begins offering his own reflections on Hope's first criminal case, one in which a long-time client has been arrested for murdering his wife and daughters. While his nameless acquaintance rambles on, Hope has an epiphany: "To this man, the tragedy was only a murder mystery, and he recounted it to me as such now, reducing it to the level of a whodunit" (136). With his chilling details, bold language, and relentless portraits of dysfunctional families, McBain blocks any attempt to turn human tragedy into intellectual, aesthetic experiences. If Ross Macdonald was the first mystery writer to explore explicitly and in detail the psyche through a framework of Freudian psychology, McBain has carried that exploration even further.

In recasting classic fairy tales as detective stories, he has drawn on the value of those tales as symbolic reenactments of inevitable human and psychological conflicts to demonstrate their continuing power to touch our imaginations. In *The Uses of Enchantment,* Bruno Bettelheim discusses the therapeutic value of such tales for children: "There is general agreement that myths and fairy tales speak to us in the language of symbols representing unconscious content. Their appeal is simultaneously to our conscious and unconscious mind, to all three of its aspects —id, ego, and superego—and to our need for ego ideals as well. This makes it very effective; and in the tales' content, inner psychological phenomena are given body in symbolic form" (36). McBain has recognized that the individual and social fears and beliefs that such stories represent continue through life.

Ironically, these tales normally associated with childhood allow McBain to verge into socially forbidden criminal and erotic worlds. This allows him to explore in great detail adultery, prostitution, incest,

bondage, pornographic films, topless bars, sexual mutilation and dis-
memberment, the genital mutilation of children, and sexual variations of
all kind—*menages a trois, a quatre, a cinq, ad infinitum.* What a client
says about a mental asylum—"Sexual fantasies tend to run rampant
here" (*Snow White* 14)—holds just as true of the novels.

In the process of defamiliarizing these European fables and adapting
them to contemporary American landscapes and mores, McBain allows
characters in his stories to point out the cruelty and violence permeating
the stories. In *Jack and the Beanstalk,* for example, Matthew Hope's current lover, a woman almost two decades older than himself, expresses
her objection while bantering about her age: " 'Pretending to be
Grandma,' I said. 'Shame on you.' 'It was the *wolf* who pretended to be
Grandma.' 'It's the wolf right here in bed with you,' I said, and bared my
teeth. 'I hate fairy tales; I think they're designed to frighten children,'
she said" (155). And to some extent she is right. Disagreeing with Bettelheim's argument that such tales have a beneficial effect upon children by
allowing them to recognize their impulses and desires as normal, critics
like Maria Tartar have encouraged restricting exposure to the stories.
Tartar indicts the genre for much the same reason that McBain turned to
it: "The heroes and heroines of canonized fairy tales are marked as tar-
gets of virtually unmediated interfamilial jealousy or resentment. The
victims of violence have no trouble turning into agents of revenge, and it
is astonishing to see how vigorously and adeptly fairy tale protagonists
punish their oppressors (who take on the mask of stepsister, witch, or
ogre) and derive pleasure from their agony" (169).

Within McBain's revision of the canon, the titles prove both ambiguous and deceptive. In some cases, he expects his audience to know the
story and so merely provides occasional allusions. In the first novel of
the series, for example, Hope's client's first wife and her children nickname the second wife *Goldilocks.* Apparently assuming that the audience
has enough familiarity with the story, McBain uses the image sparsely,
as when a daughter from the first marriage complains about one from the
second marriage "Sleeping there in my bed" (173). For the second
story's more obscure title, *Rumpelstiltskin,* he introduces a German
woman who illustrates children's books to explain the origin of the
name:

> "But you *must* know Rumpelstiltskin, *nein?*"
> "Well, sure," I said, not at all sure any more.
> "It is about a German *Muller*—how do you say it in English? A man who
> owns the mill and he grinds the grain there, do you know? *Ein Muller.* Anyway
> he tells the king that his daughter can spin gold out of straw. The king takes her

to his castle and locks her in a room and asks her to do this or else she will die. To spin the gold into straw, eh? Which of course she cannot do. But a dwarf appears to her, and tells her he can do it for her, for a price, and she gives him her necklace to spin the whole room of straw into gold. Well the king is of course astonished, and he locks her in a *bigger* room the next night with even *more* straw in it. . . . [T]he dwarf once again appears, and this time she gives him her ring, and he does it for her, he spins all the straw into gold. Well, the king is truly amazed, and he takes her to the biggest room in the castle, and it too is filled with straw, and he tells her that if she can spin all this into gold by morning, he will marry her. She is crying and crying, and she doesn't know what to do until the dwarf again appears—but she has no more jewelry to give him, she has already given him the last of her jewelry. So she promises the dwarf if she becomes queen, she will give him her firstborn child. They seal the bargain, and he turns all the straw into gold, and she becomes queen of all the land." (188)

And at the end, Hope explicitly draws the connection between the novel's title and its story of the murder of Vicky Miller, the appropriately named rock and roll queen, and the kidnapping and murder of her child. The murderer, a member of her band equally appropriately called Wheat, had "taken the basic straw of Victoria Miller's meager talent and turned it into the pure gold of three-million copy albums" (224). When a police detective wonders aloud about the crime—"Killed two people and wrecked his own life. How does that happen to somebody, Matthew? Man who used to be a giant in his profession."—Hope has the final insight: " 'He was a dwarf inside' " (229-30).

However, in many cases the title proves misleading. In *Goldilocks*, for example, both murderer and victim are blondes, leaving a question about the true goldilocks. The apparent beast of *Beauty and the Beast* may be that book's most beautiful character, just as in the original story the beast's exterior conceals a prince. *Snow White and Rose Red* turn out to be the same character, while in *Jack & the Beanstalk*, there are two different Jacks, the son trying to buy a field to grow snapbeans and the daughter's boyfriend looking for a quick fortune. In a similar play on the same name, the Jack responsible for the intricately connected *The House That Jack Built* appears to be the murder victim, Jonathan Parrish, but proves to be Jacob Brechtmann, founder of a distinguished brewing chain.

As the series progressed, McBain found even more subtle and ironic ways to use his originals. In *Cinderella*, the prostitute Jenny Santoro's fairy godmother, a remote and fussily aging gay male, prepares her to run a con on a chubby Latin drug dealer with a taste for wealthy, naive

Midwestern girls. As he discusses her wardrobe, McBain allows the monologue to reveal a key character's value system while developing the fairy tale imagery:

> What he called it was a triumph of illusion over reality
> Or something.
> We're going to turn you into a Wasp princess from Denver, Colorado, he told her. Daughter of a rich rancher. Spoiled rotten, there's nothing any man on earth can possibly give you. It'll flatter Pudgy to death to think you *might*, if he minds his fat little spic manners, actually deign to *talk* to him. . . .
> Jewelry. . . . Something for just here, do you see? Right where the cleavage begins. Draw his eyes to the bust, not that you need any help darling, don't be offended. . . . I want you to come into the lounge all starry-eyed and aghast, virtually *popping* out of the gown, tits, tits, *wonderful,* looking for someone who *should* be there but isn't, Miss Colorado who's been stood up, searching the room, Oh my goodness where *is* he, slippers that look as though they're made of glass, they do wonderful things with plastic nowadays. (103-04)

And after the main story concludes, as Jenny finds herself confronted by another of the furies from her past, McBain's Cinderella reflects with the last lines of the novel: "And she thought—as he locked the door behind him—*They always let me in the ballroom but they never let me dance*" (186).

The titles often control subplots as well as the main story. *Puss in Boots* not only describes the plot of a pornographic film that initiates the main plot but suggests the sexual awakening of Hope's daughter. And *The House That Jack Built* provides a symbol for the intricacies of both the central murder and Hope's partner's wife's affair. In that novel, the eighth in the series, McBain suggests the reach of his title by beginning each chapter with verses from the fairy tale and ending with a retelling of the original tale in its incrementally cumulative style. In doing so, he not only integrates it into all aspects of his story but also reflects the evolutionary nature of both his plots and his series. He returns to a simpler form of this technique six years later in *There Was a Little Girl*, using the rhymes of this well-known song as the titles of his seven chapters.

Part of McBain's appeal lies in the humor at the edges of his nightmares and in his continual experimentation. He will occasionally have characters use the idea of fairy tales ironically. The female director of a skin flick titled *Puss in Boots* in the novel with that title selects a French pseudonym "which intimated great sexual knowledge and which also referred back to the source of the fairy tale, the writer Charles Perrault. Not all fairy tales were written by Grimm" (125). As Hope searches for the director a little later in the novel, he encounters a skeptical motel manager: "This is a fairy tale, right" Kim said. "She checks out without collecting? And you come looking to pay for her? Come on, mister" (Puss 133). And he can toy with his story's imagery. In *Three Blind Mice* when McBain introduces Patricia Demming, who will become both his rival as a prosecutor and his lover, "She looked like a drowned rat" (23).

This interest in experimentation extends to McBain's approach to the point of view within his novels. As Hope's character evolves, he moves from observer to participant. From the beginning, however, his clients' lives parallel his own. The crimes he investigates all have their sources in the fragmentation of nuclear or extended families and all reflect, on some level, the chaos in Hope's own life. His first novel, for example, begins with his preparing to ask his wife, Susan, for a divorce in order to be free to marry the woman with whom he is having an affair. He soon finds himself defending a man trapped by the consequences of his adulteries. The series traces his liaisons with a variety of women, all complicated by his devotion to his daughter, Joanna, a precocious thirteen-year-old when the novels begin, and his continuing relationship with Susan. McBain clearly emphasizes columnist Sally Bryant Quinn's ironic observation that marriages end but divorces last forever.

By the fourth novel, *Jack and the Beanstalk*, Hope becomes involved in two bloody fistfights before being shot by a fleeing suspect. Ironically, as he becomes more involved in his cases, the novels' point of view moves from the first person to a shifting third person. By the fifth novel, *Snow White,* the first person had become an awkward device in conveying the parallel stories that would converge at the end. The interrogations, dialogue, and documents that offered some opportunity for multiple perspectives had clearly proved too limiting. While Hope tells the story of his attempt to have a young woman whom he loves declared mentally competent, he needs to leap forward to provide information about a parallel investigation by the police into the death and mutilation of a stripper, a case he will not learn about until late in the story.

The first two novels with these shifting third person narrators (*Cinderella* and *Puss in Boots*) begin with the point of view of a person about to be murdered. For the tenth novel, *Mary, Mary*, McBain shifts back to Hope's first person with a second character's first person commentary occasionally interposed along with the most extensive trial testimony in any of his novels. By the following book, *There Was a Little Girl*, McBain relies primarily on third person narratives except for the intermittent first person memories and reveries of a comatose and wounded Hope.

As Hope, now "a bit crotchety" (6), slowly recovers from the physical and psychological effects of those wounds in his latest adventure,

Gladly the Cross-Eyed Bear, his creator returns to first-person narrative while signaling a possible new direction for the series. The shift in focus suggested by the new title, a shift from the fairy tales associated with childhood to the toys associated with children, parallels more emphasis on childishness in the motives of the characters, a greater objectification or separation between the main plot and subplot, and a more ironic ending than in the earlier novels.

As a character, Hope has a clearly defined but not overly intrusive sense of morality. Hope's worldly, cynical partner, Frank Summerville, frequently mocks the curious innocence of his essential credo: "defending only people you think are innocent" (*Three Blind Mice* 51). When a lover asks him why he did not sleep with her provocative daughter who had attempted to seduce him, he answers that "there were some things a person just didn't do if he expected to live with himself ever again" (*Jack and the Beanstalk* 151). After he begins a relationship with the prosecutor of his client in *Mary Mary*, he immediately explains to the client the potential legal and ethical implications of his sexual adventure.

Hope expresses his integrity primarily through his search for truth. Although he might claim, "It's not my job to find a killer. I only have to show that my man didn't do it" (*Three Blind Mice* 131), he becomes so involved with his cases that he invariably solves the crime. Despite recognizing the inherent complexity of life—"I sometimes think all of life is *Rashomon*. . . . *Rashomon* is about variations of the truth. It is about reality and the different ways in which reality can be perceived, It is about the nature of verity and falsehood" (*Gladly the Cross-Eyed Bear* 270)—he can never allow questions to go unanswered or mysteries to go unresolved. Puzzling through them becomes his mission; in *Beauty and the Beast*, he confesses, "I hate mysteries" (94). His response to witnesses or criminals who have grown tired of his interrogations is invariably some variation on a comment in his first book, "I want to know why" (*Goldilocks* 163). In McBain's stories most characters begin by lying. Puzzling through the mazes people construct to conceal the motives lurking behind their actions invariably reveals not only the criminal but the coded meaning behind the title.

From the earliest European explorations, Florida's southwest coast has recorded Western people's attempts to impose elusive visions on the new world's shores. A modern conquistador, circus magnate John Ringling, sought to immortalize himself in Sarasota by building both a Florentine villa dedicated to European art and a mansion modeled on the Doge's Palace in Venice and named for himself, Ca'd'Zan or the House of John. Ringling's legacy, part of the persistent attempts by explorers, settlers, and developers to define and control the state's physical, social, and cultural environment, has created the confusion between dream and reality that marks modern Florida. Sorting through the results of that legacy, Ed McBain has identified the myths at the core of our dreams as the fantasies of childhood. In translating those myths into mysteries, he has created a rich body of fiction that locates our final horrors in our failure to understand ourselves and outgrow the illusions of our youth.

Note

I am indebted to Dianne L. Walton's honors thesis at Rollins, "Fairy Tales, Fantasy, and Freud" (1995), for its insights into the literary and psychological value of fairy tales.

Works Cited

Bettelheim, Bruno. *The Uses of Enchantment: The Meaning and Importance of Fairy Tales*. New York: Random, 1989.

Fiedler, Leslie. *Love and Death in the American Novel*. New York: Stein, 1966.

McBain, Ed. *Beauty and the Beast*. New York: Holt, 1982.

——. *Cinderella*. New York: Holt, 1986.

——. *Gladly the Cross-Eyed Bear*. New York: Warner, 1996.

——. *Goldilocks*. New York: Arbor, 1978.

——. *The House That Jack Built*. New York: Holt, 1988.

——. *Jack and the Beanstalk*. New York: Holt, 1984.

——. *Mary, Mary*. New York: Warner, 1992.

——. *Puss in Boots*. New York: Holt, 1987.

——. *Rumpelstiltskin*. New York: Viking, 1981.

——. *Snow White and Rose Red*. New York: Holt, 1985.

——. *There Was a Little Girl*. New York: Warner, 1994.

——. *Three Blind Mice*. New York: Arcade, 1990.

Tartar, Maria. *Off with Their Heads: Fairy Tales and the Culture of Childhood*. Princeton: Princeton UP, 1992.

10

North Florida Noir:
A Southern Perspective

Steve Glassman

"The map says it's part of Florida," Geoffrey Norman's ex-con pro-tagonist Morgan Hunt says in *Sweetwater Ranch*, "but [Pensacola] is about nine hundred miles away—and a few million miles in spirit—from what most people think of when they hear the word Florida: Miami, Fort Lauderdale, and Palm Beach" (5).

North Florida Noir country occupies the top half of the Florida peninsula—I-4, which runs from Tampa to Daytona Beach, works fine as the dividing line—and all the panhandle, an area sometimes not so jokingly said to be Georgia with a Florida zip code. The perception is that the locale remains overwhelmingly rural—even if that perception overlooks the fact that the largest city in the United States—if you go by square miles of incorporation—industrial, big-shoulders Jacksonville is included here. And then there are other population centers: Pensacola with its military personnel, Gainesville and Tallahassee with their megauniversities and in the latter's case, the state capital. Then too there are populous counties without any urban centers, notably Pinellas County, at least the Pinellas County of thirty or so years ago we will deal with here.

Morgan Hunt is right in saying none of these places have much in common with the polyglot Gomorrah squatting on the lower east coast, where those pagan rites of annual renewal known as the Orange Bowl are celebrated. When there was speculation Florida State might first be invited to that most hallowed of south Florida shrines, the local folks claimed FSU fans would arrive in Babylon with a ten dollar bill in one pocket and a copy of the Ten Commandments in the other—and leave town without breaking either.

Is it possible, then, for noir writing to flourish in a bastion of human perfectibility such as north Florida? Luckily, for noir devotees the Deep South has its own independently derived dark traditions—traditions which have proven so fertile in a literary way that they've yielded one

135

Nobel laureate and goodness knows how many Pulitzer and other lesser prizes. Unfortunately, the noir writers working these fields in north Florida have not—yet, anyway—achieved a like degree of acclaim. Nor, so far as that goes, have they matched the celebrity of crime writers plying the coasts of lower Florida.

Fame is a fickle mistress, sometimes bestowing but as often withholding her affections from the deserving. The writers I will examine here are in their various ways among the elect. Some have been fleetingly embraced by Lady Fortuna. Others are still being enticed by the promise of the laurel wreath. But for the purpose here, I am less interested in notoriety than whether a writer has made any noir innovations of note and/or done anything with the ever so fertile promise of the north Florida soil. I shall begin my investigation in the extreme southwest part of our area, then I will levitate up and over to Lake County then on up to the Jacksonville area, from where I'll go west into the panhandle, ending up in Pensacola. Coincident with the geographical organization is a temporal one, the first writers I deal with reached their apogee thirty or so years ago and are now long dormant; the later ones are still active.

The name of Frederick Clyde Davis might not spring immediately to mind in connection with north Florida detective fiction. Substituting the nom de plume Stephen Ransome probably doesn't help matters much. Davis was born in St. Joe, Missouri, in 1902, and like so many early noir writers perfected his craft by grinding out up to a thousand stories—*a year*—for *Black Mask, Detective Tales, Dime Mystery* and others. He wrote dozens of novels under several pseudonyms, but it was with Stephen Ransome's mostly Florida-based thrillers that he gained the most notoriety. Davis died in 1977 having received no major awards or recognition.

Davis earned his spurs in the pulps and it shows. Though the Stephen Ransome crime novels were published under Dodd, Mead's Red Badge imprint, a hardback series that featured Agatha Christie and G. K. Chesterton among others, his contributions to this series sometimes require an extra measure of suspended disbelief. For instance, take *Without a Trace*. An inventor has stolen from him a vial of ink that can be used to alter certified checks. The inventor, a college professor, abandons his tenured post and lams it to Florida to support his nubile daughter in poverty as a yard man, for no better reason it would seem than to service the plot.

Similar weaknesses are shown in characterization, the sense of morality and locale. His most sympathetic character, Ross Quarent, the state attorney, is pretty much the standard issue, vanilla-flavored square-jaw of mid-century commercial fiction. Even his most impressive character, crack investigator Lee Barcello, is defined best by the reactions of others to his ant-bird method of stirring things up. The sense of morality Ransome imbues his novels with is curiously Victorian given the times, the sixties and seventies. In terms of locale, the Ransome novels could as well have been set in Canada as the Sunshine State.

When Stephen Ransome was good, he was very good indeed. Although never a fabulously successful bestseller, Ransome anticipated two techniques that were to bring enormous fame to others.

The character who appears most frequently in his Florida novels is Lee Barcello, the head investigator in the state attorney's office. While never a main or even viewpoint character, Barcello is a fixture, the man whose wits the protagonist's are matched against. With a stock detective protagonist, Marlowe or Perry Mason, the author is forced to make the foil dim but sympathetic like Chandler's Berney Olds, or buffoonish like Perry Mason and Paul Drake's nemesis, Hamilton Burger.

But the characteristic protagonist of a Ransome novel is a guiltless but perhaps not totally innocent man trapped by a turn of events. Blake Carden in *The Night, the Woman* is only trying to help his brother out of a jam when he finds himself accused of the murder it appears his brother has committed. Brice Sawyer in *The Sin File* has started out to clear the name of his wife's live-in kid sister, but he finds himself entangled in a murder, the contamination from which could ruin his precarious livelihood as a building contractor. And in *Alias his Wife,* Ross Quarent, then the assistant state attorney and nominally Barcello's boss, learns a blackmailer has found Quarent is an unwitting bigamist. The blackmailer is murdered and the last person near the dead man is Quarent himself.

Now who is this Barcello who is trying to ferret out, if not the truth, then at least a conviction? "That's Barcello," Quarent tells his neighbors in *Trap #6.*

By staying away he's getting the effect he wants—he's wearing on your nerves. Meanwhile, believe me, he's not sitting around watching television soap operas. He's digging, undermining you. When he does come at you, it'll be at a strategic moment and he'll be so genuinely polite you won't realize he's putting you through his own patented brand of wringer. This morning he gave me the most painful beating of my life merely by turning his back on me. . . . In his own gentle way that man can be brutal. (80-81)

In short, one of television's most famous detectives, Columbo, bears more than a passing resemblance to Lee Barcello. There are differences.

Barcello is a sharp dresser and uncommonly handsome—as opposed to Columbo's unmade-bed sort of wardrobe—but both investigators have idiosyncratic if strikingly similar ways of breaking a case. Davis's Ransome series appeared from the fifties through the seventies. Although his novels are out of print and hard to find today, in his time he was widely read. It seems unlikely that the resemblance to America's favorite tube detective in the seventies was completely coincidental.

One classic thriller model, as exemplified by Hitchcock's *39 Steps* and *The Fugitive,* opens with the protagonist unjustly accused of a crime. The rest of the story hinges on what is known in some circles as the idiot plot—in the sense that protagonist acts like an idiot by running off "to try to clear his name." The strong element here allows immediate reader sympathy; we are led to believe at the outset the man has been unjustly accused. The weak element is that the protagonist stretches credibility by attempting do the virtually impossible: to conduct an investigation of a crime he has been accused of while evading the authorities.

Davis gives this thriller formula his own twist. He starts with the protagonist, a middle-class male, in a sensitive profession—Ross Quarent, the assistant state attorney with electoral ambitions; in other novels, protagonists Brice Sawyer, developer of a subdivision with sagging prospects; and Blake Carden, lawyer and scion of old Judge Carden. Then ever so slowly each finds himself drawn toward an accusation of criminal wrongdoing and, what is even worse, to the middle-class situation, scandal. For instance, Blake Carden withdraws thousands of dollars in cash from his bank account; the money is passed on to his brother without a receipt. When Blake asks for an explanation, he gets a demand for thousands more dollars instead. In the evening Blake sees his brother's sailboat glide toward the yacht of a local siren moored in the bay. In hopes of learning his brother's secret, Blake cranks up his skiff and motors to the yacht, where he finds the siren cut from ear to painted toenails. To make matters worse, the siren was a client of Blake—one with whom he had an extremely audible disagreement which investigator Lee Barcello overheard in the waiting room earlier that same afternoon. Blake's boat is identified by a passing cutter and his brother refuses to come forward, and Blake, loyal sibling, will not implicate his brother.

By beginning with the merest hint of a criminal problem in the life of a man whose middle-class credentials are otherwise impeccable and then gradually drawing the noose tighter, Davis has developed an instrument with Torquemadean power. It is hard to restrain yourself from jumping occasionally to your feet as you speed through these thirty-year-old page turners. A similar technique of turning the story back on the protagonist was adopted by Scott Turow in his highly successful recent blockbuster, *Presumed Innocent.*

Whether Turow was actually influenced by Davis's Stephen Ransome is a moot question, but some contemporary crime writers are cognizant of Davis. As Bill Pronzini, author of many detective novels, has pointed out, his best work "is notable for its sensitive handling and excellent characterization" (444). Although officially a resident of Pennsylvania, it's obvious that Davis spent a great many winters in the Pinellas County area and that he made a worthwhile contribution to Florida literature noir.

"Well, this isn't the greatest novel ever written, nor the best story ever told," the *Best Sellers'* reviewer said on publication of *The Last Boat out of Cincinnati,* whose author, Don Tracy, also shows a keen awareness of Pinellas County (Howley 159). "But it has a lot in its favor." Those sentiments might serve as Don Tracy's literary epitaph. He may not have been the greatest novelist—even Florida noir novelist— but he has a lot to recommend him.

Tracy was born in Connecticut in 1905 and gradually worked his way down the eastern seaboard. By the early thirties he was a reporter in Baltimore. After sojourns in New York and the army during World War II, he immigrated to Clearwater where he became, by his own estimation, one of the few persons in the United States to make a fulltime living by freelance writing, churning out a variety of local-color historicals (*Chesapeake Cavalier, Crimson Is the Eastern Shore*), crime novels (*The Hated One* and *The Big Blackout*), paperback originals under house pseudonyms and nonfiction books such as *What You Should Know About Alcoholism.* He died in 1977. As a long time writer of historicals, Tracy's strongest suit as a novelist and often the best feature of his books is the local environment.

In mainstream *Bazzaris,* set in the fictional Greek sponging community of Rovalla somewhere to the north of Tarpon Springs, Tracy demonstrates a welter of knowledge about the locale—told in the voices of its inhabitants. This is Big Jim Burnside speaking:

I've seen carriages and carryalls lined up for two blocks around the station, bringing people that was leaving down to the station and picking up just as many folks that was coming in from all over the country, far away as Chicago. The river was full of skiffs, them days, and every hotel had a launch with a canopy that used to take folks on trips up the Chellafia and show them the gators and sea cows and ibis, all gone now, except for a few gators . . . and fish—man, you couldn't put a hook in the water without coming up with a five-pound trout or twenty-pound redfish. Yes, sir, Rovalla had *class* back then, before the Greeks come in and ruined it. (60-61)

Even more impressive is the astonishing amount of Greek Tracy throws around in this novel—and the technical knowledge he shows of sponge diving, Greek style, which had been obsolete for about a generation when he brought the novel out. The deckhand

who strip[ped] off Gus's diver's suit, had cried, *'Porrurus topos!'* This was the term for the purple skin spot that signalled oxygen in the bloodstream and a case of the bends unless the proper procedure was followed. Gus had cursed, remembering that the cigarette the line-tender had thrust between his lips when the faceplate was unlocked had been sharp and acid-tasting, a sure sign of trouble. So Gus had donned his diver's gear again and been lowered to thirty fathoms. There he spent an additional hour for each fathom of lift, until he finally reached the top again, ravenous, craving tobacco, and with every muscle aching from the long ordeal. (35)

A great deal of the power of his Florida noir novels *The Big Blackout* and *The Hated One* derives from setting. *The Hated One* is one of that curious subgenre of the post–World War II South, the lawyerly civil rights saga, a sort of hard-boiled *To Kill a Mockingbird* or *Intruder in the Dust*. This time it is the story of a young black woman accused of carrying-on with and murdering the state attorney of the mythical north Florida county of Tangerine. But the novel derives strength from sources other than place, notably its characterization. The stock characters of southern genre fiction are represented—but with convincing twists. There is Brigadier-General Edmund Ruffin MacWhalen the Third (Ret.) "Besides running Tangerine County politics and owning nearly all the worthwhile property in that part of Florida, he was a Southern Gentleman, God help us all, and if anything was more sacred to him than his own infallibility, it was the MacWhalen name" (15). Naturally, there is the judge who if not crooked then at least understands too well his sacred duty to preserve the prerogatives of the propertied class. Judge Thrace's "little rosebud mouth set in that jowled, sagging white face and he pursed it into a smile that any lawyer who'd ever appeared before him knew was more dangerous than a scowl. It was the sneer of a pitiless man of power who had only contempt for the weakling and the wrong-doer and if there had ever been compassion around that little mouth, the years had rubbed it off" (42). And finally, of course, there is the over-weight, flush-faced sheriff. "Even before I looked at him I knew he still carried his giant's body as erect as a man of forty and that he still had a full, thick crop of white curly hair under his wide-brimmed Stetson; that the perpetual flush of his bronzed skin still warned of the high blood pressure that would kill him some day" (34).

But the ultimate power of Don Tracy's novels stems from the protagonist's attainment of self-realization, not to say redemption. Don Tracy's lead characters are, all of them, wounded birds. "There peering back at me," the narrator-protagonist of *The Hated One* says of the figure in the mirror behind the bar, stood Frank Coombs "onetime attorney-at-law, onetime bright young man, onetime husband of the beautiful Blanch Humphries Coombs, but presently part-time bill collector, part-time gas station attendant, fulltime ginhead" (11-12).

The landscape of Don Tracy's Florida is chillingly corrupt. Who engineered the drunken Frank Coombs's downfall? As it turned out, poor Frank has plenty of help. There is Miss Elsie, the elderly girl Friday who obligingly keeps a pint in her desk drawer and who "judiciously administered belts of straight liquor [while] somehow contriv[ing] to make it seem dirty, smelly, evil *alcohol* was not involved" (21). Frank thinks the purpose of Miss Elsie's shots is to tone his trembling body into shape for court. In actual fact, she is dosing him while his lawyer partner steals the firm from under the mostly comatose Frank's nose. His wife is in on the conspiracy. She ends up with Frank's family estate, Spring Bayou. And his former best friend, Jack Taggart, whose reputation Frank sets out to restore, has helped himself to Frank's wife and a share of the plunder. The corruption goes on and on. Ultimately, though, Tracy stops short of a complete indictment of southern and American society.

Sheriff Taggart, it turns out, is an all-right guy whose vigilance has faded with age, and the race problem is fobbed off, Faulkner-style, as an issue that the local institutions can satisfactorily deal with. In the end the dried-out Frank Coombs gets a girl. But even if *The Hated One* ends on an upbeat note that taxes the writing abilities of its author and the credibility of the reader, this is a powerful noir novel.

The Big Blackout, a lesser but deserving novel, features an alcoholic, cracker charter-boat captain with a wife, Midge, and an infant son, Bongo. The protagonist is already on the twelve-step program, but even at that he is barely able to stave off attempts by the cops to frame him. In the bargain, his best friend, the widow of his dead and drug-smuggling partner, attempts to have him assassinated by big-city goons for her sins. It's our loss that both *The Big Blackout* and *The Hated One* have long been out of print. With luck you might find *The Hated One* lurking in the stacks of a local library. It's worth the attention of any noir fan.

Due east of Tangerine County lies Lake County square in the middle of the peninsula, just north of the fold. Lake is among the most beautiful of Florida counties. The topography undulates in a most unFlorida-like manner thanks to the central ridge that runs through it like a spine. Being a Florida county, naturally, it has its moss-hung swamps and stands of pine flatwoods. But characteristically it has lakes. There are big lakes, such as the chain of lakes that spawn the Oklawaha River, and there are small lakes to be seen from every rise. Bordering many of those lakes are groves of the stateliest of fruit trees, which scent the air in spring with excruciatingly sweet perfume and adorn the view most of the rest of the year with Christmas tree-like ornaments. The towns of Lake County must seem to tourists speeding through to the Sodoms and Gomorrahs farther south like perfect exercises in Jeffersonian America. Its communities include an all-American registry of place names, Leesburg, Groveland, Tavares, Eustis, Mount Dora, Umatilla. None is very large and all are clean and well fed and spacious but without offensive Trimalchian opulence. Yes, through the windshield of a speeding car, Lake County must have promised, even in 1949, a veritable vision of paradise.

It's not likely that the men on the Bull Gang, many with their feet shackled, standing in the ditch as those cars buzzed by, would have agreed with that assessment. They had counted off as they passed through the gate of S.R.D. Camp #93 just down the road. After a quick formation the prisoners were loaded into the cage truck and "the last man was certain to be kicked in the ass by the Walking Boss" a gentleman or at least a free man who, rain or shine, never removed his mirror sunglasses (*Cool Hand Luke* 7).

As incongruous as it may seem, pastoral Lake County, that Jeffersonian emerald, was the setting of Donn Pearce's Florida noir classic, *Cool Hand Luke*. But is it as incongruous as at first blush it appears, that a book about one of the most violent of American institutions, the chain gang, should be set there? Running yin- and yang-like through American ideology are two paradoxical ideas. Both are celebrated in middle-school civics classes. The more lauded is known as Democracy. In a significant way America gave the world that institution, which recognizes the equality of all individuals. And for better or for worse, we also aided immeasurably in the modern-day formulation of the doctrine of Capitalism, which celebrates the triumph of unbridled individualism. In its earlier incarnations capitalism was the motive force for bringing alien men in chains to these shores and organizing them into gangs to plant cotton and harvest rice. It only took a cataclysmic war to produce the conditions under which the Fourteenth Amendment could finally be ratified. That amendment abolished all forms of involuntary servitude—with the exception of penal servitude.

In the deep South, penal servitude was, naturally, modeled after that ever abundant paradigm, the slave plantation. Knowing a good spot of capitalism when they saw it, the states even rented out gangs of men to private contractors. This enterprise was carried on in the Sunshine State until about twenty-five years ago when a chain gang left out in a hurricane washed away. The resulting stink caused the lawmakers in Tallahassee to adopt a system of incarcerating its prisoners more consistent with that of the northern states.

The biographical snippet for Donn Pearce in *Contemporary Authors* reads: "Born 1928, in Croydon, Pa. Education: Attended high school in New York, NY. Politics: None. Religion: None. Career: U. S. Merchant Marine, officer, 1945-65, except for a period in a Florida State Prison" (625). What fate, aside from a health calamity or radical isolation, could be worse to the middle-class mind than exile to a chain gang? Yet, ironically, some of the most stirring testaments to the unquenchable nature of the human soul have been set in prisons or prison-like conditions. Solzhenitsyn's gulag novels, Warner Brothers' Paul Muni chain-gang films, James Jones's sagas of enlisted men bound together by authority and war.

The grim realism, not to say naturalism, of this story is held at bay by the engaging personality of Lloyd Douglas, whose prison handle is "Cool Hand Luke." He's an amiable drifter. Although a war hero, the man is prone to acts of petty, even senseless, rebellion. The system knows what to do with him, lock him up. Inside, he's no more tractable than on the outside. He challenges authority at every opportunity. And he has a knack of winning by losing. There is only one way this story can turn out. In the end the system beats Luke by killing him—or Luke wins by making the system murder him, depending on how optimistic you can be.

Cool Hand Luke is a memorable addition to the literature of incarceration. More important, it is a story that was enacted uncounted times in Florida's past—on the antebellum plantation, and, later, in the work farms and turpentine camps—all of them institutions that were vital to the making of this state. It is a shame that the guise this story is best known in, the Paul Newman movie which Pearce co-scripted, was set in a sort of generic Southern state, and seemed to have been filmed in California. The director, Stuart Rosenburg, liked the shock effect of juxtaposing the wide open prairies of the west with the chain men slaving in fenced ditches. A careful cinematographer could have achieved—I believe—an even more haunting effect by contrasting the brutality of the chain gang against the beauty of the orange groves in the lake country of the central ridge. The mere thought chills the blood.

Jacksonville is a city of bridges, as anyone who has ever had to cross the broad Saint Johns River several times to get just a few miles farther down on the same bank can attest. Larry Humes's *Bridge to Nowhere* is not only a whodunit but also a how-was-it-done. The city museum is burgled. The treasure of an ancient Spanish galleon salvaged in the Keys is made off with. The perpetrator is pursued by police to the middle of a rainbow bridge spanning the tidewater Saint Johns, where s/he abandons the car and leaps from the bridge. A passing freighter pulls no body from the water. In fact, the crew reports they saw nothing amiss.

Investigative reporter Brad Norris turns up a link between the ship and the supposed burglar. But then as his investigation broadens, he begins to root out all sorts of unusual links. He noses around Saint Pete. He goes down to the Keys and interviews a Mel Fisher-like treasure hunter. He overnights on the treasure hunters' boat. He ogles the treasure-hunting crew. He meets a female journalist from up north. He ogles her. She ogles him. Still he has gotten no closer to solving the puzzle of the bridge.

Humes's book does what many infinitely more successful noir novels fail to do. It teases the reader with a genuine puzzle. How did that burglar take the leap from a highrise bridge and presumably live to tell about it? Even better, the central mystery of the story is organic to the locale in which it is set, Jacksonville, the city of bridges. Moreover, Humes displays a commendable knowledge and love of Florida.

Mickey Friedman's first crime novel, *Hurricane Season,* was published in the early eighties about the time Humes brought out his bridge mystery. Friedman's book, set in a panhandle saltwater community, was a hard one for critics to make sense of. "'A novel with murder' is a fairly accurate description of Mrs. Friedman's [book] which portrays inbred, suspicious, nasty people," Newgate Callendar said in the crime column for the *New York Times Book Review.* "She has adopted an unusual format. Many of the beginning chapters are two or three page cameos, background or character sketches leading to—what?" the puzzled reviewer wonders. Then he goes on to tot up the various zanies and crazies Friedman parades before us: "We learn all about the town and its industry, moonshining. We meet a religious fanatic and a mixed-up girl who has slept with half the men in town. We discover a local war in which two competing distillers are ready to exterminate each other. They play tough down there. Then there is the lady that runs the story near the ferry. She is the one who figures things out." Ultimately, Callendar ends with what seems a qualified nod of approval. "If nothing else, Mrs. Friedman has written a murder mystery that in many respects breaks the mold, and that happens only two or three times a year."

Callendar's consternation is understandable because, for a novel of detection, *Hurricane Season* is to a great extent clueless. Many characters populate this fairly slim (195-page) volume—and more of them than a reader can easily keep in mind take a turn at telling the story. The author doesn't bother introducing any characters of import until ten pages—five percent of the book—have elapsed. These characters, however, are engaged in the eminently interesting business of conducting an illicit affair, one that the woman thinks should become a licit affair through the agency of divorce and marriage. Unfortunately before the messy consequences of this undertaking can be fully savored, the temptress is promptly killed off.

Then enters out of the blue a student from the Baptist seminary who has tied up the temptress with fishing line in an effort to reform her—and confesses to killing her. Not only do we have a murderer who has no motive (let alone a fictive necessity) for the killing, we have an investigator in the way of Woody the sheriff who refuses to investigate. So his mother-in-law, Lily, undertakes an investigation of her own.

Then as though the novel wasn't spreading thin enough, Lily becomes suspicious of Josh, a young man who is camped on an uninhabited section of an island out in the Gulf. All that is a red herring because it turns out Josh is a revenue agent infiltrating a moonshiner's camp over there. He becomes fast friends with Lily and the closest thing to a male lead in the gerrymandered plotline of the book. His love interest, Sue Nell, is—aha, finally—the third corner of the original love triangle. She engages in even more tortured love geometry when she allows her compass to get involved with Josh's protractor. After a great deal of digression at southern small-town socials that have nothing to do with the story, Sue Nell, the real murderer, puts a pistol in her mouth and blows her brains out.

Callendar was not the only contemporary reviewer who exhibited reserve vis-à-vis the suspense element of this book. Jean White writing in the *Washington Post Book Review* agrees that *Hurricane Season* "is not your usual mystery novel" (qtd. in "Friedman" 180). But she was grateful that it isn't. "What makes [it] special is its extraordinary sense of place. The backwater land of Florida pervades the story. These are people and a way of life that few of us have met before." In other words the development that some might consider digressive is what makes this a book worthy of note to White. *Los Angeles Times* reviewer Carolyn See expands on that theme. "*Hurricane Season* leaves the reader with the itch, a yearning to go into every little ratty dime store with fly-specked windows in every little forgotten town across the country and see what's really going on" (qtd. in "Friedman" 180).

Friedman, unlike Don Tracy and most of the others discussed here, came by her sense of place by birth. She was born Michaele Thompson in Dothan, Alabama, in 1944 and moved to the Florida panhandle as a youngster. She claimed in an interview, somewhat tongue in cheek, that she adopted the mystery genre because "it provides a form for a writer to play with. Limitations can be liberating" (qtd. in "Friedman" 180). In her case they are very liberating because she hardly pays any attention to the traditional form at all, at least in *Hurricane Season.*

In the eleven years between *Hurricane Season* and Friedman's fictional return to the Gulf coast, she produced five novels among which is *Magic Mirror,* a fairly straightforward murder mystery. Georgia Lee, the first-person narrator, forsakes Bay City, Florida, and with Twinkie, her cat, jets off to Paris where she dodges the most noir of French gangsters and ultimately recovers a mirror that once belonged to Nostradamus (which unfortunately turns out to be a fake.) By hewing to first-person point of view, the plotline is reined in, in a wholly uncharacteristic way. While not particularly innovative, the book achieves its considerable effects by writing that is superb—witty, knowledgeable, ironic. Arguably, Friedman has the most raw writing talent of all the novelists discussed here.

But writing about the South seems to make Friedman Faulknerian. In her homecoming to the panhandle novel, *Riptide,* she goes at it, *Hurricane Season*-like again. There is the attenuated, not to say horizontal, storyline. The plethora of characters include Isabel, an expatriate St. Elmoite (she had emigrated to New York), her aunt, an old boyfriend, his mate and his jealous wife, a lawyer, a murdered marine patrol officer, an undercover cop, a convict in the big house who is connected only by having his wife shacked up with the narc, most of whom are viewpoint characters somewhere along the line—or rather the nonlinear storyline.

Then there is the other big house, the manse rotting in the background of the trailer Isabel is to inherit. In so many ways it seems like Frenchman's Bend revisited. The name of the family estate, Cape Cache, is even evocative of Faulkner's hamlet. There's buried treasure in the story and a genealogical hunt for one River Pete that would do proud the heart of any Daughter of the American Confederacy.

There is one difference between *Riptide* and Faulkner's *Hamlet* and even *Hurricane Season. Riptide* doesn't work. This isn't to say the book is an outright flop on the mystery level; it's a fine workaday story. But the novel hasn't the power of *Hurricane Season,* which took advantage of the diffuse storyline to examine the institutions of one of the most interesting periods of American history, the postwar, pre–Civil Rights South. *Riptide* has no such pretensions. For instance, the killer turns out to be a hippie deckhand. He's a drifter but neither his rootlessness nor anonymity is tied into any deeper social realm, or even discussed.

Critics and novelists enjoy a symbiotic relationship; although interdependent, they are mutually consuming. The novelist offers a tusk, and the critic demands it be a trunk or a tail. As novels of detection, Mickey Friedman's books are sometimes out of control. They are also somewhat uneven in quality. But this is a women with formidable talent. If she has already written her best Florida noir, she has left a fine testament. My guess, though, is there is better to come.

The far western tip of the Florida panhandle is Morgan Hunt country in the same sense that Fort Lauderdale—at the other end of the state—is Travis McGee's territory. Somehow all this doesn't seem to have been an accident. As everyone who has even a passing interest in noir fiction knows, McGee is outrageously iconoclastic. Schooled in the University of Hard Knocks, the curriculum for which is darkly alluded to rather than openly stated, McGee looms taller, or at any rate, stronger than any cracker psychopath John D. MacDonald ever matched him with in single combat. He lives on a houseboat in close proximity to his shaggy bear of an economist sidekick, Meyer. He tools around in a sixty-year-old Rolls Royce that has been converted to a pickup truck. Supposedly he makes his living as a salvage consultant, by retrieving, for a whopping 50 percent fee, debts that otherwise cannot be collected. In actual fact, he just seems to go around lending a helping hand to the crippled and downtrodden, and especially, McGee never misses a chance to resuscitate a fractured damsel with a mercy kiss.

Geoffrey Norman's Morgan Hunt did his hard time in a Deep South slammer (the Harvard of universities of hard knocks) for murdering a man who had abused his sister. Championed by Nat Semmes, a do-gooder lawyer, Hunt saved a fair share on his legal bills which he amused himself by speculating with in the stock market while in the steel hotel. Now on the outside, Hunt has himself a coon dog by the name of Jubal Early, a house on a sluggish river (the Perdido—"lost" in Spanish) loaded with bass and bream, and a Cajun girlfriend, by the name of Miss Jessie Beaudraux who is "beautiful without being flawless, not like one of those mass-produced models who look like they could have been milled by the thousands on some kind of computer-controlled machine" (*Sweetwater Ranch* 41). Also, he has an enormous moral debt to his social-crusading lawyer, which he discharges by conducting investigations, gratis.

Geoffrey Norman is an enormously prolific magazine writer, churning out pieces on a production-line basis for the likes of *Forbes, Playboy, Outside, Modern Maturity, Self, National Geographic* among other magazines. He has written about fishing guides in the Florida Keys, gone quail hunting with Winston Groom, the author of *Forest Gump,* and shot turkey and duck for these publications. He has also interviewed David Mamet and knocked out think pieces.

Nor is there any doubt that Geoffrey Norman knows the people and the area of the country he writes about. Here's a sample of rural southern:

Like most people she showed her roots in a crunch. Now trying to defend herself, you could hear the red clay and weathered board and a chinaberry tree in her voice. And that was a partial explanation for a lot of what had happened to her. Real country people have a hard time with the bright lights and the kind of life that doesn't start until the sun has gone down. (*Sweetwater Ranch* 32)

And that other southern institution, the military, the part anyhow that has stripes on its sleeves Norman demonstrates a gut knowledge of. Sergeant Hollibird had

an inch of bristling hair cover[ing] his scalp and the contours of his skull showed through his tightly stretched skin. He was lean but well muscled. He wore a green T-shirt, fatigue pants, and mirror-polished jump boots . . . . Hollibird['s] eyes narrowed into slits, and his smile shifted into a sneer. You could see he liked to fight and that before the night was over he'd find the fight he needed. I planned to be somewhere else when it happened." (*Sweetwater Ranch* 114-16)

Morgan Hunt is a straight-line descendant of Travis McGee. But is he a worthy successor to noir fiction's best-known protagonist in these past thirty years? Norman develops engaging plots. He writes with authority. His characters are as well drawn and as interesting (arguably) as MacDonald's. Is it possible that an Elvis impersonator could be a better artist than Elvis himself ever was? Of course, it is. Well, then is it possible that he could ever lay serious claim to the king's crown? That's the burden Morgan Hunt and Geoffrey Norman labor under, at least to some of us die-hard MacDonald fans who hear familiar but not wholly welcome echoes in his fiction. One cannot help pondering what would happen if Norman looked inward, at the personalities and places he knows so well and let them generate a noir style of his own.

Works Cited

Callendar, Newgate. Rev. of *Hurricane Season*. *New York Times Book Review* 27 Nov. 1983: 28.

Friedman, Mickey. *Hurricane Season*. New York: Dutton, 1983.

——. *Magic Mirror*. New York: Viking, 1988.

——. *Riptide*. New York: St. Martin's, 1994.

"Friedman, Michaele Thompson." *Contemporary Authors*. Vol. 111. Detroit: Gale, 1984. 179-80.

Howley, Edith C. "Tracy, Don. *The Last Boat Out of Cincinnati*." *Best Sellers* 15 July 1970: 159.

Humes, Larry R. *Bridge to Nowhere*. South Yarmouth: Curley, 1980.

Norman, Geoffrey. *Blue Chipper*. New York: Morrow, 1992.

——. *Sweetwater Ranch*. New York: Dell, 1992.

"Pearce, Donn." *Contemporary Authors*. First Revision, Vols. 13-16. Detroit: Gale, 1975.

Pearce, Donn. *Cool Hand Luke*. New York: Scribner, 1965.

Pronzini, Bill. "Davis, Frederick C(lyde)." *Twentieth-Century Crime and Mystery Writers*. Ed. John M. Reilly. New York: St. Martin's, 1980.

Ransome, Stephen. *Alias His Wife*. New York: Dodd,1965.

——. *Meet in Darkness*. New York: Dodd, 1964.

——. *The Night, The Woman*. New York: Dodd, 1962.

——. *The Sin File*. New York: Dodd, 1965.

——. *Trap # 6*. New York: Doubleday, 1971.

——. *Without a Trace*. New York: Doubleday, 1962.

Tracy, Don. *Bazzaris*. New York: Ravenna/Trident, 1965.

——. *The Big Blackout*. Roslyn: Black, 1959.

——. *The Hated One*. New York: Simon and Schuster, 1963.

——. *Honk if You've Found Jesus*. New York: Putnam, 1974.

11

Subtropical Film Noir

Ellen Smith

Just as Moliere's M. Jourdain was surprised to learn from his tutor that he had been speaking prose all his life, so too might some of Hollywood's directors, actors, and writers have been surprised to learn from French students of film that they were creating film noir. But there has long been a French connection to such films; not only are there *Diaboliques* and *Breathlesses*, but the name itself is probably derived not only from nocturnal scenes and black-and-white film stock but also from a series of popular novels in French, the *Serie Noire*, which turn out to be chiefly translations of Hammett, Chandler, and Cain.

In addition, as Alain Silver and Elizabeth Ward's huge volume *Film Noir: An Encyclopedic Reference to the American Style* says, such movies are "a black slate on which the culture could ascribe its ills and in the process produce a catharsis to help relieve them" (1). Their introduction to the hundreds of films discussed in their book provides some necessary definitions and descriptions of the form. The central characters, they say, tend to be ambitious criminals paired against the even more typical normal person who is "assailed by the twists of fate of an irrational universe" (2). Frequently a veteran returning from World War II and affected by the horrors of battle and of the Bomb, he is alienated, disaffected, yet capable of loyalty to friends. In addition, he often becomes involved with a woman, with whom he becomes so obsessed that he will agree to commit such a crime as killing her husband—or arranging for someone else to do so.

The characters in film noir live in a world that is "contemporaneous, usually urban, and almost always American in setting. The few exceptions involve either urban men in a rural locale or Americans abroad. There is a narrative assumption that only natural forces are in play; extraordinary circumstances are either logically elucidated or left unexplained—no metaphysical values are adopted" (3).

Although the war may have provided the source of the disaffected state of the protagonists, the directors of films about them profited from some technological innovations developed because of that very war.

Better lenses, smaller dollies, more sensitive film made shooting on location, especially at night, far easier and cheaper (2). The films also profited from the German "refugees"—Fritz Lang, Max Ophuls, Otto Preminger, to name a few—whose techniques of German Expressionism contributed to the visual language of the noir mode. The "children of Caligari" had mastered "oddly angled shots; a chiaroscuro frame inscribed with wedges of light or shadowy mazes, truncated by foreground objects, or punctuated with glinting headlights bounced off mirrors, wet surfaces, or the polished steel of a gun barrel" (3).

Yet Silver and Ward contend that film noir is a "unique example of a wholly American film style" (1) and one that ended before 1960, not reaching a specific conclusion but diminishing gradually (6). They do allow, though, that film noir is not dead; versions such as *The Grifters* and *The Big Easy* attempt "to resurrect the noir sensibility" (6).

Generally speaking, aficionados of film noir would expect to see settings like Melrose, Mulholland, or Market—and those who go down those mean streets to have names like Marlowe or Muni. Despite its reputation as the Sunshine State, though, Florida can make a real claim to a successful hosting of film noir. Too many sleazy deals are consummated away from the sunshine; too many beautiful women reveal the serpent beneath. And the state can sometimes produce a hero—even if somewhat tarnished—who attempts to right things in the end.

Although by far the greatest number of films noir were shot on California's or New York's mean streets, one of the most indelibly noir images in the entire corpus is in *Key Largo* (1948) when Edward G. Robinson, a cigar clamped in his toad-like mouth, sits in a bathtub, attempting to cool off with a fan directed toward his sweaty body. About this image, James Agee said that the director, John Huston, "can make an unexpected close-up reverberate like a gong. The first shot of Edward G. Robinson in *Key Largo*, mouthing a cigar and sweltering naked in a tub of cold water, is one of the most powerful and efficient 'first entrances' of a character on record" (328).

Considering how well *Key Largo* met the needs of the genre, it seems surprising that more films were not set in this state. It has a perfect gangster in Robinson, whose character, Johnny Rocco, is even more complex because of his political affiliations during World War II. As Carrie Rickey has put it, "Edward G. Robinson as Johnny Rocco . . . was politically undesirable, humiliated at having been deported during the war 'like I was a dirty Red or something.'" Rocco, she points out, presages movie mobsters who will follow, especially in fifties movies like *On the Waterfront* and *The Garment Jungle*, which "suggest that gangsters are communists and that they are infiltrating unions" (Rickey 9).

But there is an elegiac tone to even Rocco and his henchmen; they're clearly a dying breed. They find themselves at a jumping-off place—and they are dispatched by the perfect noir hero, Humphrey Bogart. As Frank McCloud, he is in Richard Schickel's description,

a man who has known better days, now seeking respite from the world (and the exactions of a liberal conscience) by making a visit to an isolated hotel in the Florida keys. His mission is to bring consolation to the widow (Lauren Bacall) and father (Lionel Barrymore) of his wartime friend, who was killed beside him in the Italian campaign. He feels he has done his bit in the fight against fascism and is uninterested in taking arms against the breed in its native form, as personified by Edward G. Robinson. (232)

Eventually, however, he becomes *engagé:* he pilots a boat and manages to kill Rocco en route to Cuba. He himself is, predictably but not fatally, wounded; he returns to the widow, with whom he has fallen in love.

Besides the splendid gangster Robinson and the disillusioned yet heroic Bogart, *Key Largo* contains other elements that place it firmly in the top rank of film noir. The setting, mainly in the claustrophobic lobby of a seedy hotel at the end of the road, is made even more intense by the prevailing weather—either the sweltering calm before the storm or that handy narrative device in various Florida fictions, a hurricane.

The other characters, too, fit right in. There is the good girl, Lauren Bacall, smoky, embittered over the loss of her husband but seeing the worth of Frank McCloud. The other female role, Rocco's alcoholic girlfriend Gaye Dawn, earned Claire Trevor an Academy Award for best supporting actress. Rocco's cruelty toward her is truly shocking, as when he forces her to sing "Moanin' Low" and then denies her the drink he had promised her. James Agee describes the offhand way that John Huston directed her: "When Claire Trevor, starting work in *Key Largo*, asked for a few pointers, he told her,

"You're the kind of drunken dame whose elbows are always a little too big, your voice is a little too loud, you're a little too polite. You're very sad, very resigned. Like this" he said, for short, and leaned against the bar with a peculiarly heavy, gentle disconsolateness. It was the leaning she caught onto (though she also used everything he said); without further instruction of any kind, she took an Oscar for her performance. (326-27)

Much talent went into this production. Besides the actors and director mentioned above, the screenplay was adapted from a play by Maxwell Anderson (and, according to Agee, much improved). Max

Steiner did the musical score; Jay Silver Heels, who was to gain a degree of fame later, played one of the Osceola Brothers. And the special effects were suitably horrific.

Strictly speaking, Howard Hawks's *To Have and Have Not* does not take place on Florida's soil—or even very much on the waters surrounding it. Also, its noir elements are far less numerous than in the previously mentioned Bogart/Bacall movie. But it is based on Ernest Hemingway's 1937 novel about Harry Morgan, the Key West fishing guide and sometime smuggler; his blowzy wife, Marie; the rich people in their yachts, which are docked nearby; and assorted Key West characters.

The story goes that, as Howard Hawks explained it, "Ernest Hemingway and I were very good friends. . . . I said to him, 'I can make a picture out of your worst story.' He said, 'What's my worst story?' I said, 'Why that goddamned piece of junk called *To Have and Have Not*'" (Rothman 70).

Make a picture out of it he did, and change it he did. The setting, for example, is not Key West in the thirties but Martinique during the early days of World War II—though Harry Morgan's boat is still the Queen Conch registered in Key West. Lauren Bacall's "Slim" is a far cry from the novel's frumpy Marie, though Hawks explained that the movie shows an earlier stage of their relationship (Rothman 71) (an explanation rather hard to accept, given that the novel was set in the thirties and the film in the forties). The film brings in a whole new group of characters, including M. and Mme. de Bursac, members of the French Resistance. We begin to see the influence of another Bogart film here. But at least the de Bursacs do not lead a choral sing of the "Marseillaise," and pianist Hoagy Carmichael is in the picture, but is never asked to "play it again." Also, the film clearly has a happy ending, with Walter Brennan and Lauren Bacall trucking off screen with Harry Morgan (Bogart), who has returned alive from his anti-Nazi heroics.

The route from the novel's setting in Florida waters during the Depression to the French island of Martinique in the forties is a fascinating demonstration of how movies get made—a combination of friendship, film studio politics, and even State Department fears. Hawks believed that the part of Hemingway's novel that could best transfer to film was the first section, "One Trip Across," which presents Harry Morgan smuggling revolutionaries out of Cuba—a promising noir plot idea. As it turned out, Hemingway had already sold the screen rights of the novel to Howard Hughes. Since Hughes never developed a screenplay, Warner Brothers paid him $92,000—and then allowed Hawks to make the film.

Screenwriter Jules Furthman wrote a preliminary version more closely tied to the Hawks-Hemingway scenario, with Morgan piloting a boat between Florida and Cuba. But, as Gene Phillips relates, "When Hawks submitted this version of the script to the Office of the Coordinator of Inter-American Affairs . . . he was advised that the State Department feared that a motion picture which depicted insurrection and smuggling in Cuba would place a strain on Cuban-American relations and the United States could not afford to alienate an ally while World War II was still being waged." The solution? Hawks set the film in "wartime Martinique, a French island under the control of the pro-Nazi Vichy government" (51).

The closest similarity to the novel occurs in the first part of the film, where Harry takes out the rich businessman Mr. Johnson for some sport fishing. The rich American is a condensed version of the novel's haves in their expensive yachts at Key West—an often criticized section of the novel, though it does show Hemingway's attempt at social criticism, since the rest of the inhabitants of Key West are clearly have-nots. It also helps set up a noir mood, since the rich would-be deep-sea fisherman, upon losing Harry's expensive fishing gear, shows his innate cheapness and dishonesty by refusing to reimburse the owner. Harry himself, as Raymond Chandler has defined the hero, is "not himself mean"; his code of honor includes a code of sportsmanship that does *not* include skipping town rather than paying one's debts.

But perhaps the most striking difference is what happens to Harry in the two versions. As he nears death, the novel's Harry manages to gasp out that "No matter how, a man alone ain't got no bloody fucking chance" (Hemingway 225). The movie's Harry leaves the scene ringed by friends. Eddy the "rummy" (Walter Brennan), "Slim" (who has taught us how to whistle), and Harry leave the scene together, as Hoagy Carmichael is sitting at the piano, playing again.

Pauline Kael has referred to the film's "simplemindedness and slick professionalism." But she also considers those same qualities "so refreshing that the tawdry forties may seem like a golden age. They weren't, but the characters were defined: if a man was perverse, you knew he was a Nazi" (*Kiss Kiss* 453-54).

Two interesting bits of film trivia are connected to *To Have and Have Not*. For one, the film is partly the work of two winners of the Nobel Prize for literature. William Faulkner worked on the film script—in Hollywood, not Oxford, Mississippi. Also, it is frequently reported that Lauren Bacall's throaty singing was in reality her lip-synching to Andy Williams's voice. Phillips's *Hemingway and Film* says there is "no factual justification" to this rumor, though Pauline Kael (in the collection of her reprinted criticism named *Kiss Kiss Bang Bang*) and others have "perpetuated this myth" (59).

Despite the promising beginning of Florida film noir with *Key Largo* and, even with its changes to a new setting and a happy ending in *To Have and Have Not*, it is surprising that more of such films were not set here. California, New York, and at times New Orleans tended to be the settings of choice for the vast number of films noir. However, there have been some set here that deserve wider distribution and greater praise.

Perhaps because he was born in Florida, Victor Nuñez has made some films that convey the atmosphere of Florida as well as anyone could possibly do it. His *Ruby in Paradise* (1993), though it does not fit into the noir category, does a fine job of capturing the atmosphere of Panama City during the off season. Nuñez, who also wrote the screenplay, creates the mood of the empty beaches and the shops full of tawdry T-shirts and shell bric-a-brac. The visual quality of the sky and sand calls to mind the light that pervades Edward Hopper's lonely New England beaches. Yet Nuñez' story is one of self-fulfillment and earned independence, as Ruby (played well by Ashley Judd) leaves her rural Tennessee to become a woman who knows herself and what she can do.

Nine years earlier, in 1984, Nuñez transferred John D. MacDonald's *A Flash of Green* to film for the television show *American Playhouse*. The subject is one of MacDonald's best: a fundamentally decent man, a reporter in a small town on the west coast of Florida, who gets involved with a questionable land development. Watching the character become slowly corrupted is painful—and Nuñez handles it well, as does Ed Harris, perfectly cast as the reporter. It is unfortunate that it is hard to find a copy of the film; it deserves to be better known.

As it turned out, several years later Ed Harris was cast in another film set in Florida that is firmly in the film noir tradition. *China Moon*, though filmed in 1991, was not released until 1994. A stranger to Florida might wonder about just how much sunshine does shine in this state, since it is filmed in velvety, murky gloom—and even the interior shots all seem to take place at night. The Harris character lives in a suitably run-down trailer but is attracted—as had been many of his California brothers in noir—to a wealthy woman, Madeleine Stowe, who lives in a huge white house with an impressively columned front porch.

She is also married to a successful man, played, surprisingly enough, by the British actor Charles Dance. This is a neat bit of casting, since he can act roles that are admirable (as in the television series *The Jewel and the Crown*) but also quite corrupt (as in *White Mischief*). White-suited and equipped with a Southern accent, he is clearly the one to be killed.

Here the plot begins to sound not just like an homage to movies we're familiar with, but a too-close imitation of them: *Double Indemnity*, *Body Heat* (more of which later). Though Ed Harris plays the role of a small-town policeman with his usual skill, though we watch him being drawn into the web of the dark and beautiful Madeleine Stowe, though the plot twists are fun if predictable, and even though the sordid settings convince, we would still have to say that the film fails to satisfy. Familiarity may not breed contempt in this case, but it may be hard to stifle a yawn.

In attempting to name the best-known example of film noir in a Florida setting, many might mention *Scarface*, Brian De Palma's 1983 remake of the 1932 film starring Paul Muni. In his version De Palma transferred the Chicago mob scene to the world of the Cuban drug dealers in Miami.

Yet a search of Silver and Ward's monumental *Film Noir: An Encyclopedic Reference to the American Style* does not reveal any discussion of the film among the hundreds of films covered, except for the occasional mention of the earlier version. Appendix A to the volume provides the editors' justification for the rejection, as well as an important set of distinctions they make between film noir and what they consider *Scarface*: a gangster film.

Despite the esthetic merits of some gangster films, they argue, such films should be excluded: "The concept of a complex protagonist with an existential awareness of his situation excludes the gangster film." Although "the gangster film and film noir share several narrative and iconic characteristics, most obviously crime, violence, and the urban environment . . . [t]he fundamental difference between the gangster film and film noir is that of narrative attitude" (323). The gangster film "never lost its demented idealism," while "characters populating film noir are either corrupt or morally ambiguous" (324).

In addition, the violence in the gangster film is "almost flamboyant, and graced with a staccato rhythm," while "the noir film's use of violence is more controlled and ultimately more brutal." And "most gangster films have an eventual restoration of order, a redemption, in a sense of social values," whereas films noir conclude more ambiguously. Silver and Ward do allow that earlier gangster films like the original *Scarface* contain "pre-noir" characteristics—camera work, nocturnal settings, the revenge plot motif, expressionistic lighting—yet, they conclude, distinctions between the two "must be made, and, once made, must be applied as consistently as possible" (324-25).

It may be that Brian De Palma was attempting to remake the earlier classic into a film that more closely approaches the noir genre. In setting his *Scarface* in contemporary Miami, with its violence and glitz, and in choosing as the central character a Marielito, an immigrant in the 1980 boat lift from Cuba, who wants to make it big in America, he set in motion some genuine noir possibilities. However, several critics have given varying judgments about the success of De Palma's directorial intent and Oliver Stone's script.

Roger Ebert views the film in a positive light, especially the character Tony Montana, played by Al Pacino. This movie, he says, "is one of those special movies, like *The Godfather*, that is willing to take a flawed, evil man and allow him to be human." He also contends that De Palma and Stone "have created a gallery of specific individuals and one of the fascinations of the movie is that we aren't watching crime-movie clichés, we're watching people who are criminals" (632).

But Pauline Kael, who had been one of De Palma's greatest partisans, comes down hard on virtually all aspects of the film. She is particularly rough on Tony Montana—who, were he in a genuine film noir, would be a combination of integrity and the capacity for corruption—but is here "a cigar butt in a bird's eye view of an ashtray . . . such a coked-up dullard that many of us in the audience—especially women—may lose all interest in him" (*State* 105). Kael concludes, "*Scarface* is a lazy, druggy spectacle—manic yet exhausted, with De Palma entering into the derangement and trying to make something heroic out of Tony's emptiness and debauchery" (106). Leonard Maltin's *1996 Movie and Video Guide* administers the final kick: "This film wallows in excess and unpleasantness for nearly *three hours* and offers no new insights except that crime doesn't pay" (1,139).

Two other films could be said to fit—although loosely—into the category of Florida film noir. Burt Reynolds assigned himself the task of directing and an excellent cast, including Candice Bergen, George Segal, Charles Durning, and Alex Rocco, in a version of Elmore Leonard's *Stick*. The novel provides the perfect matrix for a film noir: an ex-con returns to Florida from prison in another state to seek revenge for the death of a friend. Needing a job, he is drawn into the household and the world of a wealthy South Florida "businessman" whose business is drugs and whose partners are singularly nasty. The novel develops his noir character and moral dilemmas.

Unfortunately, the film cannot be considered to have achieved the success that the novel did. It was first released in 1984, then again in 1985 after having been brought back for some reworking. But even that didn't help: it is now resting on video store shelves—a just reward for its being judged "incredibly boring" (Maltin 1246).

Elmore Leonard's *Cat Chaser* (1989), also, did not fare well on its journey to film. Again with a good cast, including Kelly McGillis, Peter Weller, Frederic Forrest, and Charles Durning, it was never released to commercial theaters. The novel provides many opportunities for a film that would follow the noir tradition. The central character, George Moran, is living the life of a lazy Florida motel owner, forgetting his past in the Marines as he sits by the pool of the Coconut Palms, "where there isn't a single palm tree" (Leonard 10). But a beautiful femme fatale draws him in to a trip to the Dominican Republic and the memory of—and reenactment of—a shooting. His last question in the text is the finely ambiguous "I don't have a lawyer. You think I'm gonna need one?" It is unfortunate that the storytelling and the issues Leonard brings up cannot be appreciated on the big screen.

Two films that combine Florida and gangsters and potentially noir subjects also have turned out to be two of the most delightful films of recent years.

In 1959, *Some Like It Hot* introduced Jack Lemmon and Tony Curtis as two hapless musicians in Chicago who, needing to have their rattle-trap car fixed, just happen to be in the garage where the St. Valentine's Day Massacre takes place. Needing a job and, even more desperately, a way out of town, they take the only work available, in an all-girl orchestra heading south on a train to Florida.

One problem with the setting is that, as anyone familiar with San Diego knows, "Florida" in the movie is the truly astonishing Hotel del Coronado. ("That place could obviously not exist," an early reviewer is rumored to have said.) However, besides its spectacular architecture, it has the requisite sand, palm trees, and wealthy older folks, so it suffices for Florida. Besides, where else could a couple on the lam from Chicago go quickly in February—and be able to wear the high heels, chic dresses, and cloche hats their new roles require?

Naturally they are pursued by the mob; as in the typical gangster movie, the bad guys are brought to justice. But Lemmon and Curtis do experience some parodically noir dilemmas. Their ambiguity may not be so much moral as sexual, though; the struggles Lemmon undergoes when Marilyn Monroe, a.k.a. Sugar Kane ("jello on springs") crawls into his Pullman berth exemplify excruciating comic pain. Tony Curtis adopts a disguise, as well. He is a blazer-clad Cary Grant trying to win the femme fatale Sugar, who, unlike Barbara Stanwyck or Mary Astor, couldn't be sweeter—even though she leads him close to danger.

The ambiguous noir ending is converted in this movie into what is one of the funniest ending lines of any movie ever made. Jack Lemmon's gender, it appears, will remain bent when Joe E. Brown tells him that "Nobody's perfect."

Jonathan Demme's *Married to the Mob* (1988) also takes the noir and gangster modes and makes a marvelous hash of them. Dean Stockwell, brilliant as mob capo Tony "The Tiger," has Michelle Pfeiffer's husband, Alec "The Pickle" Baldwin, killed for reasons the French would understand; it's a crime of passion. Alec is caught *in flagrante* with Tony's girl—although Tony also has the hots for Alec's wife. Fearing for her life and her virtue, the Pfeiffer character escapes to a tacky apartment in Manhattan, is linked up with government agent Matthew Modine, but then is convinced by the forces of justice to go to Miami with the mobster.

The setting for the Florida scenes provides a perfect backdrop for the comic parody. The hotel where the assignation is to take place, with its gilded mirrors, swags, and ornate furniture, is glitz to the nth degree. It should be said that this film really parodies the gangster more than the noir film, but its presentation of Michele Pfeiffer, a heroine with hesitations, dilemmas, and a final heroic engagement—not to mention a perfect New York accent—does parody certain noir heroes.

Although *Midnight Cowboy* and *Godfather II* do not fit perfectly into the category of film noir, they contain scenes set in Florida that demonstrate how the setting can be used to exemplify qualities that are much in the noir tradition.

John Schlesinger's *Midnight Cowboy* (1969) cannot be considered film noir, although the character of Joe Buck (Jon Voight), the innocent would-be hustler from Texas and Ratso Rizzo (Dustin Hoffman), the street kid from New York, would easily find a place in a more traditional film noir. In addition, the honest presentation of prostitution, homosexuality, and the drug-ridden *dolce vita* crowd in New York would fit, as would the random and shocking acts of violence, like Joe's gagging a shy homosexual with a telephone. But the main narrative movement of the film is more internal, toward the bonding of the two major characters.

Part of the bonding is accomplished through the shared dream of Florida as a kind of paradise. The dream sequence in which the gimpy-legged Ratso is able to race on the sandy beach with beautiful girls is poignant, especially since it contrasts so strongly with the reality of their lives in the more squalid parts of Manhattan. The closest to Florida that Ratso gets is, of course, only partway on the bus, but he does arrive with Joe Buck's arm around his shoulder so the other passengers will not realize that he has died.

Florida also appears in a key scene in Francis Ford Coppola's *Godfather, Part II* (1974). All three *Godfathers* are not pure film noir, nor are they just gangster movies. Perhaps the best way to classify them is to accept Pauline Kael's judgment: what Coppola reached with the (first two) *Godfather* movies is "the place where genre is transcended and what we're moved by is an artist's vision" (*Taking It All In* 227).

In Part II, Michael Corleone, played by Al Pacino, has already achieved ascendancy in the New York Mafia as *capo di tutti capi*. He has done so in the extraordinary final scene of Part I, in which his serving as godfather to his first nephew in a meticulously filmed church service is juxtaposed against the meticulously prepared and violent deaths of his major rivals. But in Part II there is still further opposition, chiefly in the form of Hyman Roth (played by Lee Strasberg), the film's homage to Meyer Lansky. Michael wants control over Florida and the money and power that come with mob connections in the Caribbean, particularly Batista's Cuba.

So he travels to South Florida to visit Roth. It is typical of Coppola's vision of the life of mafiosi that he shows them living in such ordinary places with ugly bourgeois furniture and interior decoration. The mundane and everyday exist side by side with violence: in Part I, Clemenza teaches Michael how to make spaghetti sauce while the "soldiers" have "gone to the mattresses" in a gang war. Here, the powerful, wealthy Roth lives in a small cinder-block house on an ordinary street with inexpensive rattan chairs. His blonde wife, in her fifties-style crinoline petticoats and full skirt, serves sandwiches on a tray. Roth offers Michael advice— which Michael comes to realize is, ultimately, betrayal. But along with administrative counsel, Roth also praises the virtue of watching baseball, the All-American game.

Of recent Florida films the one that fits the film noir formula best is Lawrence Kasdan's *Body Heat* (1981). Dealing with the All-American film noir game of killing a nasty husband, it is clearly best of the recent class. Stephen Schiff calls it "certainly the best imitation of a film noir since *Chinatown* seven years before. . . . [It] isn't muffled and somber and period-bound like the remake of *The Postman Always Rings Twice* . . . it's thoroughly entertaining and its self-consciousness only enhances its hypnotic aura" (33). Silver and Ward contend that *Postman* "evokes the noir sensibility much more powerfully than many of the films which followed it" (400).

From the very beginning we know we're in noir territory. To the accompaniment of a seductive saxophone and a backdrop of flickering candle flames alternating with the curves of a woman's body, the Art Deco letters of the screen credits announce the title and the actors and set the dominant tone.

We soon meet Ned Racine, played by William Hurt. He is an incompetent lawyer who makes just enough money to eat once a month in a fancy restaurant—if he doesn't order an appetizer. At his first appearance he is watching a distant fire while an unnamed woman reproaches him for his inattentiveness and starts to get dressed. In a scene shortly thereafter, he is instructed by the judge on how he should handle the case he is currently pleading. Soon after that, he is joshed by his friend Lowenstein (played by an almost unrecognizable Ted Danson), who suggests that he "stop using your incompetence as a weapon."

That incompetence will be used as a weapon later on, but it takes Racine a while to discover how. Meanwhile, at an outdoor concert where the town has gone to get away from the heat, he sees a stunning woman —dressed in white, as always—walk past him. He follows her, tries out a variety of lines, and seems not to be getting anywhere. The dialog here can be seen as parodic sexy noir (especially her line "You're not too smart; I like that in a man"), but it is great fun, and William Hurt and Kathleen Turner (as Matty Walker) are obviously making the most of it. He buys her a cherry-flavored snow cone to cool off; she spills it on her blouse; he goes for a damp paper towel as she murmurs an inviting *double entendre*. When he returns, she is gone.

But it is not long before he does follow her to her home. She plays her extremely successful game of hard to get, and he breaks a window to get to her. From that point on, he unwittingly does everything she has planned for him to do. They kill her husband, a truly slimy sort played by Richard Crenna. But then things begin to fall apart. It takes a while for Ned to realize that he is being set up in a really big way. Finally, when in prison and he has time to think it all out, he comes up with the solution—proved by pictures in a high-school yearbook. In the last scene the black widow Matty Walker is lying on a cushioned chair at a magnificent beach in Brazil, apparently escaping scot-free. But the audience hopes that justice may be achieved after the curtain comes down and the lights come up.

Anyone who lives in Florida would surely enjoy the film. The feel of a small town on a south Florida beach is just right, from the jumble of buildings on main street to the smoky place called Stella's where everyone meets for coffee or iced tea. Matty's beautiful home in modified Spanish style, overhung with Spanish moss and choked with vegetation, is photographed in velvety murk. In fact, the film almost turns into black and white during the night scenes, especially in the fog that descends on the night when Matty and Ned kill her husband. A clever use of black and white, also, appears in the chessboard squares on the floor of her bathroom, and with the black bathtub with ball-and-claw feet. The title says it all; even the local police chief predicts all kinds of evildoing that will result from the heat wave. The one thing that doesn't ring true is that, even in 1981, virtually every house and building in Florida *did* have air conditioning. But one can't count the bullets in a six-shooter. And all that sweating adds to the atmosphere.

Not everyone has approved of *Body Heat*. Pauline Kael, for example, complains about Kathleen Turner's remoteness and William Hurt's being "too tight and held in" (*Taking* 256). The talk, she says, has "an echo-chamber effect" (255). That, I think, is why it can be so appealing. We're hungry for stylish noir—and the musical accompaniment, the Bogart dialog, the excellent supporting characters, Mickey Rourke and Ted Danson, the changes from light to dark to light again, those wind chimes—all these not only evoke films past but are entertaining in their own right. They create the style Lawrence Kasden intended.

The relationship between Matty and Ned, deeply immoral, is also developed with a sense of homage to the past. At one point she gives him a fedora just like the ones Bogart wore. Ned tries it on only once, then tosses it to the top of a hatrack. Later he shows that he realizes what the true gift of that femme fatale really was: "That was her one special gift. She was relentless."

Though the plot lines do follow the formula, the intricacy of the twists and turns is still a delight, especially today, when the well-made plot seems to be an object of disdain to so many scriptwriters and directors. Everything fits in. And, at the very last, when "Matty" is on the beach, her current companion—young and male, though we see only his back—speaks first in Portuguese, then translates, "It is hot." She replies, "Yes."

Works Cited

Agee, James. *Agee on Film*. New York: Beacon, 1950.

Bailey, John, dir. *China Moon*. With Ed Harris, Madeleine Stowe, and Charles Dance. 1994.

Coppola, Francis Ford, dir. *The Godfather, Part II*. With Al Pacino, Robert DeNiro, John Cazale, and Lee Strasberg. 1974.

Demme, Jonathan, dir. *Married to the Mob*. With Michelle Pfeiffer, Matthew Modine, and Dean Stockwell. 1988.

De Palma, Brian. *Scarface*. With Al Pacino, Steven Bauer, Michelle Pfeiffer, and Robert Loggia. 1983.

Ebert, Roger. *Roger Ebert's Video Companion: 1995 Edition*. Kansas City: Andrews and McMeel, 1994.

Ferrara, Abel, dir. *Cat Chaser*. With Kelly McGillis, Peter Weller, and Frederic Forrest. 1989.

Hawks, Howard, dir. *To Have and Have Not*. With Humphrey Bogart, Lauren Bacall, and Walter Brennan. 1944.

Hemingway, Ernest. *To Have and Have Not*. New York: Scribner, 1970.

Huston, John, dir. *Key Largo*. With Humphrey Bogart, Lauren Bacall, and Edward G. Robinson. 1948.

Kael, Pauline. *Kiss Kiss Bang Bang*. New York: Bantam, 1969.

——. *State of the Art*. New York: Dutton, 1985.

——. *Taking It All In*. New York: Holt, 1984.

Kasdan, Lawrence, dir. *Body Heat*. With William Hurt, Kathleen Turner, and Richard Crenna. 1981.

Leonard, Elmore. *Cat Chaser*. New York: Avon, 1982.

Maltin, Leonard, ed. *1996 Movie and Video Guide*. New York: Signet, 1995.

Nuñez, Victor. *A Flash of Green*. With Ed Harris, Blair Brown, and Richard Jordan. 1984.

——. *Ruby in Paradise*. With Ashley Judd. 1993.

Phillips, Gene D. *Hemingway on Film*. New York: Frederick Ungar, 1980.

Reynolds, Burt, dir. *Stick*. With Candice Bergen, George Segal, and Charles Durning. 1985.

Rickey, Carrie. "On Mob Rule." *They Went Thataway: Redefining Film Genres*. Ed. Richard T. Jameson. San Francisco: Mercury House, 1994. 4-11.

Rothman, William. "To Have and Have Not Adapted a Novel." *The Modern American Novel and the Movies*. Ed. Gerald Peary and Roger Shatzin. New York: Frederick Ungar, 1978. 70-79.

Schickel, Richard. *Schickel on Film*. New York: William Morrow, 1989.

Schiff, Stephen. "Body Heat." *They Went Thataway: Redefining Film Genres*. Ed. Richard T. Jameson. San Francisco: Mercury House, 1994. 31-35.

Schlesinger, John, dir. *Midnight Cowboy*. With Dustin Hoffman and Jon Voight. 1969.

Silver, Alain, and Elizabeth Ward, eds. *Film Noir: An Encyclopedic Reference to the American Style*. Woodstock: Overlook, 1992.

Wilder, Billy, dir. *Some Like It Hot*. With Jack Lemmon, Tony Curtis, Marilyn Monroe, and Joe E. Brown. 1959.

12

A Bibliography of Florida Mysteries, 1895-1996

Maurice O'Sullivan and Lynne Phillips

Aarons, Edward S. [See Edward Ronns.]

Adams, Eustace Law. *Gambler's Throw*. New York: Longmans, 1930.

Aguero, Vincent H. *Two Promises to Keep*. New York: Exposition, 1965.

Ahern, Jerry, and Sharon Ahern. *Miamigrad*. New York: Pocket, 1987.

Albert, Marvin. [See Albert Conroy.]

Allen, Lydia H. *Glorious Misadventure*. Philadelphia: Dorrance, 1941.

Alter, Robert Edmond. *Carny Kill*. Greenwich: Fawcett, 1966.

———. *Swamp Sister*. 1966. Berkley: Creative Arts, 1986.

Anderson, V. S. *Storm Front*. New York: Doubleday, 1992.

Ard, William. [See also Ben Kerr.] *All I Can Get*. Derby: Monarch, 1959.

———. *Mr. Trouble*. New York: Rinehart, 1955.

———. *The Root of His Evil*. New York: Rinehart, 1957.

Ayres, E. A. *Hour of the Manatee*. New York: St. Martin's, 1994.

Banko, Daniel. *Very Dead with a Twist*. New York: Dutton, 1975.

Barry, Mike. *Miami Marauder*. New York: Berkley, 1974.

Barth, Richard. *Deadly Climate*. New York: St. Martin's, 1988.

Beatty, Elizabeth. *The Jupiter Missile Mystery*. New York: Avalon, 1960.

———. *River in the Sun*. New York: Avalon, 1958.

Bechevet, Lydia de. *Mystery of the Twisted Man*. New York: Grafton, 1927.

Becker, Stephen. *Juice*. New York: Simon and Schuster, 1958.

Beechcroft, William. *Position of Ultimate Trust*. New York: Dodd, 1981.

Bennett, Robert D. *Rendezvous 2.2*. New York: Fawcett Gold Medal, 1986.

Biggers, Earl Derr. *Love Insurance*. Indianapolis: Bobbs-Merrill, 1914.

Bowen Nan. *Hear No Evil*. New York: Macmillan, 1968.

Brace, Timothy. [Theodore Pratt.] *Murder Goes Fishing*. New York: Dutton, 1936.

———. *Murder Goes in a Trailer*. New York: Dutton, 1937.

———. *Murder Goes to the Dogs*. New York: Dutton, 1938.

Bracken, Steve. *Delfina*. Greenwich: Fawcett, 1962.

Bragunier, Mordina Floyd. [See Mordie Floyd.]

Braly, Malcolm. *The Master*. New York: Warner, 1973.

Brent, R. L. *Liquidator*. New York: Charter, 1974.

Brewer, Gil. *And the Girl Screamed*. Greenwich: Fawcett, 1944.

——. *Pay It Hard*. Derby: Monarch, 1960.

——. *The Red Scarf*. New York: Mystery House, 1958.

——. *Three Way Split*. Greenwich: Fawcett, 1960.

Brody, Marc. [William C. Williams.] *Teaser Set to Kill*. Australia: Horwitz, 1958.

Brown, Carter. *Graves I Dig!* New York: New American Library, 1960.

Buchanan, Edna. *Act of Betrayal*. New York: Hyperion, 1996.

——. *Contents Under Pressure*. New York: Hyperion, 1992.

——. *Miami, It's Murder*. New York: Hyperion, 1994.

——. *Nobody Lives Forever*. New York: Random, 1990.

——. *Suitable for Framing*. New York: Hyperion, 1995.

Buchanan, Jack. *Miami War Zone*. New York: Jove, 1988.

Buffett, Jimmy. *Where Is Joe Merchant?* New York: Harcourt, 1992.

Caidin, Martin. *Maryjane Tonight at Angels Twelve*. Garden City: Doubleday, 1972.

——. *Three Corners to Nowhere*. New York: Bantam, 1975.

Caillou, Alan. *Swamp War*. New York: Pinnacle, 1973.

Carmichael, Fred. *Said the Spider to the Fly*. New York: French, 1987.

Carrier, Warren Pendleton. *Bay of the Damned*. New York: Day, 1957.

Carter, Nick. [Ralph Hayes.] *Danger Key*. New York: Universal-Award, 1966.

——. *Operation Moon Rocket*. New York: Universal, 1968.

Chaber, M. E. *The Bonded Dead*. New York: Holt, 1971.

Chambers, Dana. *The Case of Caroline Animus*. London: Hale, 1951.

——. *Darling, This Is Death*. London: Hale, 1951.

Chambers, Elwyn Whitman. *Keys to Dry Tortugus*. New York: Doubleday, 1940.

Chambers, Whitman. *Bright Star of Danger*. New York: Doubleday, 1940.

——. *Dry Tortugas*. New York: Doubleday, 1940.

Chandler, Bryn. *Behind the Badge*. New York: Ballantine, 1984.

Charteris, Leslie. *The Saint in Miami*. Garden City: Doubleday, 1940.

Chase, Elaine Raco. *Dangerous Places*. New York: Bantam, 1987.

——. *Dark Corners*. New York: Bantam, 1988.

Chase, James Hadley. [Rene Brabazon Raymond.] *Believe This . . . You'll Believe Anything*. London: Hale, 1975.

——. *Believed Violent*. London: Hale, 1975.

——. *A Can of Worms*. London: Hale, 1979.

——. *An Ear to the Ground*. London: Hale, 1968.

——. *Have a Change of Scene*. London: Hale, 1973.

——. *Like a Hole in the Head*. London: Hale, 1970.

——. *So What Happens to Me*. London: Hale. 1974.

——. *The Soft Centre*. London: Hale, 1964.

——. *Strictly for Cash*. London: Hale, 1951.

——. *There's a Hippie on the Highway*. London: Hale. 1970.

——. *Want to Stay Alive?* London: Hale, 1971.

——. *The Way the Cookie Crumbles*. London: Hale, 1965.

——. *Well Now, My Pretty*. London: Hale, 1967.

——. *You Can Say That Again*. London: Hale, 1980.

Chase, Josephine. *The Mark of the Red Diamond*. Philadelphia: Penn, 1929.

Chelton, John. *My Deadly Angel*. New York: Fawcett, 1955.

Christian, A. G. *Harani Trail*. New York: Doherty, 1988.

Churchill, Luanna. [John Karl Dughman and Frieda Mae Dughman.] *Grinning Ghoul*. New York: Lenox Hill, 1974.

——. *Shades and Shadows*. New York: Lenox Hill, 1973.

Claymore, Tod. [Hugh Cleverly.] *Reunion in Florida*. New York: Penguin, 1955.

Clayton, John Bell. *Six Angels at My Back*. New York: Macmillan, 1952.

Cleverly, Hugh. [See Tod Claymore.]

Cline, C. Terry. *Missing Persons*. New York: Arbor, 1981.

——. *Reaper*. New York: Fine, 1989.

Cody, Liza. *Backhand*. New York: Doubleday, 1992.

Cody, Patrick. *A Fool's Death*. New York: Crown, 1993.

Cohen, Octavius Roy. *Child of Evil*. New York: Appleton, 1936.

Colby, Robert. *Kim*. Derby: Monarch, 1962.

——. *Make Mine Vengeance*. New York: Avon, 1959.

——. *Murder Mistress*. Sydney: Phantom, 1959.

——. *Quaking Widow*. Sydney: Phantom, 1958.

Collins, Stuart. *Burndown*. New York: Knightsbridge, 1990.

Colver, Alice Mary (Ross). *The Look-Out Girl*. New York: Penn, 1928.

Comfort, Iris. *Echoes of Evil*. Garden City: Doubleday, 1977.

——. *Shadow Masque*. Garden City: Doubleday, 1980.

Conners, Thomas. *Combat Zone—Miami*. Miami: Floridiana, 1978.

Conroy, Albert. [Marvin Albert.] *Blood Run!* New York: Lancer, 1973.

——. *Strangle Hold!* New York: Lancer, 1973.

Conty, Jean-Pierre. *Big Secret, Suzuki*. New York: International, 1969.

Conway, Norman. *The Omega Operation*. N.p.: Canyon, 1974.

Cooper, Courtney Riley. *Action in Diamonds*. Philadelphia: Penn, 1942.

Coram, Robert. *America's Heroes*. New York: New American Library, 1990.

——. *Narcs*. New York: New American Library, 1988.

Corrigan, Mark. *Love for Sale*. London: Laurie, 1954.

Coxe, George Harmon. *Inland Passage*. New York: Knopf, 1949.

——. *Never Bet Your Life*. New York: Alfred Knopf, 1952.

Crabb, Ned. *Ralph; or, What's Eating the Folks in Fatchakulla County*. New York: Morrow, 1979.

Crawford, Max. *Six Key Cut*. New York: Atheneum, 1986.

Creasey, John. *Murder, London-Miami*. New York: Scribner, 1969.

Crews, Lary. *Extreme Close-Up*. New York: Lynx, 1989.

——. *Kill Cue*. New York: Lynx, 1988.

——. *Option to Die*. New York: Lynx, 1989.

Crockett, Linda. *Sandman*. New York: Tor, 1990.

Cullimore, Alan. *Good Place to Hide*. New York: Tor/Tom Doherty, 1988.

Daly, Carroll John. *The Hidden Hand*. New York: Clode, 1929.

Daniels, Dorothy. [See Suzanne Somers.]

Davis, Frederick Clyde. [See Stephen Ransome.]

Davis, Maggie. *Miami Midnight*. New York: Bantam, 1989.

Dean, Robert George. *Layoff*. New York: Scribner, 1942.

Deane, Jim. *Moon Over Miami*. New York: New American Library, 1975.

DeBorchgrave, Arnaud. *Monimbo*. New York: Simon and Schuster, 1983.

Dent, Lester. *Lady Afraid*. Garden City: Doubleday, 1948.

Derrick, Lionel. *Cryogenic Nightmare*. Los Angeles: Pinnacle, 1978.

——. *Demented Empire*. New York: Pinnacle, 1976.

DeWitt, Jack. *Murders on Shark Island*. New York: Liveright, 1941.

Dexter, Pete. *The Paperboy*. New York: Random, 1995.

Dietrich, Robert. *Be My Victim*. New York: Dell, 1956.

Dixon, Franklin. *Mystery of Smuggler's Cove*. New York: Wanderer/Simon and Schuster, 1980.

Doyle, James T. *Epitaph for a Loser*. New York: Walker, 1988.

Drake, Alison. [Trish Janeshutz McGregor.] *Black Moon*. New York: Ballantine, 1989.

——. *Fevered*. New York: Ballantine, 1988.

——. *Tango Key*. New York: Ballantine, 1988.

Dresser, Davis. [See Brett Halliday.]

Du Bois, Theodora. *Rogue's Coat*. New York: American Mercury, 1949.

Dughman, John Karl, and Frieda Mae Dughman. [See Luanna Churchill.]

Duncan, Lois. *Point of Violence*. Garden City: Doubleday, 1966.

Eberhart, Mignon (Good). *Another Man's Murder*. Roslyn: Black, 1957.

——. *Unidentified Woman*. New York: Random, 1943.

——. *The White Dress*. New York: Random, 1945.

Edwards, Jane. *Terror by Design*. New York: Avalon, 1990.

Ellin, Stanley. *The Bind*. New York: Random, 1970.

——. *Star Light, Star Bright*. New York: Random, 1979.

Ely, Wilmer. *The Boy Chums Crossing in Florida Waters*. New York: Burt, 1914.

Ernst, Paul. *Lady, Get Your Gun*. New York: Mill/Morrow, 1955.

Evans, Elaine. *Shadowland*. New York: Magnum, 1970.

Faherty, Robert. *Better Than Dying*. Garden City: Doubleday, Doran, 1935.

Feegal, John R. *Autopsy*. New York: Avon, 1975.

——. *Death Sails the Bay*. New York: Avon, 1978.

Fickling, G. G. *Bombshell*. New York: Pyramid, 1964.

Fisher, David E. *The Last Flying Tiger*. New York: Scribner, 1976.

Floyd, Mordie. [Mordina Floyd Bragunier.] *Secret of Saraband*. New York: Couregy, 1961.

Flynn, J. M. *Surfside 6*. New York: Dell, 1962.

Foley, Rae. *Wild Night*. New York: Dodd, 1960.

Foster, Richard. *Bier for a Chaser*. London: Muller, 1960.

——. *Too Late for Mourning*. London: Muller, 1961.

Frank, George. [See George F. Worts.]

Frazer, Robert Cain. *Mark Kilby and the Miami Mob*. New York: Pocket, 1960.

Freemantle, Brian. *Charlie Muffin's Uncle Sam*. London: Cape, 1980.

Friedman, Mickey. *Hurricane Season*. New York: Dutton, 1983.

——. *Magic Mirror*. New York: Viking, 1988.

——. *Riptide*. New York: St. Martin's, 1994.

Fuller, William Hanscom. *Back Country*. New York: Dell, 1954.

——. *Brad Dolan's Miami Manhunt*. New York: Dell, 1958.

——. *Girl in the Frame*. New York: Dell, 1957.

——. *Goat Island*. New York: Dell, 1954.

——. *The Pace That Kills*. New York: Dell, 1956.

Gibson, Walter. [See Maxwell Grant.]

Glendinning, Richard R. *Terror in the Sun*. New York: Fawcett, 1952.

——. *Who Evil Thinks*. Greenwich: Fawcett, 1952.

Gora, Michael. *Blood Coast*. Smithtown: Exposition, 1980.

Gordon, Alison. *Night Game*. New York: St. Martin's, 1992.

Goulart, Ron. *The Wisemann Originals*. New York: Walker, 1989.

Grafton, Sue. *B. Is for Burglary*. New York: Holt, 1985.

Granger, Bill. *Schism*. New York: Pocket, 1982.

Grant, Maxwell. [Walter Gibson.] *City of Ghosts*. New York: Street and Smith, 1939.

——. *Crime Over Miami*. New York: Street and Smith, 1940.

——. *Crime Stronghold*. New York: Street and Smith, 1941.

——. *Death Diamonds*. New York: Street and Smith, 1942.

——. *Dictator of Crime*. New York: Street and Smith, 1941.

——. *Five Keys to Crime*. New York: Street and Smith, 1945.

——. *The Yellow Band*. New York: Street and Smith, 1937.

Grave, Stephen. *China White*. N.p.: Star, 1986.

——. *The Florida Burn*. New York: Avon, 1985.

——. *Hellhole*. N.p.: Star, 1987.

——. *Probing by Fire*. N.p.: Star, 1987.

——. *The Razor's Edge*. N.p.: Star, 1986.

——. *The Vengeance Game.* New York: Avon, 1985.

Green, Alan. *What a Body!* New York: Simon and Schuster, 1949.

Green, Edith Pinero. *Sneaks.* New York: Dutton, 1979.

Greig, Maysie. *The High Road.* New York: Arcadia, 1954.

——. *The Reluctant Cinderella.* New York: Avalon, 1952.

——. *Stopover in Paradise.* Garden City: Doubleday, Doran, 1938.

Greth, Roma. *Nightmare!* Chicago: Dramatic , 1961.

Grippando, James. *The Pardon.* HarperCollins, 1994.

Gunter, Archibald Clavering. *Don Blasco of Key West.* New York: Home, 1896.

Hagen, Patricia. *Dark Journey Home.* New York: Avon, 1974.

Hale, Arlene. *The Season of Love.* Boston: Little, Brown, 1971.

——. *The Stormy Sea of Love.* New York: New American Library, 1976.

Hale, Christopher. *He's Late This Morning.* Garden City: Doubleday, 1949.

——. *Murder in Tow.* Garden City: Doubleday, Doran, 1943.

Hale, Jennifer. *Beyond the Dark.* New York: Berkley, 1978.

——. *House of Strangers.* New York: Prestige, 1972.

——. *House on Key Diablo.* N.p.: Beagle, 1974.

——. *Stormhaven.* New York: Lancer, 1970.

Hall, Adam. *The Quiller Barracuda.* New York: Morrow, 1990.

Hall, James. *Bones of Coral.* New York: Knopf, 1991.

——. *Buzz Cut.* New York: Delacorte, 1996.

——. *Gone Wild.* New York: Delacorte, 1995.

——. *Hard Aground.* New York: Delacorte, 1993.

——. *Mean High Tide.* New York: Delacorte, 1994.

——. *Tropical Freeze.* New York: Warner, 1989.

——. *Under Cover of Daylight.* New York: Delacorte, 1987.

Halleran, Tucker. *A Cool, Clear Death.* New York: St. Martin's, 1984.

Halliday, Brett. [Davis Dresser.] *At the Point of a .38.* New York: Dell, 1974.

——. *The Blonde Cried Murder.* New York: Torquil, 1956.

——. *Blood on Biscayne Bay.* Chicago: Ziff Davis, 1946.

——. *Blood on the Black Market.* New York: Dodd, Mead, 1943.

——. *Blood on the Stars.* New York: Dodd, Mead, 1948.

——. *Blue Murder.* New York: Dell, 1973.

——. *Bodies Are Where You Find Them.* New York: Holt, 1941.

——. *Call for Michael Shayne.* New York: Dodd, Mead, 1949.

——. *The Corpse Came Calling.* New York: Dodd, Mead, 1942.

——. *Count Backwards to Zero.* New York: Dell, 1971.

——. *Counterfeit Wife.* Chicago: Ziff Davis, 1947.

——. *Date with a Dead Man.* New York: Dodd, Mead, 1959.

——. *Dead Man's Diary, and Dinner at Dupre's.* New York: Dell, 1945.

——. *Death Has Three Lives.* New York: Torquil, 1955.

——. *Die Like a Dog.* New York: Dodd, Mead, 1960.

——. *Dividend on Death*. New York: Holt, 1939.

——. *Dolls Are Deadly*. New York: Dodd, Mead, 1960.

——. *Fit to Kill*. New York: Dodd, Mead, 1954.

——. *Fourth Down to Death*. New York: Dell, 1970.

——. *Framed in Blood*. New York: Dodd, Mead, 1951.

——. *Guilty As Hell*. New York: Dodd, Mead. 1967.

——. *The Homicidal Virgin*. New York: Dodd, Mead, 1961.

——. *I Come to Kill You*. New York: Dell, 1971.

——. *Killers from the Keys*. New York: Dodd, Mead, 1961.

——. *Lady Be Bad*. New York: Dell, 1969.

——. *Last Seen Hitchhiking*. New York: Dell, 1974.

——. *Marked for Murder*. New York: Dodd, Mead, 1945.

——. *Mermaid on the Rocks*. New York: Dell, 1967.

——. *Michael Shayne's 50th Case*. New York: Dodd, Mead, 1964.

——. *Michael Shayne's Long Chance*. New York: Dodd, Mead, 1944.

——. *Michael Shayne's Triple Mystery* ("Dead Man's Diary," "A Taste for Cognac," "Dinner at Dupre's"). New York: Ziff Davis, 1948.

——. *Million Dollar Handle*. New York: Dell, 1976.

——. *Murder and the Married Virgin*. New York: Dodd, Mead, 1944.

——. *Murder and the Wanton Blonde*. New York: Torquil, 1958.

——. *Murder in Haste*. New York: Dodd, Mead, 1961.

——. *Murder Is My Business*. New York: Dodd, Mead, 1945.

——. *Murder Spins the Wheel*. New York: Dodd, Mead, 1966.

——. *Murder Wears a Mummer's Mask*. New York: Dodd, Mead, 1943.

——. *Never Kill a Client*. New York: Dodd, Mead, 1962.

——. *Nice Fillies Finish Last*. New York: Dell, 1965.

——. *One Night with Nora*. New York: Torquil, 1953.

——. *Pay-Off in Blood*. New York: Dodd, Mead, 1953.

——. *The Private Practice of Mike Shayne*. New York: Holt, 1940.

——. *A Redhead for Mike Shayne*. New York: Dodd, Mead, 1964.

——. *She Woke to Darkness*. New York: Torquil, 1954.

——. *Shoot the Works*. New York: Torquil, 1957.

——. *Shoot to Kill*. New York: Dodd, Mead, 1964.

——. *Six Seconds to Kill*. New York: Dell, 1970.

——. *So Lush, So Deadly*. New York: Dell, 1968.

——. *Stranger in Town*. New York: Torquil, 1955.

——. *Target: Mike Shayne*. New York: Dodd, Mead, 1959.

——. *A Taste for Violence*. New York: Dodd, Mead, 1949.

——. *This Is It, Michael Shayne*. New York: Dodd, Mead, 1950.

——. *Tickets for Death*. New York: Holt, 1941.

——. *Too Friendly, Too Dead*. New York: Dodd, Mead, 1963.

——. *The Uncomplaining Corpses*. New York: Holt, 1940.

——. *Violence Is Golden*. New York: Dell, 1968.

——. *Weep for a Blonde*. New York: Torquil, 1957.

——. *What Really Happened*. New York: Dodd, Mead, 1952.

——. *When Dorinda Dances*. New York: Dodd, Mead, 1951.

——. *Win Some, Lose Some*. New York: Dell, 1976.

Hamilton, Donald. *The Intimidators*. Greenwich: Fawcett, 1974.

——. *The Intriguers*. New York: Ballantine, 1972.

——.*The Shadowers*. Greenwich: Fawcett, 1964.

Haring, Dan. *The A. O. Caper*. Sydney: Cleveland, 1976.

——. *Big-Time Caper*. Sydney: Cleveland, n.d.

——. *Countdown to Murder!* Sydney: Cleveland, n.d.

——. *Dames Come Deep Freeze*. Sydney: Cleveland, n.d.

——. *Don't Die on Me, Diana*. Sydney: Cleveland, n.d.

——. *The Filthy Ones*. Sydney: Cleveland, 1977.

Harrington, William. *Scorpio 5*. New York: Coward, 1975.

Harrison, Jim. *A Good Day to Die*. New York: Delta, 1973.

Harrison, Whit. [Harry (Benjamin) Whittington.] *Strip the Town Naked*. Boston: Beacon, 1960.

Hayes, Joseph Arnold. *No Escape*. New York: Delacorte, 1982.

Hayes, Ralph. [See Nick Carter.]

Healy, Jeremiah. *Rescue*. New York: Pocket, 1995.

Heatter, Basil. *Scarred Man*. Greenwich: Fawcett, 1973.

Heyman, Evan Lee. *Miami Undercover*. New York: Popular Library, 1961.

Hiaasen, Carl. [See also William D. Montalbano.] *Double Whammy*. New York: Warner, 1987.

——. *Native Tongue*. New York: Warner, 1991.

——. *Skin Tight*. New York: Warner, 1989.

——. *Stormy Weather*. New York: Knopf, 1995.

——. *Strip Tease*. New York: Alfred A. Knopf, 1993.

——. *Tourist Season*. New York: Warner, 1986.

Higgins, Joan. *A Little Death Music*. New York: Dodd, Mead, 1987.

Hild, Jack. *Firestorm U.S.A.* Toronto: Worldwide, 1987.

Hill, Kim. *Death on Demand*. Sun Lakes: Horton, 1985.

Hillgarth, A. *What Price Heaven?* New York: Houghton, 1929.

Hilton, John Bux. *The Sunset Law*. New York: St. Martin's, 1982.

Himmel, Richard. *I'll Find You*. London: Fawcett, 1950.

Hinchman, Jane. *Dreamspinner*. New York: Walker, 1986.

Hirschfield, Burt. *Key West*. New York: Morrow, 1978.

Hoffman, Alice. *Turtle Moon*. New York: Putnam, 1992.

Holden, Larry. *Hide-Out*. New York: Elon, 1953.

Holley, Helen. *Blood on the Beach*. New York: Mystery, 1946.

Houston, Margaret Bell. *Yonder*. New York: Crown, 1955.

Hoyt, Richard. *Marimba*. New York: Tor, 1992.

Huber, Frederick Vincent. *Axx Goes South*. New York: Walker, 1989.

Humes, Larry. *Bridge to Nowhere*. New York: Leisure, 1980.

Hunt, E. Howard. *From Cuba with Love*. [Ring Around Rosy.] c.1964. New York: Pinnacle, 1974.

Hunter, Evan. [See Ed McBain.]

Hunter, R. Wilkes. *Net of Fear*. Sydney: Horwitz, 1965.

Hurst, Edward H. *Mystery Island*. Boston: Page, 1907.

Jakes, John (William). [See Alan Payne.]

Janeshutz, Trish. [T. J. Macgregor. See also Allison Drake.] *Hidden Lake*. New York: Ballantine, 1987.

——. *In Shadow*. New York: Ballantine, 1985.

Janson, Hank. *Bewitched*. London: Moring, 1957.

——. *Hell's Angel*. London: Moring, 1956.

——. *Milady Took the Rap*. South Carolina: Janson, 1951.

Johnson, James Leonard. *The Nine Lives of Alphonse*. Philadelphia: Lippincott, 1968.

Johnston, Velda. *The White Pavilion*. Boston: Hall, 1974.

Jordan, Leonard. [Leonard Levinson.] *Operation Perfidia*. New York: Warner, 1975.

Kallen, Lucille. *Blue Pearl*. New York: Hyperion, 1994.

——. *C. B. Greenfield: The Piano Bird*. New York: Ballantine, 1985.

Kane, Henry. *My Darlin' Evangeline*. New York: Dell, 1961.

Karr, Lee. *Dark Cries of Gray Oaks*. New York: Kensington, 1989.

Kastle, Herbert. *Miami Golden Boy*. New York: Geis, 1969.

Katzenbach, John. *In the Heat of the Summer*. New York: Atheneum, 1982.

——. *Just Cause*. New York: Putnam, 1992.

——. *The Shadow Man*. New York: Ballantine, 1995.

——. *The Traveler*. New York: Putnam, 1987.

Kaufmann, Lane. Waldo. New York: Lippincott, 1960.

Keene, Day. [See also William Richards.] *Miami 59*. New York: Dell, 1965.

Kelley, Lamar. *That's No Way to Die*. New York: Pyramid, 1970.

Kendrick, Baynard Hardwick. *Blood on Lake Louisa*. New York: Greenburg, 1934.

——. *Death Beyond the Go-Thru*. New York: Doubleday, Doran, 1938.

——. *The Eleven of Diamonds*. New York: Greenburg, 1936.

——. *Flight from a Firing Wall*. New York: Simon and Schuster, 1966.

——. *The Iron Spiders*. New York: Greenburg, 1936.

Kennedy, Barbara. *The Uninvited Guest*. New York: Fawcett, 1981.

Kerr, Ben. [William Ard.] *Damned If He Does*. Toronto: Popular Library, 1956.

——. *Shakedown*. New York: Holt, 1952.

King, Rufus. *The Case of the Redoubled Cross*. Garden City: Doubleday, 1949.

——. *The Faces of Danger*. Garden City: Doubleday, Doran, 1964.

——. *Malice in Wonderland*. Garden City: Doubleday, 1958.

——. *Murder Masks Miami*. Garden City: Doubleday, Doran, 1939.

——. *Murder on the Yacht*. Garden City: Doubleday, Doran, 1932.

King, Terry Johnson. *Noose of Red Beads*. New York: Abelard, 1968.

Kingsley, Bettina. *Blind Chance*. New York: Dell, 1974.

Kinnie, Jamie. [See Andre Sax.]

Knight, Kathleen Moore. *The Silent Partner*. Garden City: Doubleday, 1951.

Knotts, Raymond. [Gordon Volk.] *And the Deep Blue Sea*. New York: Farrar, 1944.

Koenig, Joseph. *Floater*. New York: Mysterious, 1986.

Koperwas, Sam. *Easy Money*. New York: Morrow, 1983.

LaFrance, Marston. *Miami Murder-Go-Round*. Cleveland: World, 1957.

Lanham, Edwin. *Passage to Danger*. New York: Harcourt, 1961.

Lariar, Lawrence. *The Day I Died*. New York: Appleton, 1952.

Latimer, Jonathan. *The Dead Don't Care*. New York: Doubleday, Doran, 1938.

Law, Janice. *The Shadow of the Palms*. Boston: Houghton, 1979.

Lederer, Mira. *Adriatic Formula*. New York: Leisure, 1980.

Leonard, Elmore. *Cat Chaser*. New York: Arbor, 1982.

——. *Glitz*. New York: Warner, 1985.

——. *Gold Coast*. New York: Arbor, 1980.

——. *LaBrava*. New York: Arbor, 1983.

——. *Maximum Bob*. New York: Delacorte, 1991.

——. *Pronto*. New York: Delacorte, 1993.

——. *Split Images*. New York: Arbor, 1982.

——. *Stick*. New York: Arbor, 1983.

Leslie, John. *Havanna Hustle*. New York: Pocket, 1994.

——. *Killing Me Softly*. New York: Pocket, 1994.

Lesser, Milton. *Violence Is Golden*. New York: Bouregy, 1956.

Leventhal, Stan. *The Black Marble Pool*. New York: Amethyst, 1990.

Levine, Paul. *False Dawn*. New York: Bantam, 1993.

——. *Fool Me Twice*. New York: Morrow, 1996.

——. *Mortal Sin*. New York: Morrow, 1994.

——. *Night Vision*. New York: Bantam, 1991.

——. *Slashback*. New York: Morrow, 1995.

——. *To Speak for the Dead*. New York: Bantam, 1990.

Levison, Eric. *Ashes of Evidence*. Indianapolis: Bobbs-Merrill, 1992.

——. *The Eye Witness*. Indianapolis: Bobbs-Merrill, 1921.

——. *Hidden Eyes*. Indianapolis: Bobbs-Merrill, 1920.

Lewis, Jack. *A Night for Evil*. London: Challenge, 1967.

Lindsay, Jeffrey P. *Tropical Depression*. New York: Fine, 1994.

Lockridge, David. *Encounter in Key West*. Philadelphia: Lippincott, 1966.

Lockridge, Richard, and Francis Lockridge. *Death by Association*. Philadelphia: Lippincott, 1952.

——. *Murder by the Book*. Philadelphia: Lippincott, 1963.

Lockwood, Ethel. *The Haunted Hammock*. New York: Lenox Hill, 1973.

Lordahl, Jo Ann. *Those Subtle Weeds*. New York: Ace, 1974.

Lurie, Alison. *The Truth About Lorin Jones*. New York: Avon, 1988.

Lutz, John. *Bloodfire*. New York: Holt, 1991.

——. *Burn*. New York: Holt, 1995.

——. *Flame*. New York: Holt, 1990.

——. *Hot*. New York: Holt, 1992.

——. *Kiss*. New York: Holt, 1988.

——. *Scorcher*. New York: Holt, 1987.

——. *Spark*. New York: Holt, 1993.

——. *Torch*. New York: Holt, 1995

——. *Tropical Heat*. New York: Holt, 1986.

Lynch, Miriam. *The Silken Web*. New York: Bouregy, 1961.

MacDonald, John D. *April Evil*. New York: Dell, 1956.

——. *The Brass Cupcake*. New York: Fawcett, 1950.

——. *Bright Orange for the Shroud*. Greenwich: Fawcett, 1965.

——. *The Crossroads*. New York: Simon and Schuster, 1959.

——. *Darker Than Amber*. New York: Fawcett, 1966.

——. *Dead Low Tide*. New York: Fawcett, 1953.

——. *A Deadly Shade of Gold*. Greenwich: Fawcett, 1965.

——. *The Deadly Welcome*. Greenwich: Fawcett Publications, 1959.

——. *The Deep Blue Good-by*. New York: Fawcett, 1964.

——. *The Dreadful Lemon Sky*. Philadelphia: Lippincott, 1975.

——. *Dress Her in Indigo*. Greenwich: Fawcett, 1969.

——. *The Drowner*. Greenwich: Fawcett, 1963.

——. *The Empty Copper Sea*. Philadelphia: Lippincott, 1978.

——. *A Flash of Green*. New York: Simon and Schuster, 1962.

——. *Friend of the Family*. Greenwich: Fawcett, 1975.

——. *The Girl in the Plain Brown Wrapper*. Greenwich: Fawcett, 1968.

——. *The Girl, the Gold Watch & Everything*. Greenwich: Fawcett, 1962.

——. *The Green Ripper*. New York: Lippincott, 1979.

——. *The Long Lavendar Look*. Greenwich, CT Fawcett, 1970.

——. *Murder in the Wind*. New York: Dell, 1956.

——. *One Fearful Yellow Eye*. Greenwich: Fawcett, 1966.

——. *Pale Grey for Guilt*. Greenwich: Fawcett, 1968.

——. *A Purple Place for Dying*. Philadelphia: Lippincott, 1964.

——. *The Quick Red Fox*. Greenwich: Fawcett, 1964.

——. *The Scarlet Ruse*. New York: Lippincott, 1973.

——. *A Tan and Sandy Silence*. Greenwich: Fawcett, 1972.

——. *The Turquoise Lament*. Philadelphia: Lippincott, 1973.

——. *Where Is Janie Gantry?* New York: Fawcett, 1961.

MacGregor, T. J. [See also Trish Janeshutz and Allison Drake.] *Blue Pearl*. New York: Hyperion, 1994.

——. *Dark Fields*. New York: Ballantine, 1986.

——. *Death Fields*. New York: Ballantine, 1991.

——. *Death Sweet*. New York: Ballantine, 1988.

——. *Kill Flash*. New York: Ballantine, 1987

——. *Kin Dread*. New York: Ballantine, 1990.

——. *Mistress of the Bones*. New York: Hyperion, 1995.

——. *On Ice*. New York: Ballantine, 1989.

——. *Spree*. New York: Ballantine, 1992.

——. *Storm Surge*. New York: Hyperion, 1993.

Mackenzie-Lamb, Eric. *Labyrinth*. New York: Morrow, 1979.

Macklin, Mark. *The Thin Edge of Mania*. New York: Ace, 1956.

MacLean, Alistair. *Fear in the Sky*. Garden City: Doubleday, 1961.

MacMahon, Thomas Patrick. *Jink*. New York: Simon and Schuster, 1971.

Malina, Fred. *Some Like 'Em Shot*. New York: Mill/Morrow, 1949.

Maling, A. *Loophole*. New York: Harper, 1971.

Manson, Will. *The Deadly Game*. N.d.: Caravelle, 1967.

Marchant, Bessie. *The Secret of the Everglades*. London: Blackie, 1902.

Marlowe, Dan J. *The Name of the Game Is Death*. Greenwich: Fawcett, 1962.

——. *Never Live Twice*. Greenwich: Fawcett, 1964.

——. *Operation Whiplash*. Greenwich: Fawcett, 1973.

Marlowe, Stephen. [See C. H. Thames.]

Martin, Absalom. *Kastle Krags: A Story of Mystery*. New York: Duffield, 1922.

Matthiessen, Peter. *Killing Mr. Watson*. New York: Random, 1990.

Mayfield, Serena. *The Lonely Terror*. New York: Pocket, 1973.

McBain, Ed. *Beauty and the Beast*. New York: Holt, 1982.

——. *Cinderella*. New York: Holt, 1986.

——. *Gladly the Cross-Eyed Bear*. New York: Warner, 1996.

——. *Goldilocks*. New York: Arbor, 1978.

——. *The House that Jack Built*. New York: Holt, 1988.

——. *Jack and the Beanstalk*. New York: Holt, 1984.

——. *Mary, Mary*. New York: Warner, 1992.

——. *Puss in Boots*. New York: Holt, 1987.

——. *Rumpelstiltskin*. New York: Viking, 1981.

——. *The Sentries*. New York: Simon and Schuster, 1965.

——. *Snow White and Rose Red*. New York: Henry Holt, 1985.

——. *There Was a Little Girl*. New York: Warner , 1994.

——. *Three Blind Mice*. New York: Arcade, 1990.

McDonald, Cherokee Paul. *Gulf Stream*. New York: Warner, 1988.

——. *The Patch*. New York: Popular Library, 1986.

McDowell, Mike. *Cold Moon over Babylon*. New York: Avon, 1980.

McGuane, Thomas. *Ninety-Two in the Shade*. New York: Farrar, 1973.

McKernan, V. *Osprey Reef*. Chicago: Carroll, 1990.

McKnight, Bob. *The Bikini Bombshell*. New York: Ace, 1959.

——. *Drop Dead, Please*. New York: Ace, 1961.

——. *The Flying Eye*. New York: Ace, 1961.

——. *Homicidal Handicap*. New York: Ace, 1963.

——. *Kiss the Babe Goodbye*. New York: Ace, 1960.

——. *Murder Mutuel*. New York: Ace, 1958.

——. *Secret Sinners*. London: Merit, 1960.

——. *A Slice of Death*. New York: Ace, 1960.

——. *A Stone Around Her Neck*. New York: Ace, 1962.

——. *Swamp Sanctuary*. New York: Ace, 1959.

McLendon, J. *Deathwork*. Philadelphia: Lippincott, 1971.

Merchant, Bessie. *The Secret of the Everglades*. London: Blackie, 1902.

Merkin, Robert. *The South Florida Book of the Dead*. New York: Morrow, 1982.

Merle, Robert. *The Day of the Dolphin*. Greenwich: Fawcett, 1969.

Messman, Jon. *A Bullet for the Bride*. New York: Pyramid, 1972.

Metcalfe, Whitaker. *Two Weeks Before Murder*. New York: Arcadia, 1959.

Michaels, Jan. [Jan Milella.] *The Only Witness*. Ontario: Harlequin, 1987.

Millella, Jan. [See Jan Michaels.]

Montalbano, William D., and Carl Hiaasen. *Powder Burn*. New York: Atheneum, 1981.

——. *Trap Line*. New York: Atheneum, 1982.

Morgan, Stanley. *Too Rich to Live*. New York: Fawcett, 1979.

Murphy, Dallas. *Apparent Wind*. New York: Pocket, 1991.

Murphy, John. *The Long Reconnaissance*. New York: Double-day, 1970.

Murphy, Warren. *Death Sentence*. New York: Penguin, 1990.

Murray, Max. *The Sunshine Corpse*. London: Joseph, 1954.

Muse, Patricia. *Eight Candles Glowing*. New York: Ballantine, 1976.

Neely, Esther Jane. *Chateau Laurens*. Cammeray (N.S.W.): Horwitz, 1979.

Nehrbass, Arthur F. *Dead Easy*. New York: Dutton, 1993.

Nelson, Mildred. *The Island*. New York: Pocket, 1973.

Norman, Geoffrey. *Blue Chipper*. New York: William, 1993.

——. *Deep End*. New York: Morrow, 1994.

——. *Midnight Water*. New York: Dutton, 1983.

——. *Sweetwater Ranch*. New York: Atlantic Monthly, 1991.

O'Rourke, William. *Criminal Tendencies*. New York: Dutton, 1987.

Pace, Tom. *The Afternoon of a Loser*. New York: Harper, 1970.

——. *Fisherman's Luck*. New York: Harper, 1971.

Packard, Frank L. *Four Stragglers*. New York: Burt, 1923.

Page, Celia. *Resort Hotel*. Garden City: Doubleday, 1942.

Paine, Ruth D. [See Celia Page.]

Pairo, Preston. *Winner's Cut*. New York: Richardson, 1986.

Palmer, Thomas. *The Transfer*. New Haven: Ticknor, 1982.

Palmtag, Dinah. *Starling Street*. New York: Dell, 1973.

Parker, Barbara. *Blood Relations*. New York: Dutton, 1996.

——. *Suspicion of Guilt*. New York: Dutton, 1995.

——. *Suspicion of Innocence*. New York: Dutton, 1994.

Patti, Paul. *Silhouettes*. New York: St. Martin's, 1990.

Patton, Cliff. *Fatal Analysis*. New York: Kensington, 1988.

Payne, Alan. [John (William) Jakes.] *This'll Slay You*. New York: Ace, 1958.

Pearce, Donn. *Cool Hand Luke*. New York: Scribner, 1965.

Pendleton, Don. *Hammerhead Reef*. New York: Worldwide, 1985.

——. *Miami Massacre*. New York: Pinnacle, 1970.

——. *Paramilitary Plot*. New York: Worldwide, 1982.

——. *Thermal Thursday*. New York: Pinnacle, 1979.

——. *WhiteLine War*. Toronto: Worldwide, 1990.

——. *Wild Card*. Toronto: Worldwide, 1990.

Philbrick, W. R. *The Crystal Blue Persuasion*. New York: New American Library, 1988.

——. *The Neon Flamingo*. New York: New American Library, 1987.

——. *Tough Enough*. New York: New American Library, 1989.

Plumb, Charles. *A Murderous Move*. New York: Tower, 1981.

Polk, James K. *The Camellia Caper*. New York: Vantage, 1978.

Pope, Edith. *Colcorton*. New York: Scribner, 1944.

Powell, Richard Pitts. *And Hope to Die*. New York: Simon and Schuster, 1947.

——. *Shark River*. New York: Simon and Schuster, 1950.

——. *Shell Game*. New York: Simon and Schuster, 1950.

——. *A Shot in the Dark*. New York: Simon and Schuster, 1952.

Pratt, Theodore. [See also Timothy Brace.] *Mercy Island*. New York: Knopf, 1941.

——. *Without Consent*. Greenwich: Fawcett, 1962.

Price, Wesley. *Death Is a Stowaway*. New York: Godwin, 1933.

Provost, Gary. *Without Mercy*. New York: Pocket, 1990.

Putre, John Walter. *Death among the Angels*. New York: Scribner, 1991.

Ramm, Carl. *Florida Firefight*. New York: Dell, 1984.

Randisi, Robert. *Hard Look*. New York: Walker, 1993.

Ransome, Stephen. [Frederick Clyde Davis.]. *Alias His Wife*. New York: Dodd, 1965.

——. *The Hidden Hour*. New York: Dodd, 1966.

——. *I'll Die for You*. Garden City: Doubleday, 1959.

——. *Meet in Darkness.* New York: Dodd, Mead, 1964.

——. *Men in Her Death.* Garden City: Doubleday, 1956.

——. *The Night, The Woman.* New York: Dodd, 1962.

——. *One Man Jury.* New York: Dodd, 1964.

——. *The Sin File.* New York: Dodd, 1965.

——. *So Deadly My Love.* Garden City: Doubleday, 1957.

——. *Trap #6.* New York: Doubleday, 1971.

——. *Without a Trace.* New York: Doubleday, 1962.

Rea, Margaret Lucile Paine. *Blackout at Rehearsal.* Garden City: Doubleday, Doran, 1943.

——. *Death Walks the Dry Tortugas.* Garden City: Doubleday, Doran, 1942.

Reach, James. *Murder Over Miami.* New York: French, n.d.

Read, Opie. *On the Suwanee River.* Chicago: Laird, 1895.

Reilly, Helen (Kieran). *Lament for the Bride.* New York: Random, 1951.

Reiss, Bob. *Flamingo.* New York: St. Martin's, 1990.

Richards, William. [Day Keene.] *Dead Man's Tide.* New York: Graphic, 1953.

Robert, Sandor. [See S. Robert Tralins.]

Robins, Elizabeth. *The Secret That Was Kept.* New York: Harper, 1926.

Robinson, Kevin. *Mall Rats.* New York: Walker, 1992.

——. *A Matter of Perspective.* New York: Walker, 1993.

——. *Split Seconds.* New York: Walker, 1991.

Roche, Arthur Somers. *In the Money.* New York: Dodd,1936.

——. *The Pleasure Buyers.* New York: Macmillan, 1925.

Rohde, William L. *Uneasy Lies the Head.* New York: Ace, 1957.

Rohmer, Sax. *The Moon Is Red.* London: Jenkins, 1954.

Rome, Anthony. *The Lady in Cement.* London: Hale, 1962.

——. *Miami Mayhem.* New York: Pocket, 1960.

Ronns, Edward. [Edward S. Aarons.] *Dark Destiny.* Kingston: Quinn, 1950.

——. *I Can't Stop Running.* Sydney: Phantom, 1953.

Rosenberger, Joseph. *Project Andromeda.* New York: Lorevan, 1988.

Runyon, Damon. *Runyon a La Carte.* New York: Pocket, 1946.

Russell, Charlotte Murray. *Murder Steps In.* Garden City: Doubleday, Doran, 1942.

Russo, John. *Living Things.* New York: Warner, 1988.

Sanchez, Thomas. *Mile Zero.* New York: Knopf, 1989.

Sanders, Lawrence. *McNally's Caper.* New York:Putnam, 1993.

——. *McNally's Luck.* New York: Putnam, 1994.

——. *McNally's Puzzle.* New York: Putnam, 1996.

——. *McNally's Risk.* New York: Putnam, 1993.

——. *McNally's Secret.* New York: Putnam, 1993.

——. *McNally's Trial.* New York: Putnam, 1995.

——. *Sullivan's Sting.* New York: Putnam, 1990.

Sanford, Jerome. *Miami Heat*. New York: St. Martin's, 1991.

Sapir, Richard, and Warren Murphy. *Kill or Cure*. N.p.: Pinnacle, 1973.

Sarto, Ben. *Miami for Murder*. N.p.: Modern Fiction, 1954.

Sax, Andre. [Stephen Soitos and Jamie Kinney.] *Salt Cat Bank*. Nashville: Charter, 1980.

Scarpetta, Frank. *Mafia Massacre*. New York: Belmont, 1974.

Schley, Sturges Mason. *Dr. Toby Finds Murder*. New York: Random, 1961.

Serrian, Michael. *Night Runners*. New York: Paperjacks, 1987.

Shaara, Michael. *The Herald*. New York: McGraw, 1981.

Shames, Laurence. *Florida Straits*. New York: Simon and Schuster, 1992.

——. *Scavenger Reef*. New York: Dell, 1994.

——. *Sunburn*. New York: Little, Brown, 1995.

——. *Tropical Depression*. New York: Hyperion, 1996.

——. *Virgin Heat*. New York: Hyperion, 1997.

Shapiro, Milton J. *The Hawk*. New York: Ace, 1975.

Shedd, George Clifford. *The Lady of Mystery House*. New York: Macauley, 1917.

Singer, N. *Diamond Stud*. New York: Manor, 1976.

Singerman, Philip. *Prancing Tiger*. New York: Morrow, 1994.

Smith, Mitchell. *Sacrifice*. New York: Dutton, 1996.

Smith, Robert Kimmel. *Sadie Shapiro in Miami*. New York: Simon & Schuster, 1977.

Soitos, Stephen. [See Andre Sax.]

Somers, Suzanne. [Dorothy Daniels.] *Romany Curse*. N.p.: Belmont, 1971.

Spillane, Mickey. *The By-Pass Control*. New York: Dutton, 1966.

Springer, Charlotte, and Bob Springer. *Smuggler's Moon*. New York: Exposition, 1954.

Sproul, Kathleen. *The Mystery of the Closed Car*. New York: Dutton, 1935.

Standiford, Les. *Deal on Ice*. New York: HarperCollins, 1997.

——. *Deal to Die For*. New York: HarperCollins, 1995.

——. *Done Deal*. New York: HarperCollins, 1993.

——. *Raw Deal*. New York: HarperCollins, 1994.

Stanford, Don. *Bargain in Blood*. N.p.: Gold Medal, 1951.

Sterling, Sterling. *Dead Right*. New York: Lippincott, 1956.

Stewart, Anne. *Regatta Moon*. New York: Phoenix , 1937.

Stivers, Dick. *Miami Crush*. Toronto: Worldwide, 1987.

Stone, A. *Fighting Byng: A Novel of Mystery, Intrigue, and Adventure*. New York: Britton, 1919.

Stone, Elna. *Dark Masquerade*. New York: Prestige, 1973.

Strange, John Stephen. *The Strangler Fig*. Garden City: Doubleday, Doran, 1930.

Striker, Francis H. *The Clue of the Cypress Stump*. New York: Grosset, 1948.

Striker, Randy. *The Deep Six*. New York: New American Library, 1981.

——. *Everglades Assault*. New York: New American Library, 1982.

——. *Key West Connection*. New York: New American Library, 1981.

Taylor, Matt, and Bonnie Taylor. *Neon Dancer*. New York: Walker, 1991.

——. *Neon Flamingo*. New York: Dodd, 1989.

Terhune, Albert Payson. *Black Caesar's Clan*. New York: Doran, 1922.

——. *The Secret of Sea-Dream House*. New York: Harper, 1929.

Thacker, Cathy Gill. *Fatal Amusement*. Toronto: Harlequin, 1988.

Thames, C. H. [Stephen Marlowe.] *Violence Is Golden*. New York: Bouregy, 1956.

Thayer, Lee. *Five Bullets*. New York: Dodd, 1944.

——. *The Jaws of Death*. New York: Dodd, 1946.

Thomas, D. *Gulf Coast Run*. New York: Leisure, 1980.

Thompson, W. Crawford. *Suitcase Full of Money*. N.p.: Curtis, 1973.

Toole, W. D., Jr. *Death in Deep Shadows*. Philadelphia: Stickley, 1977.

Tracy, Donald. *The Big Blackout*. Roslyn: Black, 1959.

——. *Flats Fixed—Among Other Things*. New York: Pocket , 1974.

——. *The Hated One*. New York: Simon and Schuster, 1959.

——. *Honk If You've Found Jesus*. New York: Putnam, 1974.

Tralins, S. Robert. [Sandor Robert.] *Ring-a-Ding UFO's*. New York: Belmont, 1967.

Trocheck, Kathy Hogan. *Crash Course*. New York: HarperCollins, 1997.

——. *Lickety-Split*. New York. HarperCollins, 1996.

Van Siller, Hilda. *The Lonely Breeze*. Garden City: Doubleday, 1965.

——. *The Mood for Murder*. Garden City: Doubleday, 1966.

Volk, Gordon. [See Raymond Knotts.]

Walker, Irma. *The Murdoch Legacy*. Indianapolis: Bobbs-Merrill, 1975.

Walker, Robert W. *Razor's Edge*. New York: Windsor, 1989.

Ware, Judith. *The Faxon Secret*. New York: Paperback Library, 1966.

Wass, Albert. *Deadly Fog at Deadman's Landing*. Astor: Danubian, 1979.

Watson, Sterling. *Deadly Sweet*. New York: Pocket, 1994.

——. *Weep No More My Brother*. New York: Morrow, 1978.

Weinman, Irving. *Easy Way Down*. New York: Ballantine, 1991.

Wellen, Edward. *An Hour To Kill*. New York: St. Martin's, 1993.

Welles, Elizabeth. *The Spaniard's Gift*. New York: Pocket, 1977.

Werry, Richard R. *Casket for a Lying Lady*. New York; Dodd, 1985.

Westcott, C. T. *Half a Klick from Home*. New York: Charter, 1990.

Westlake, Donald E. *Trust Me on This*. New York: Mysterious, 1985.

Wetlaufer, Susy. *Judgment Call*. New York: Morrow, 1992.

Wheatley, Dennis. *Murder off Miami*. London: Hutchinson, 1936.

White, Lionel. *Flight into Terror*. New York: Dutton, 1955.

White, Randy Wayne. *Captiva*. New York: G. P. Putnam's Sons, 1996.

——. *The Heat Islands*. New York: St. Martin's, 1992.

——. *The Man Who Invented Florida*. New York: St. Martin's, 1993.

——. *Sanibel Flats*. New York: St. Martin's, 1990.

Whited, Charles. *The Brandon Affair*. New York: New American Library, 1976.

Whiteley, L. S. *Snakes in the Garden*. New York: Walker, 1990.

Whitney, Phyllis Ayame. *Dream of Orchids*. Garden City: Doubleday, 1985.

——. *Poinciana*. Garden City: Doubleday, 1980.

Whittington, Harry. *The Humming Box*. New York: Ace, 1956.

Whittington, Henry Benjamin. [See Whit Harrison.]

Wilder, Robert. *Walk with Evil*. Greenwich: Fawcett, 1957.

Willeford, Charles. *The Burnt Orange Heresy*. New York: Vintage/Random, 1971.

——. *Miami Blues*. New York: St. Martin's, 1984.

——. *New Hope for the Dead*. New York: St. Martin's, 1985.

——. *Sideswipe*. New York: St. Martin's Press, 1987.

——. *The Way We Die Now*. New York: Random,1988.

Willey, Gordon Randolph. *Selena*. New York: Walker, 1993.

Williams, Charles. Aground. New York: Viking, 1960.

——. *All the Way*. New York: Dell, 1958.

——. *Go Home, Stranger*. Greenwich: Fawcett, 1954.

——. *Man on the Run*. Greenwich: Fawcett, 1958.

——. *The Sailcloth Shroud*. New York: Viking, 1960.

——. *Talk of the Town*. New York: Dell, 1958.

Williams, Joy. *Breaking and Entering*. New York: Vintage, 1981.

——. *State of Grace*. New York: Scribner, 1986.

Williams, William C. [See Marc Brody.]

Wilson, Karen Ann. *Copy Cat Crimes*. New York: Berkley, 1995.

——. *Eight Days Flying*. New York: Berkley, 1994.

Wilson, Sloan. *The Greatest Crime*. New York: Arbor, 1980.

Winchell, Prentice. *Dead Right*. Philadelphia: Lippincott, 1956.

——. *Dishonor Among Thieves*. Garden City: Doubleday, 1958.

Winston, Daoma. *The Mayeroni Myth*. New York: Pocket, 1979.

——. *Trificante Treasure*. New York: Lancer, 1968.

Winters, Mike. *Miami, One Way*. London: Weidenfeld, 1985.

Wolfe, Bernard. *In Deep*. New York: Knopf, 1957.

Woods, Sherryl. *Hot Property*. New York: Dell, 1992.

Worts, George. F. [George Frank.] *Red Darkness*. New York: Allen, 1928.

Yarnell, Duane. *Mantrap*. Greenwich: Fawcett, 1960.

Zachary, Hugh. *One Day in Hell*. N.p.: Newstand, 1961.

Contributors

Julie Brannon is an instructor at Florida State University. She often teaches a course on southern noir writers, including Carl Hiaasen.

Bill Brubaker, a professor at Florida State University, has published *Stewards of the House: The Detective Fiction of Jonathan Latimer* (Bowling Green Popular Press) and has entries in *Masters of Mystery and Detective Fiction* and *Great Women Mystery Writers*. He is currently engaged in a book-length study of Jonathan Latimer's moviescript *Film Noir*.

Sarah D. Fogle is a professor at Embry-Riddle Aeronautical University. She frequently teaches detective literature courses and has published in the field.

Steve Glassman teaches humanities at Embry-Riddle Aeronautical University. He is author of *Blood on the Moon: A Novel of Old Florida,* and an editor of *Zora in Florida* and *Florida Noir.*

Ed Hirshberg, professor of English at the University of South Florida, wrote the Twayne biography on John D. MacDonald. He has also edited *JDM Bibliophile* since 1978. "Got interested in John D. MacDonald by joining the Friday afternoon Sarasota writers' group with no agenda except drinking, talking, and playing Liars' Poker. Experienced the genesis of Travis McGee in 1964 and have been hooked ever since."

Anna Lillios, associate professor of English at the Unversity of Central Florida, has published essays on Zora Neale Hurston and other Florida authors. Currently, she is editing a Hurston issue for *The Southern Quarterly* and writing a book on Hurston.

Harold Nugent is professor emeritus of linguistics and rhetoric in the University System of New Hampshire. In addition to serving on the Monroe County Planning Commission, he is a volunteer interpretive guide for the National Key Deer and the Crocodile Lake Refuge.

Susan Nugent coordinates the English Department at Florida Keys Community College. Her recent research explores the influence of maritime history on Key West's art, music, and literature.

Maurice O'Sullivan, professor of English at Rollins College, is coeditor of *The Florida Reader, Florida Poetry,* and *The Emergence of Modern America*; he is editor of *Shakespeare's Other Lives.*

Lynne M. Phillips, an associate professor and reference librarian emerita at Rollins College, has been active in the AAUP and Central Florida library associations.

Ellen Smith is an associate professor at Stetson University. She has given numerous conference papers on the topic of Florida fiction, in particular Florida detective fiction, and has taught courses in detective fiction.

Index

185

188   Index